Use Both Sides of Your Brain

Other books by Tony Buzan

Speed Memory
Spore One
Advanced Learning and Reading—Manual

Use
Both Sides
of
Your Brain

TONY BUZAN

 *A Dutton
Paperback*

E. P. Dutton   New York

First published by the British
Broadcasting Corporation, London, 1974.
This paperback edition first published by
E. P. Dutton & Co., Inc. 1976
Copyright © 1974 by Tony Buzan
All rights reserved. Printed in the U.S.A.
First American Edition

10   9   8   7   6   5

Library of Congress Catalog Card Number: 76-11857
ISBN: 0-525-47436-6

**dedicated
to
you**

With thanks to all those whose effort and co-operation
enabled me to write this book:

Zita Albes; Astrid Andersen; Jeannie Beattie;
Nick Beytes; Mark Brown; Joy Buttery;
Bernard Chibnall; Steve and Fanny Colling;
Susan Crockford; Lorraine Gill;
Bill Harris; Brian Helweg-Larsen;
Thomas Jarlov; Trish Lillis; Hermione Lovell;
Annette McGee; Joe McMahon;
My Parents and Brother; Khalid Ranjah;
Auriol Roberts; Ian Rosenbloom;
Caitrina Ni Shuilleabhain;
Robert Millard Smith; Chris and Pat Stevens;
Jan Streit; Christopher Tatham;
Lee Taylor; Nancy Thomas;
Bill Watts; Gillian Watts.

Contents

Patterned summaries of the chapters   between pages **8** & **9**

You and this book   **10**

Your mind is better than you think   **13**
    Man's understanding of his own mind
    Interconnections of the brain's neurons
    Why our performance does not match our potential
    I.Q. tests – the limitations.
    The excellence of the brain demonstrated: the human baby

Reading – more efficiently and faster   **22**
    Reading and learning problems
    Reading and learning defined
    Why reading problems exist
    Misconceptions about reading and speed reading; how
        they arise
    The eye
    Perception during reading and learning
      Improvement for the slow reader
      Advantages of fast reading
      Advanced reading techniques
      Metronome training

Memory   **41**
    Questions on memory
    Recall during a learning period
    Recall after a learning period
    Review techniques and theory
    Review, mental ability and age
    Memory systems
      The Number-Rhyme system
    Key words and concepts in remembering

Key words – noting   **68**
    Exercise – key words; standard responses
    Key words and concepts – creative and recall
      Multi-ordinate nature of words
      Individual's interpretation of words
    Memory – a comparison between standard note
        and key word noting

Brain patterns for recall and creative thinking   83

   Exercise
   Linear history of speech and print
   Contrast: the structure of the brain
   Advanced note taking and patterning techniques

Brain patterns — advanced methods and uses   97

   Models for the brain
   Technology and new insights into ourselves: the
      hologram as a model for the brain
   Advanced brain pattern noting
   Wider application of patterning techniques
     Transforming for speeches and articles
     Note taking from lectures
     Creative pattern structure for meetings

The Organic Study Method: Introduction   108

   Problems of 'getting down' to study
   Reasons for fear and reluctance
   Reasons for fear and reluctance when approaching study
      books
   Problems arising from the use of standard study
      techniques
   New study techniques
   Study planned to suit the individual's needs

The Organic Study Method: Preparation   119

   The best use of time
   Defining the areas and amount of study
   Distribution of the student's effort
   Noting of current knowledge on the subject being studied
   Planning approach to new subject
   Defining reasons for study and goals to be achieved

The Organic Study Method: Application   130

   Study overview
   Preview
   Inview
   Review
   Summary of the Organic Study Method

Bibliography   143

The patterns on the following pages represent a new method for noting.

There are eight of them, and they summarise the chapters of the book.

In these 'brain patterns' key words are linked to each other around a main centre (in these cases, the overall theme of a chapter), and a mental picture is built up of an entire thought structure.

- Before starting to read the book, take a quick look at the chapters (commencing page 83) where the theory and method for making these patterned notes is fully outlined.

- Use the notes for each chapter as a preview of what is to come; they will make the reading of the chapter easier.

- After finishing a chapter, look at its patterns once again. This will serve as a good review, and will help you to remember what you have read.

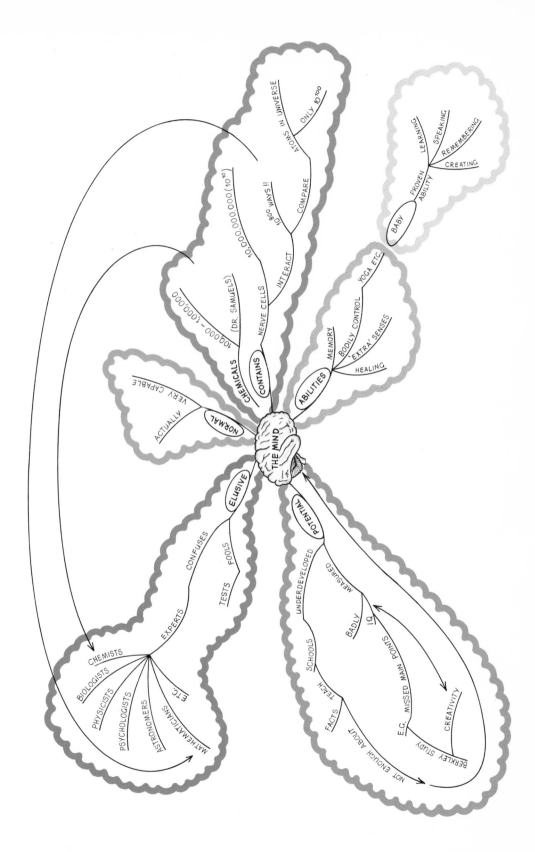

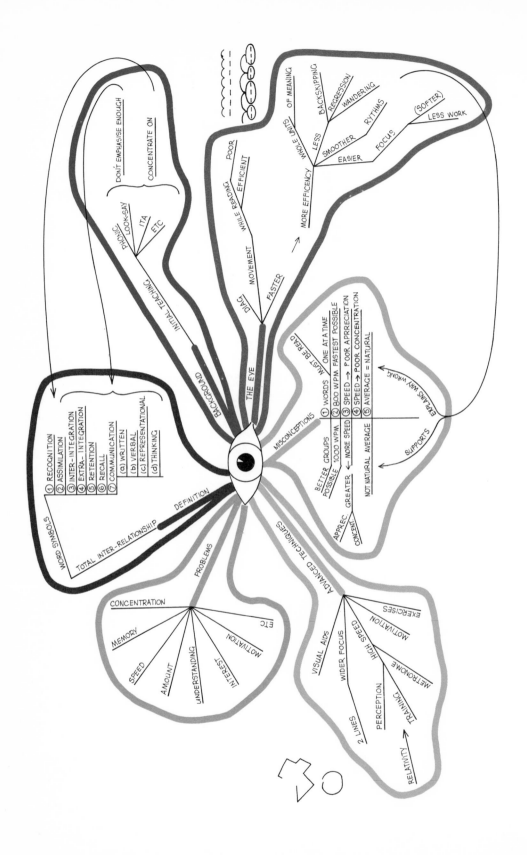

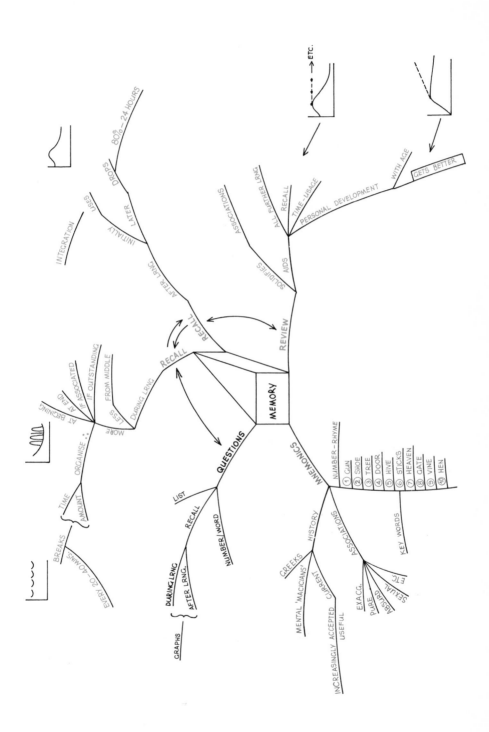

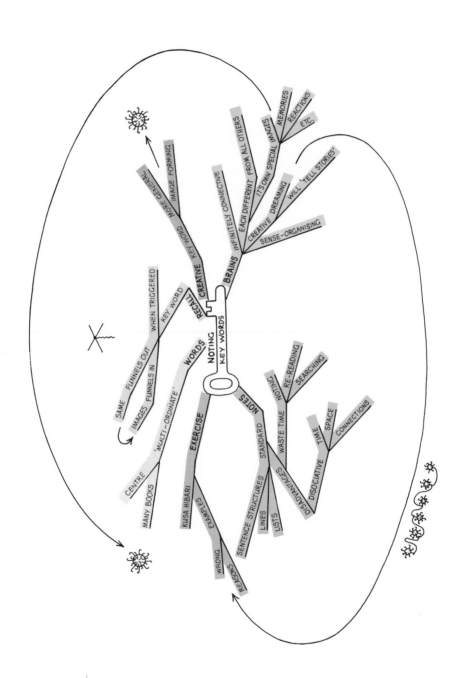

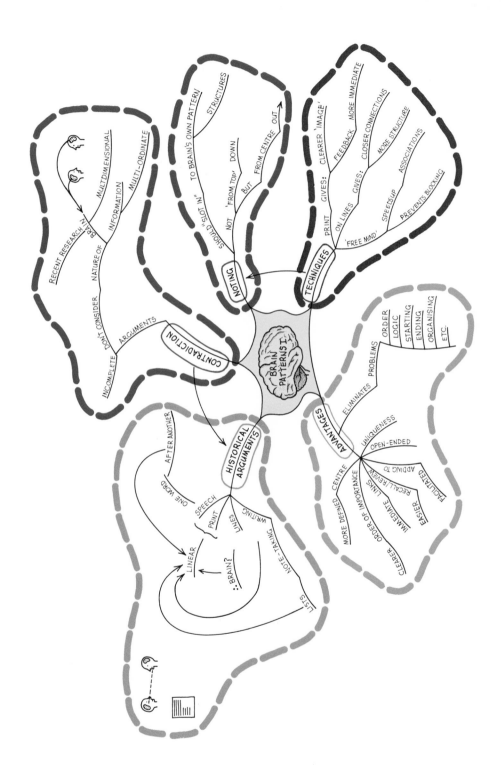

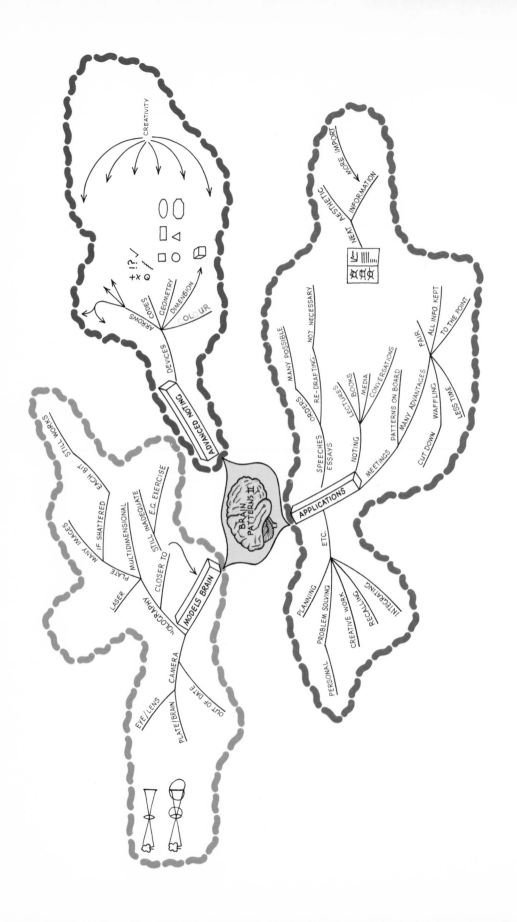

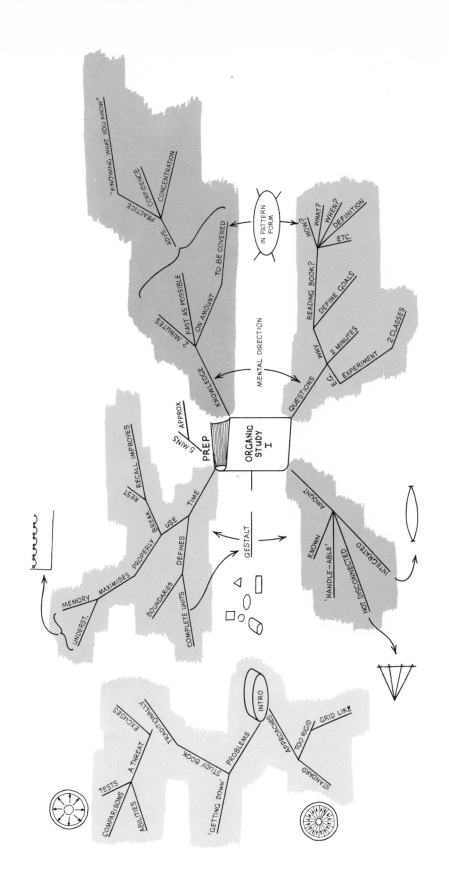

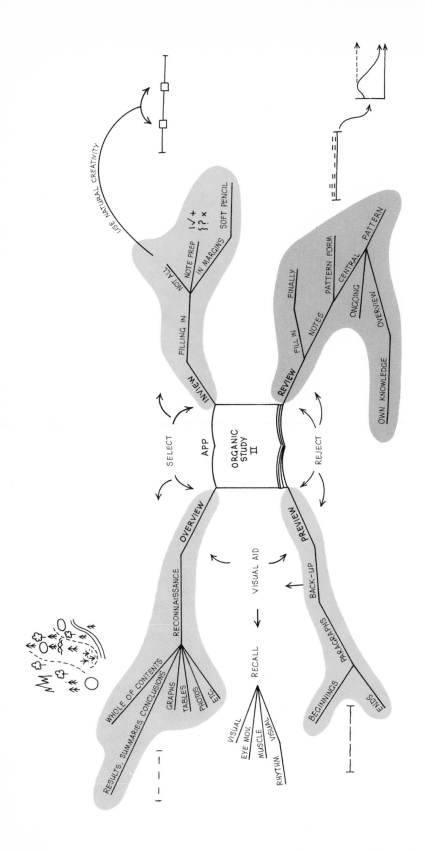

You and this book

Use both sides of your brain is written to help you do just that. By the time you have finished the book you should be able to study more effectively, solve problems more readily, read faster and more efficiently, and know generally much more about how your mind works and how to use it to the best advantage.

This introductory section gives general guide lines about the book's contents, and the ways in which these contents are best approached.

The chapters

Each chapter deals with a different aspect of your brain's functioning. First the book applies current information about the brain to the way in which our vision can be best used.

Next, a chapter explains how you can improve memory both after and during learning. In addition a special system is introduced for perfectly memorising listed items.

The middle chapters explore the brain's internal patterns. This information about how we think is applied to the way in which we use language and words for recording, organising, remembering, creative thinking and problem solving.

The last chapters deal with the Organic Study Method. Rather than being one of the simple grid methods such as the SQ3R, the Organic Study Method will enable you to study any subject ranging from English to Higher Mathematics.

Your effort

It is essential that you practice if you wish to be able to use effectively the methods and information outlined. At various stages in the book there are exercises and suggestions for further activity. In addition you should work out your own practise and study schedule, keeping to it as firmly as possible.

Personal notes

At the end of each chapter you will find pages for 'Personal Notes'. These are for any odd jottings you might wish to make during reading and can also be used when you discover relevant information after you have 'finished' the book.

The Personal Notes should also prove useful in connection with the BBC television series *Use your head*. The chapter headings and television programmes are not identical but the information in each supports and adds to the other. Much information from the programmes could be usefully recorded in your Personal Notes.

The principle underlying these pages is that *Use both sides of your brain*, being an informational book, is not simply a record of the author's personal views, but also allows the reader to criticise, comment, record and supplement the information. For this reason the book has been planned with wide margins, in which you are encouraged to add your own thoughts.

Bibliography

On page 143 you will find a special list of books. These are not just books of academic reference, but include books which will help you develop your general knowledge as well as giving you more specialised information concerning some of the areas covered in *Use both sides of your brain*.

The Time-Life books give clear and graphic accounts of such topics as Vision and the Mind, and can be used most effectively for family reading and study.

My own book, *Speed memory*, is a combination of the special memory techniques for recalling lists, numbers, names and faces, etc. It should be used in conjunction with the information from the Memory chapter.

You and yourself

It is hoped that *Use both sides of your brain* will help you to expand as an individual, and that through an increasing awareness of yourself you will be able to develop your own ways of thinking.

Each person using information from this book starts with different levels of learning ability, and will progress at the pace best suited to him. It is important therefore to measure improvement in relation to yourself and not others.

Although much of the information has been presented in connection with reading, formal noting and studying, the complete application is much wider. When you have finished and reviewed the book, browse through it again to see in which other areas of your life the information can be helpfully applied.

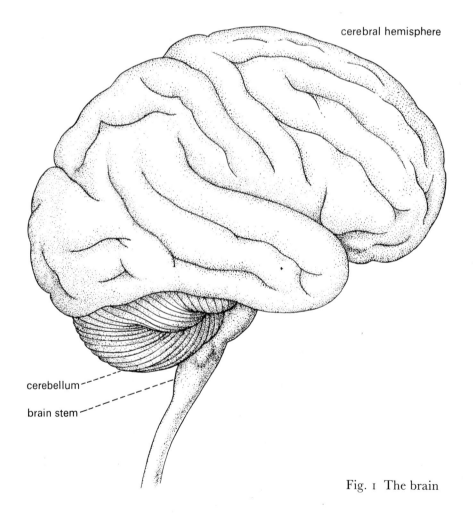

cerebral hemisphere

cerebellum

brain stem

Fig. 1 The brain

Your mind is better than you think

It is only in the last 150 years that any real progress has been made in man's understanding of his own mind, and even that progress has shown us little in comparison to what there is to be known. At the moment, despite the fact that we know the various parts of the brain, know much about the way in which chemicals change inside it, know about DNA and RNA, and know about certain experimental results under restricted conditions, we are still struggling with what must be the most elusive quarry man has ever chased.

Just when we think we have located areas where activities such as thinking, remembering and speaking are based, up pops a situation which proves that the answer is by no means certain; and just when tests seem to prove that the mind works in a given way, along comes another test which proves that it doesn't work that way at all, or along comes another human being with a brain which manages to make the test meaning-less.

What we *are* gathering from our efforts at the moment is a knowledge that the mind is infinitely more subtle than we previously thought, and that everyone who has what is ironi-cally called a 'normal' mind has a much larger ability and potential than was previously thought.

A few examples will help to make this clear.

13

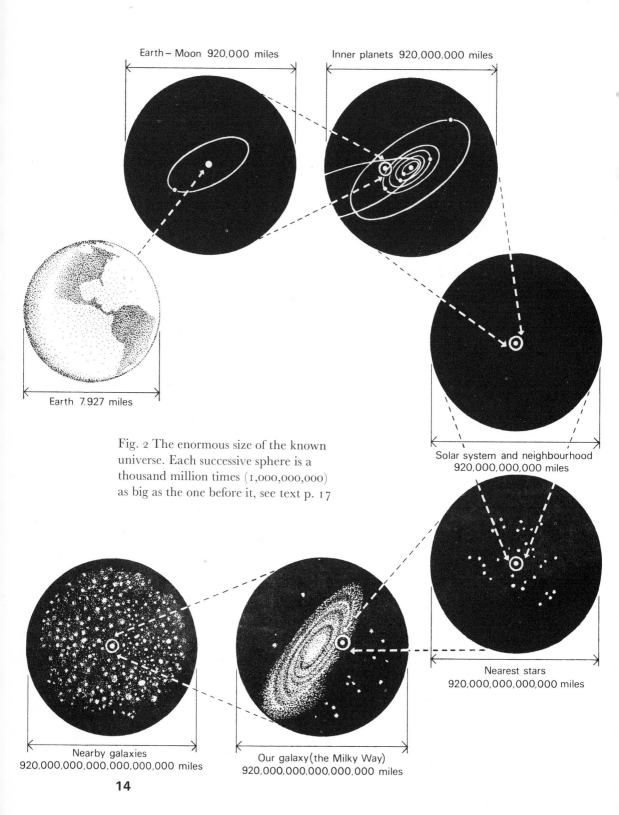

Earth – Moon 920,000 miles

Inner planets 920,000,000 miles

Earth 7,927 miles

Fig. 2 The enormous size of the known universe. Each successive sphere is a thousand million times (1,000,000,000) as big as the one before it, see text p. 17

Solar system and neighbourhood 920,000,000,000 miles

Nearest stars 920,000,000,000,000 miles

Nearby galaxies 920,000,000,000,000,000,000 miles

Our galaxy (the Milky Way) 920,000,000,000,000,000 miles

14

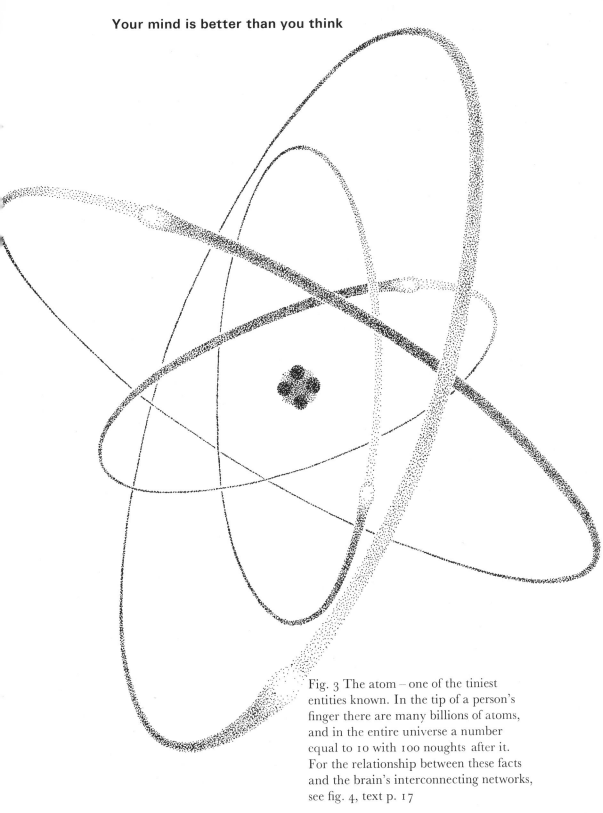

Fig. 3 The atom – one of the tiniest entities known. In the tip of a person's finger there are many billions of atoms, and in the entire universe a number equal to 10 with 100 noughts after it. For the relationship between these facts and the brain's interconnecting networks, see fig. 4, text p. 17

10,000,000,000,000,000,000,000,000,000,000,
000,000,000,000,000,000,000,000,000,000,000
000,000,000,000,000,000,000

Fig. 4a The number of atoms (one of the smallest particles we know of) in the known universe (the largest thing we know of). See text p. 17.

10,000,000,000,000,000,000,000,000,000,000,
000,000,000,000,000,000,000,000,000,000,000,
000,000,000,000,000,000,000,000,000,000,000,
000,000,000,000,000,000,000,000,000,000,000,
000,000,000,000,000,000,000,000,000,000,000,
000,000,000,000,000,000,000,000,000,000,000,
000,000,000,000,000,000,000,000,000,000,000,
000,000,000,000,000,000,000,000,000,000,000,
000,000,000,000,000,000,000,000,000,000,000,
000,000,000,000,000,000,000,000,000,000,000,
000,000,000,000,000,000,000,000,000,000,000,
000,000,000,000,000,000,000,000,000,000,000,
000,000,000,000,000,000,000,000,000,000,000,
000,000,000,000,000,000,000,000,000,000,000,
000,000,000,000,000,000,000,000,000,000,000,
000,000,000,000,000,000,000,000,000,000,000,
000,000,000,000,000,000,000,000,000,000,000,
000,000,000,000,000,000,000,000,000,000,000,
000,000

Fig. 4b The number of estimated interconnections and patterns the 10,000,000,000, individual neurons of one brain can make. See text p. 17.

16

Your mind is better than you think

Most of the more scientific disciplines, despite their apparent differences of direction, are all being drawn into a whirlpool, the centre of which is the mind. Chemists are now involved with the intricate chemical structures that exist and interact inside our heads; biologists are struggling with the brain's biological functions; physicists are finding parallels with their investigations into the farthest reaches of space; psychologists are trying to pin the mind down and are finding the experience frustratingly like trying to place a finger on a little globule of mercury; and mathematicians who have constructed models for complex computers and even for the Universe itself, still can't come up with a formula for the operations that go on regularly inside each of our heads every day of our lives.

Dr David Samuels of the Weizmann Institute recently estimated that in one average brain there are between 100,000 to 1,000,000 different chemicals reacting.

We also know that in an average brain there are 10,000,000,000 individual neurons or nerve cells. This figure becomes even more astounding when it is realised that each neuron can interact with other neurons in not just one, but many ways – it has been recently estimated that the number of interconnections may be as many as 10 with eight hundred noughts following it. To realise just how enormous this number is, compare it with a mathematical fact about the Universe: one of the smallest items in the Universe is the atom. The biggest thing we know is the Universe itself. The number of atoms in the Universe is predictably enormous: 10 with one hundred noughts after it. The number of interconnections in *one* brain makes even this number seem tiny. (See figs. 2, 3 and 4).

Other examples of the mind's abilities abound – examples of extraordinary memory feats, feats of super-strength, and unusual control of body functions defying the 'laws of science', are becoming more widespread. They are now fortunately more documented, generally recognised and usefully applied.

Even with this mounting evidence a number of people still remain sceptical, pointing to the performance of most of us, suggesting that we hardly fit the description! In response to this objection a questionnaire was given to people from all areas of life. The questions are noted below, and underneath each question is noted the reply given by at least 95 per cent. As you read ask yourself the questions.

- In school were you taught anything about how your memory functions?
  No.
- Were you taught anything about special and advanced memory techniques?
  No.
- Anything about how your eye functions when you are learning, and about how you can use this knowledge to your advantage?
  No.
- Anything about the ranges of study techniques and how they can be applied to different disciplines?
  No.
- Anything about the nature of concentration and how to maintain it when necessary?
  No.
- Anything about motivation, how it effects your abilities, and how you can use it to your advantage?
  No.
- Anything about the nature of key words and key concepts and how they relate to note taking and imagination etc?
  No.
- Anything about thinking?
  No.
- Anything about creativity?
  No.

By now the answer to the original objection should be clear: the reasons why our performances do not match even our minimum potentials is that we are given no information about what we are, or about how we can best utilise our inherent capacities.

A similar reply can be given to those who say that I.Q. tests measure our 'absolute intelligence', so therefore *they* must be right.

Apart from the fact that an I. Q. score can be significantly changed by even a small amount of well directed practice, there are other arguments against these tests:

First the Berkley Study on Creativity showed that a person whose I. Q. assessment was high was not necessarily independent in thought; independent in action; either possessed of or able to value a good sense of humour; appreciative of beauty; reasonable; relativistic; able to enjoy complexity and novelty; original; comprehensively knowledgable; fluent; flexible; or astute. Not much is left . . . .

Secondly those who argue that I.Q. does measure a wide and absolute range of human abilities are, to use the familiar expression, not able to see the wood for the trees. The test should be concerned with three major areas: 1. the brain being tested; 2. the test itself; 3. the results. Unfortunately the I.Q. protagonists have become too obsessed with numbers 2 and 3 and have left out number 1.

They have failed to realise that their tests do not test basic human ability, but measure untrained and undeveloped human performance. Their claims are much like those of an imaginary surveyor of women's feet sizes in the Orient at the time when their feet were restricted to make them small. From the crib the foot was placed in bandages until the woman was nearly full grown. This was done to stunt the growth and to produce 'dainty' feet.

To assume, however, as the surveyor might have done, that these measurements represent natural and fully developed bodily dimensions is as absurd as it is to assume that intelligence tests measure the natural dimensions of our minds. Our minds, like the women's feet, have been 'bound' by the way we have misjudged and mistrained them, and are therefore not naturally developed.

Another and perhaps the most convincing case for the excellence of the human brain, is the human baby. Far from being the 'helpless and incapable little thing' that many people assume it to be, it is the most extraordinary learning, remember-

19

ing and intellectually advanced being – even in its most early stages it surpasses the performance of the most sophisticated computers.

With very few exceptions, all babies learn to speak by the time they are two, and many even earlier. Because this is so universal it is taken for granted, but if the process is examined more closely it is seen to be extremely complex.

Try listening to someone speaking while pretending that you have no knowledge of language and very little knowledge of the objects and ideas the language discusses. Not only will this task be difficult, but because of the way sounds run into each other the distinction between different words will often be totally unclear. Every baby who has learned to talk has over-come not only these difficulties but also the difficulties of sort-ing out what makes sense and what doesn't. When he is confronted with sounds like 'koooochiekoooochiekooooooooo-aahhhhisn'tealovelelyli'ldarling!' one wonders how he ever manages to make sense of us at all!

The young child's ability to learn language involves him in processes which include a subtle control of and an inherent understanding of rhythm, mathematics, music, physics, linguis-tics, spatial relations, memory, integration, creativity, logical reasoning and thinking, etc.

The reader who still doubts his own abilities has himself learned to talk and to read. He should therefore find it difficult to attack a position of which he himself is evidence for the defence!

There really is no doubt that the mind is far more capable than has been thought. The remainder of this book will attempt to shed light on a number of the areas in which performance and self-realisation can be achieved.

Personal Notes

Reading – more efficiently and faster

Overview

- Reading and learning problems
- Reading and learning – definition – the process
- Misconceptions about reading and speed reading; why they arose
- The eye
- Perception during reading and learning
- Exercises for improving comprehension and speed

Reading and learning problems

- In the space below note *all* the problems you have with reading and learning. Be strict with yourself. The more you are able to define, the more completely you will be able to improve.

Don't catch details —
ll remember things
need to read some things faster
some slower

- Note your own definition of the word *Reading*.

Interpreting + analyzing data

Reading – more efficiently and faster

Teachers of reading and learning have noted over the past five years that in each of their classes, the same general problems arise. Below is the list of those most commonly experienced. The reader is advised to check his own against these, adding to his own list any others that apply – there will probably be quite a few.

TABLE I Areas in which reading and learning problems are commonly experienced.

vision	noting	recall
speed	retention	impatience
comprehension	age	vocabulary
time	fear	subvocalisation
amount	fatigue	typographic style
surroundings	laziness	literary style
	boredom	selection
	interest	rejection
	analysis	concentration
	criticism	back-skipping
	motivation	
	appreciation	
	organisation	
	regression	

Each of the problems in the table above is serious, and can by itself disrupt reading and learning. This book is devoted to solving these problems, the current chapter being concerned primarily with vision, speed, comprehension, time and amount, and the learning environment.

Before getting down to the more physical aspects of reading I shall first define the term properly, and in the light of this definition shall explain why the wide range of problems that exist is so universally experienced.

23

Reading defined

Reading, which is often defined as 'getting from the book what the author intended' or 'assimilating the written word' deserves a far more complete definition. It can be defined as follows:

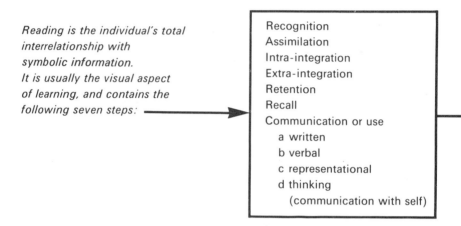

Reading is the individual's total interrelationship with symbolic information. It is usually the visual aspect of learning, and contains the following seven steps:

Recognition
Assimilation
Intra-integration
Extra-integration
Retention
Recall
Communication or use
   a written
   b verbal
   c representational
   d thinking
     (communication with self)

The definition includes consideration of most of the problems in table 1, page 23. The only problems not included are those which are, in a sense, 'outside' the reading process, 'surroundings', 'age', etc.

Why the problems exist

The reader may justifiably ask at this point why so many people experience the problems noted.

The answer lies in our approach to the initial teaching of reading. (Most of you reading this book who are over twenty-five will probably have been taught by the Phonic or Alphabet Method. Others will probably have been taught by either this or by the Look and Say Method.)

The most simplified Phonic Method teaches the child first the alphabet, then the different sounds for each of the letters

recognition

The reader's knowledge of the alphabetic symbols. This step takes place almost before the physical aspect of reading begins.

assimilation

The physical process by which light is reflected from the word and is received by the eye, then transmitted to the brain. (See fig. 5).

intra-integration

The equivalent to basic understanding, and refers to the linking of all parts of the information being read with all other appropriate parts.

extra-integration

This includes analysis, criticism, appreciation, selection and rejection. The process in which the reader brings the whole body of his previous knowledge to the new knowledge he is reading, making the appropriate connections.

retention

The basic storage of information. Storage can itself become a problem. Most readers will have experienced entering an examination room and storing most of their information during the two hour exam period! Storage, then, is not enough in itself, and must be accompanied by recall.

recall

The ability to get back out of storage that which is needed, preferably *when* it is needed.

communication

The use to which the information is immediately or eventually put; includes the very important subdivision: thinking.

in the alphabet, then the blending of sounds in syllables, and finally the blending of sounds forming words. From this point on he is given progressively difficult books, usually in the form of series graded 1 to 10, through which he progresses at his own speed. He becomes a 'silent' reader during the process.

The Look and Say Methods teach the child by presenting him with cards on which there are pictures. The names of the objects shown are clearly printed underneath them. Once a child has become familiar with the pictures and the names associated with them, the pictures are removed leaving only the words. When the child has built up enough basic vocabulary he progresses through a series of graded books similar to those for the child taught by the Phonic Method, and also becomes a 'silent' reader.

The outlines given of the two methods are necessarily brief, and there are at least fifty other methods similar to these presently being taught in England and in other English-speaking countries.

The point about these methods, however, is not that they are inadequate for achieving their aim, but that they are inadequate for teaching any child to read in the complete sense of the word.

Referring to the definition of Reading, it can be seen that these methods are designed to cover only the stage of recognition in the process, with some attempt at assimilation and intra-integration. The methods do not touch on the problems of speed, time, amount, retention, recall, selection, rejection, note-taking, concentration, appreciation, criticism, analyses, organisation, motivation, interest, boredom, surroundings, fatigue or typographic style, etc.

It can thus be seen that there is justification for the problems so widely experienced.

Recognition, it is important to note, is hardly ever mentioned as a problem, because it has been taught adequately in the early years of school. All the other problems are mentioned because they have *not* been dealt with during the educational process.

Later chapters deal with the majority of these problems. The remainder of this chapter is devoted to eye movement, comprehension and the speed of reading.

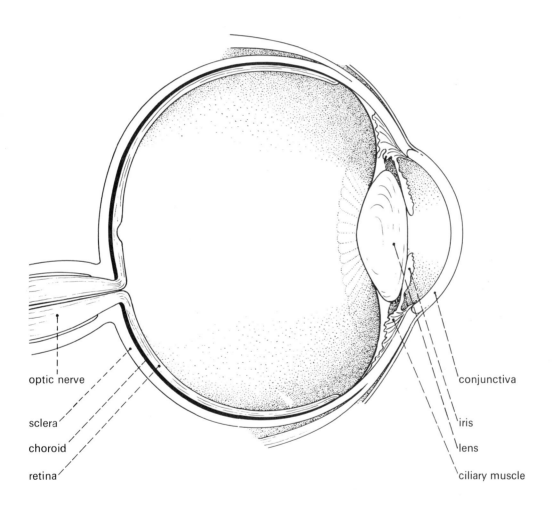

optic nerve

sclera

choroid

retina

conjunctiva

iris

lens

ciliary muscle

Fig. 5 Your eye.

Reading eye movements

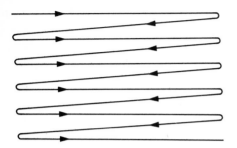

Fig. 6 Assumed reading eye movement as shown by people with no knowledge of eye movements. Each line is thought to be covered in less than one second. See text this page.

When asked to show with their forefinger the movement and speed of their eyes as they read, most people move their fingers along in smooth lines from left to right, with a quick jump from the end of one line back to the beginning of the next. They normally take between a quarter to one second for each line. (See fig. 6).

Two major errors are being made: the movement and the speed.

Even if the eye moved as slowly as one line per second, words would be covered at the rate of 600–700 words per minute (w.p.m.). As the average reading speed on even light material is 250 w.p.m., it can be seen that even those estimating slower speeds assume that they cover words much more rapidly than they really do.

If eyes moved over print in the smooth manner shown in fig. 6 they would be able to take in nothing, because the eye can see things clearly only when it can 'hold them still'. If an object is still the eye must be still in order to see it, and if an object is moving the eye must move with the object in order to see it. A simple experiment either by yourself or with a friend will confirm this. Hold a forefinger motionless in front of the eyes and either feel your own eyes or watch your friend's eyes as they look at the object. They will remain still. Next move the finger up, down, sideways and around, following it with the eyes. And finally move the finger up, down and around, holding the eyes still, or cross both hands in front of your face, at the same time looking at them both simultaneously. (If you can accomplish this last feat write to me immediately!) When objects move, eyes move with them if they are to be seen clearly.

Reading – more efficiently and faster

Relating all this to reading, it is obvious that if the eyes are going to take in words, and if the words are still, the eyes will have to pause on each word before moving on. Rather than moving in smooth lines as shown in fig. 6, the eyes in fact move in a series of stops and quick jumps. (See fig. 7).

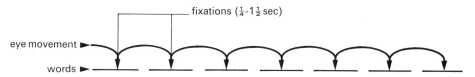

Fig. 7 Diagram representing the stop-and-start movement of the eyes during the reading process. See text this page.

The jumps themselves are so quick as to take almost no time, but the fixations can take anywhere from $\frac{1}{4}$ to $1\frac{1}{2}$ seconds. A person who normally reads one word at a time – and who skips back over words and letters is forced, by the simple mathematics of his eye movements, into reading speeds which are often well below 100 w.p.m., and which mean that he will not be able to understand much of what he reads, nor be able to read much. (See fig. 8)

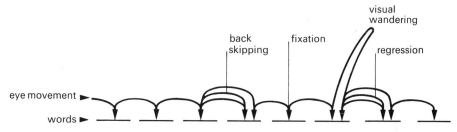

Fig. 8 Diagram showing poor reading habits of slow reader: one word read at a time, with unconscious back-skipping, visual wandering, and conscious regressions. See text this page.

It might seem at first glance that the slow reader is doomed, but the problem can be solved, and in more than one way:

Reading – more efficiently and faster

1 Skipping back over words can be eliminated, as 90 per cent of back-skipping and regression is based on apprehension and is unnecessary for understanding. The 10 per cent of words that do need to be reconsidered can be noted as explained in the chapter on Organic Study, pages 137/8.

2 The time for each fixation can be reduced to approach the $\frac{1}{4}$ second minimum – the reader need not fear that this is too short a time, for his eye is able to register as many as five words in one one-hundredth of a second.

3 The size of the fixation can be expanded to take in as many as three to five words at a time. (See fig. 9)

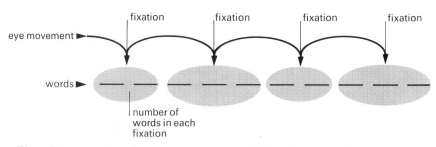

Fig. 9 Diagram showing eye movements of a better and more efficient reader. More words are taken in at each fixation, and back-skipping, regression and visual wandering are eliminated. See text this page.

This solution might at first seem impossible having explained that the mind deals with one word at a time. In fact it can equally well fixate on *groups* of words, which is better in nearly all ways: When we read a sentence we do not read it for the individual meaning of each word, but for the meaning of the phrases in which the words are contained.

Reading for example, 'the   cat
          sat   on   the
road' is more difficult than reading the cat sat   on the road.
The slower reader has to do more mental work than the faster more smooth reader because he has to add the meaning of each

30

word to the meaning of each following word. In the above example this amounts to five or six additions. The more efficient reader, absorbing in meaningful units, has only one simple addition.

Another advantage for the faster reader is that his eyes will be doing less physical work on each page. Rather than having as many as 500 fixations tightly focused per page as does the slow reader, he will have as few as 100 fixations per page, each one of which is less muscularly fatiguing.

Yet another advantage is that the rhythm and flow of the faster reader will carry him comfortably through the meaning, whereas the slow reader, because of his stopping and starting, jerky approach, will be far more likely to become bored, to lose concentration, to mentally drift away and to lose the meaning of what he is reading.

It can be seen from this that a number of the commonly held beliefs about faster readers are false:

1 *Words must be read one at a time:* Wrong. Because of our ability to fixate and because we read for meaning rather than for single words.

2 *Reading faster than 500 w.p.m. is impossible:* Wrong. Because the fact that we can take in as many as six words per fixation and the fact that we can make four fixations a second means that speeds of 1,000 are perfectly feasible.

3 *The faster reader is not able to appreciate:* Wrong. Because the faster reader will be understanding more of the meaning of what he reads, will be concentrating on the material more, and will have considerably more time to go back over areas of special interest and importance to him.

4 *Higher speeds give lower concentration:* Wrong. Because the faster we go the more impetus we gather and the more we concentrate.

5 *Average reading speeds are natural and therefore the best:* Wrong. Because average reading speeds are not natural. They are

speeds produced by an incomplete initial training in reading, combined with an inadequate knowledge of how the eye and brain works at the various speeds possible.

Advanced reading techniques

Apart from the general advice given above, some readers may be able to benefit from the following information which is usually practised in conjunction with a qualified instructor:

1 *Visual aid techniques:* When children learn how to read they often point with their finger to the words they are reading. We have traditionally regarded this as a fault and have told them to take their fingers off the page. It is now realised that it is we and not the children who are at fault. Instead of insisting that they remove their fingers we should ask them to move their fingers faster. It is obvious that the hand does not slow down the eye, and the added values that the aid gives in establishing a smooth rhythmical habit are immeasurable.

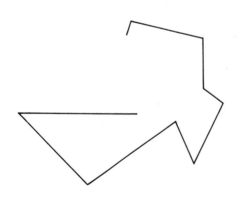

To observe the difference between unaided and aided eye movement, ask a friend to imagine a large circle about one foot in front of him, and then ask him to look slowly and carefully around the circumference. Rather than moving in a perfect circle, his eyes will follow a pattern more resembling an arthritic rectangle. (See fig. 10).

Fig. 10 Pattern showing unaided eye movement attempting to move around the circumference of a circle. See text this page.

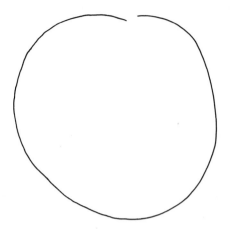

Next trace a circle in the air with your finger asking your friend to follow the tip of your finger as you move smoothly around the circumference. You will observe that the eyes will follow almost perfectly and will trace a circle similar to that shown in fig. 11.

Fig. 11 Pattern showing aided eye movement around the circumference of a circle. See text this page.

This simple experiment also indicates what an enormous improvement in performance there can be if a person is given the basic information about the physical function of the eye and brain. In many instances no long training or arduous practising is necessary. The results, as in this case, are immediate.

The reader is not restricted to the use of his forefinger as a visual aid, and can use to advantage a pen or a pencil, as many naturally efficient readers do. At first the visual aid will make the reading speed look slow. This is because, as mentioned earlier, we all imagine that we read a lot faster than we actually do. But the aided reading speed will actually be faster.

2 *Expanded focus.* In conjunction with visual aid techniques, the reader can practise taking in more than one line at a time. This is certainly not physically impossible and is especially useful on light material or for overviewing and previewing. It will also improve normal reading speeds. It is very important always to use a visual guide during this kind of reading, as without it the eye will tend to wander with comparatively little direction over the page. Various patterns of visual aiding should be experimented with, including diagonal, curving, and straight-down-the-page movements.

3 *High speed perception*. Turning pages as fast as possible attempting to see as many words per page as possible. This form of training will increase the ability to take in large groups of words per fixation, will be applicable to overviewing and previewing techniques, and will condition the mind to much more rapid and efficient general reading practices. This high speed conditioning can be compared to driving along a motorway at 90 miles an hour for one hour. Imagine you had been driving at this speed, and you suddenly came to a road sign saying 'slow to 30'. To what speed would you slow down if somebody covered your speedometer and said 'go on, tell me when you reach 30'. The answer of course would be 50 or 60 m.p.h.

The reason for this is that the mind has become conditioned to a much higher speed, which becomes 'normal'. Previous 'normals' are more or less forgotten in the presence of the new ones. The same applies to reading, and after a high speed practice you will often find yourself reading at twice the speed without even feeling the difference. (See fig. 12).

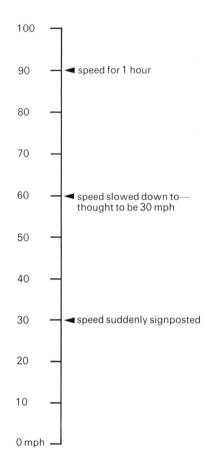

Fig. 12 Illustration showing how the mind 'gets used to' speed and motion. The same kind of relativistic 'misjudgements' can be used to advantage to help us learn to learn more adequately. See text this page.

Motivational practice

Most reading is done at a relaxed and almost lackadaisical pace, a fact which many speed reading courses have taken advantage of. They give their students various exercises and tasks, and suggest to them that after each exercise their speed will increase by 10–20 w.p.m. And so it does, often by as much as 100 per cent over the duration of the lessons. The increase, however, is often due not to the exercises, but to the fact that the student's motivation has been eked out bit by bit during the course.

The same significant increases could be produced by guaranteeing each student, at the beginning of the course, the fulfilment of any wish he desired. Performance would immediately equal those normally achieved at the end of such courses – similar to the unathletic fellow who runs a hundred metres in 10 seconds flat and jumps a 6-foot fence when being chased by a bull. In these cases motivation is the major factor, and the reader will benefit enormously by consciously applying it to each learning experience. If a decision is made to do better, then poor performance will automatically improve.

Metronome training

A metronome, which is usually used for keeping musical rhythm, can be most useful for both reading and high speed reading practices. If you set it at a reasonable pace, each beat can indicate a single sweep for your visual aid. In this way a steady and smooth rhythm can be maintained and the usual slowdown that occurs after a little while can be avoided. Once the most comfortable rhythm has been found, your reading speed can be improved by occasionally adding an extra beat per minute.

The metronome can also be used to pace the high speed perception exercises, starting at slower rates and accelerating to exceptionally fast rates, 'looking' at one page per beat.

The information on eye movements, visual aids and advanced reading techniques should be applied by the reader to each of his reading situations. It will be found that these techniques and items of advice will become more useful when applied together with information and techniques from other chapters, especially the last three dealing with the Organic Study Method.

At the end of this chapter are a series of exercises which give practice in all areas. These exercises should be done in 5 to 20-minute sessions per day, preferably before any normal reading or studying. During the first few weeks as much as half-an-hour per day can be spent profitably. As you become more practised in the exercises they need be done only when revision is felt necessary.

N.B. The formula for working out speed in w.p.m. is:

$$\text{w.p.m. (speed)} = \frac{\text{number of pages read} \times \text{number of words per average page}}{\text{number of minutes spent reading}}$$

EXERCISES

After any w.p.m. calculation enter the number on the graph on page 38.

1 Exercise eye movements over page, moving eyes on horizontal and vertical planes diagonally upper left to lower right, and then upper right to lower left. Speed up gradually day by day. Purpose – to train eyes to function more accurately and independently.

2 Read normally for 5 minutes from a book which you will be able to continue using. Record w.p.m. on continuing graph page 38.

3 Practise turning 100 pages at approximately 2 seconds per page, moving eyes very rapidly down the page. (2 × 2 min. sessions)

Exercises continued

4 a Practise as fast as you can for 1 minute, not worrying about comprehension.
   b Read with motivated comprehension – 1 minute.
   c Calculate and record w.p.m.
Repeat as time allows.

5 Use any book (light material) of your choice, preferably one in which you are interested.
   Try for as much comprehension as possible, but realise that exercise is concerned primarily with speed. In this exercise reading should continue from last point reached.
   a Practise-read for 1 minute at 100 w.p.m. faster than your highest normal speed
   b Practise-read 100 w.p.m. faster than (a).
   c Practise-read 100 w.p.m. faster than (b).
   d Practise-read 100 w.p.m. faster than (c).
   e Practise-read 100 w.p.m. faster than (d).
   f Practise-read with comprehension for 1 minute from point reached at end of (e). Calculate and record w.p.m.

6 High Speed Practice 1
   a Use any easy book. Start from the beginning of a chapter.
   b Practise-read with visual aid, three lines at a time at a *minimum* of 2,000 w.p.m. for 5 minutes.
   c Re-read to mark in 4 minutes.
   d Re-read to mark in 3 minutes.
   e Re-read to mark in 2 minutes.
   f Read on from mark, for same comprehension as at (b) for 5 minutes.

7 High Speed Practice 2
   a Use any easy book, start at the beginning of a chapter.
   b Scan for one minute, using visual aid, 4 seconds per page.
   c Practise-read from the beginning at minimum of 2,000 w.p.m. for 5 minutes.
   d Repeat this exercise when possible.

PROGRESS GRAPH

speed wpm

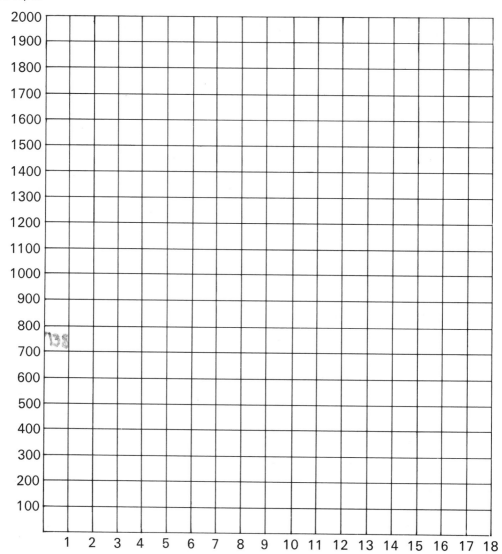

See exercises pages 36/37.

This graph should soon be complete. When it is full make
another similar one and keep it in your book.

Personal Notes

Personal Notes

Memory

Overview

- Questions on memory.
- Recall during a learning period.
- Recall after a learning period.
- Review techniques and theory.
- Memory systems – those used by the Greeks and still used by stage performers to astound audiences.
- Key words and concepts for easier methods of using language, noting, learning, thinking and remembering.

Test 1

On the right of these instructions is a list of words. Read each word on this list once, quickly, in order, and then turn to page 46 and fill in as many of the words as you can. You will not be able to remember all of them, so simply try for as many as you can. Read the complete list, one after the other. To ensure you do this properly use a small card, covering each word as you read it.

start now

Next turn to page 46, fill in as many of these items as you can, and answer the questions which immediately follow.

went
the
book
work
and
good
and
start
of
the
late
white
and
paper
Mohammed Ali
light
of
skill
the
own
stair
note
and
rode
will
time
home

Test 2

On page 47 you will find a blank graph. Fill it in with a line which represents the amount you think your memory recalls during a learning period. The vertical left-hand line marks the starting point for the learning; the vertical right-hand line marks the point when learning stops; the bottom line represents no recall at all (complete forgetting); and the top line represents perfect recall.

On the right are examples of graphs filled in by three people.

These graphs start at 75% because it is assumed that most standard learning does not produce 100% understanding or recall.

There are of course many other alternatives, so now turn to page 47 and complete the graph for the way in which you think your recall works.

Memory

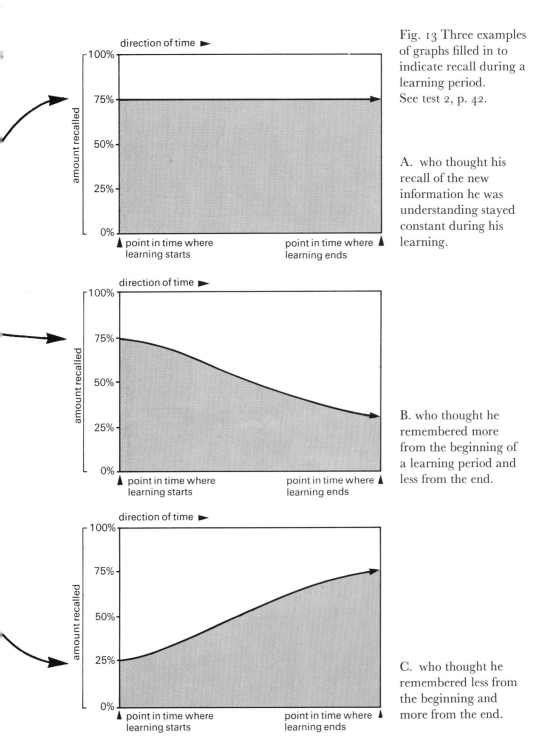

direction of time ▶

100%
75%
50%
25%
0%

amount recalled

▲ point in time where learning starts   point in time where learning ends ▲

direction of time ▶

100%
75%
50%
25%
0%

amount recalled

▲ point in time where learning starts   point in time where learning ends ▲

direction of time ▶

100%
75%
50%
25%
0%

amount recalled

▲ point in time where learning starts   point in time where learning ends ▲

Fig. 13 Three examples of graphs filled in to indicate recall during a learning period. See test 2, p. 42.

A. who thought his recall of the new information he was understanding stayed constant during his learning.

B. who thought he remembered more from the beginning of a learning period and less from the end.

C. who thought he remembered less from the beginning and more from the end.

Test 3

On page 48 is a blank graph to show the way your memory behaves *after* a learning period has been completed. The vertical left-hand line marks the end point of your learning; there is no right-hand vertical line because it is assumed that the 'afterwards' would be for a few years!; the bottom line represents no recall at all; and the top line represents perfect recall.

The graphs on the right show three people's assessment of their recall after learning.

As with Test 2 there are many alternatives, so now turn to page 48 and complete the graph in the way which most closely represents what you feel to be your normal pattern of forgetting. For the purpose of the exercise you can assume that nothing happens after your learning period to remind you of the information you learned.

Test 4

Here is a list of words next to numbers. As with Test 1 read each item once, covering the ones read with a card as you progress down the list. The purpose of this is to remember which word went with which number:

Now turn to page 48 and fill in the answers in the order requested.

4 glass
9 mash
1 watch
6 chair
10 carpet
5 paper
8 stone
3 orange
7 banana
2 sky

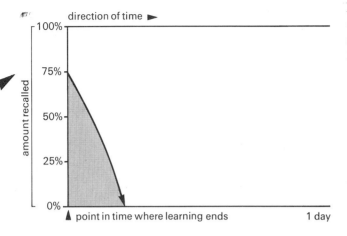

Fig. 14 Three examples of graphs filled in to show recall after a learning period has been completed.
See test 3, p. 44.

A. who thought he forgot nearly every-thing in a very short period of time.

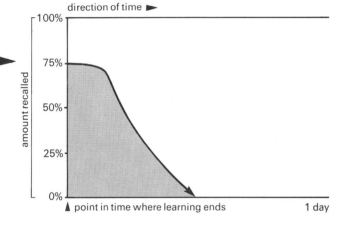

B. who thought his recall was constant for a little while and then dropped off fairly steeply.

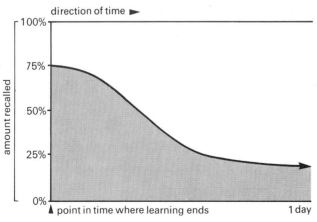

C. who thought his memory stayed constant for a while and then dropped off more slowly, levelling out at a certain point.

Test responses and further questions

Test 1: responses

When answering the questions, do not refer to the original list

1 Fill in as many of the words, in order, as you can.

2 How many of the words from the beginning of the list did you remember before making the first error?

_____

3 Can you recall any words which appeared more than once in the list? If so note them

_____

_____

4 How many of the words within the last five did you remember?

_____

5 Do you remember any item from the list which was outstandingly different from the rest?

_____

6 How many words from the middle of the list can you remember which you have not already noted in answers to previous questions?

_____

_____

_____

_____

Test 2: responses

Fill in, as demonstrated in the examples of fig. 13 page 43, the line which represents the way your memory recalls _during_ a learning period.

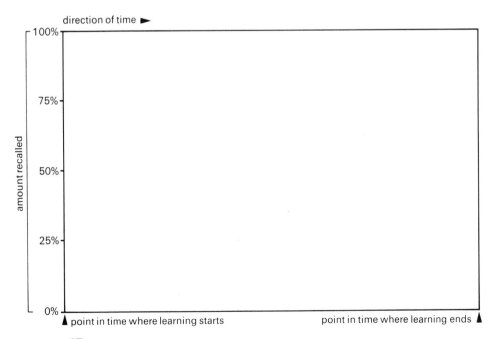

Test 3: responses

Fill in the graph below in the way you think your recall behaves after a learning period has been completed (see examples fig. 14 page 45).

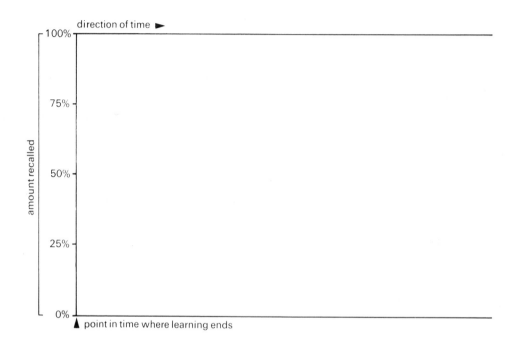

Test 4: responses

Here are the numbers 1 to 10. Fill in next to each number the word which originally appeared next to it. The numbers are not listed in same order as before. Do not refer back until you have filled in as many as you can.

1 ———————————
7 ———————————
4 ———————————
5 ———————————
6 ———————————
3 ———————————
10 ——————————
8 ———————————
2 ———————————
9 ———————————

Score_____

Recall during learning—discussion of Tests 1 and 2

Test 1 showed how recall functions during a period of learning, as long as understanding remains fairly constant (the words in the list were not 'difficult').

In this test virtually everyone has the following results: anywhere between 2 and 8 of the words at the beginning of the list are recalled; most of the words which appear more than once are recalled (in this case 'the', 'and', 'of'); one or two of the last five words are recalled; and the outstanding word or phrase is recalled (in this case Mohammed Ali); very few of the words from the middle are recalled.

This is a pattern of test scores which shows very dramatically that memory and understanding do not work in exactly the same way as time progresses – all the words were under-

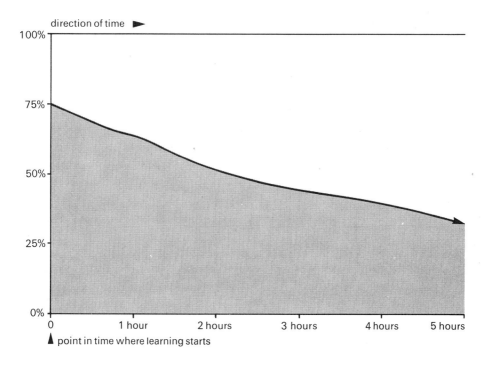

Fig. 15 As time goes on, recall of material being learned tends to get progressively worse unless the mind is given proper rests. See text pp. 49/50.

stood, but only some were recalled. The differences between the way in which memory and understanding function help explain why so many people find they don't recall very much after hours of learning and understanding. The reason is that recall tends to get progressively worse as time goes on unless the mind is given brief rests. (See fig. 15).

Thus the graph requested in Test 2 will be more complex than the simple examples given. It will probably also be more complex than the graph you have traced for your own recall behaviour during learning. Average scores from Test 1 produce a graph similar to fig. 16.

From the graph it is clear that under normal circumstances and with understanding fairly constant, we tend to recall: more at the beginning and ends of learning periods; more of items which are associated by repetition, sense, rhyming etc.; more of things which are outstanding or unique; and considerably *less* of things from the middle of learning periods.

If recall is going to be kept at a reasonable level, it is necessary to find the point at which recall and understanding work in greatest harmony. For normal purposes this point occurs in a time period of between 20 to 40 minutes. A shorter period does not give the mind enough time to appreciate the rhythm and organisation of the material, and a longer period results in the continuing decline of the amount recalled. (As graphed in fig. 17).

If a period of learning from a lecture, a book or the mass media is to take two hours, it is far better to arrange for brief breaks during these two hours. In this way the recall curve can be kept high, and can be prevented from dropping during the later stages of learning. The small breaks will guarantee eight relatively high points of recall, with four small drops in the middle. Each of the drops will be less than the main drop would have been were there no breaks. (See fig. 17).

Breaks are additionally useful as relaxation points. They get rid of the muscular and mental tension which inevitably builds up during periods of concentration.

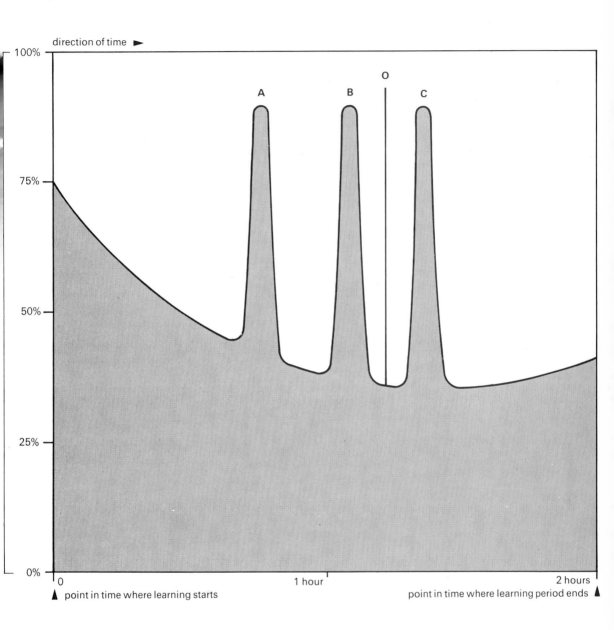

Fig. 16 *Recall during learning – breakdown*
Graph indicating that we recall more from the beginning and ends of
a learning period. We also recall more when things are associated or
linked (A, B and C) and more when things are outstanding or unique
(O). See text pp. 49/50.

51

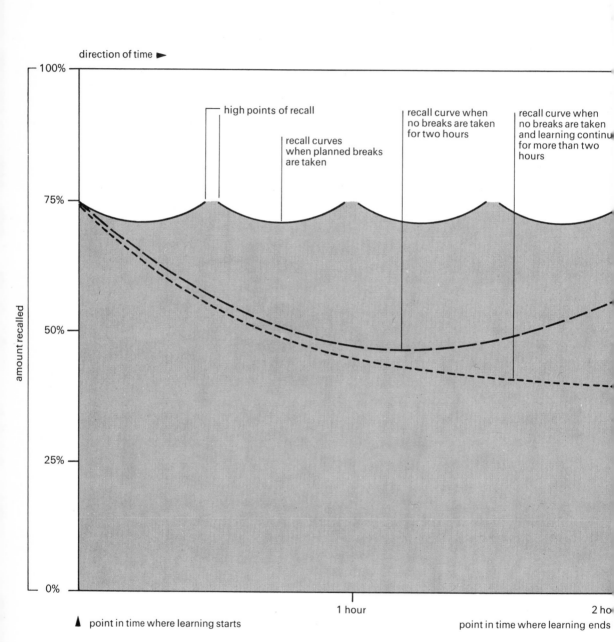

direction of time ►

high points of recall

recall curves
when planned breaks
are taken

recall curve when
no breaks are taken
for two hours

recall curve when
no breaks are taken
and learning continu
for more than two
hours

amount recalled

100%

75%

50%

25%

0%

1 hour

2 ho

▲ point in time where learning starts

point in time where learning ends

Fig. 17 *Recall during learning – with and without breaks*
A learning period of between 20–40 minutes produce the best relationship between understanding and recalling. See text pp. 49/50.

Recall after a learning period – discussion of Test 3 and answers

In Test 3 you were asked to fill in a graph indicating the way you thought your recall functioned after a period of learning had been completed. The examples on page 45 were answers many people have given when asked this question, although a much wider variety of responses overall was registered.

Apart from those graphed on page 45 – other answers included: straight lines plunging almost immediately to nothing: variations on the more rapid drop, some falling to 0%, others always maintaining some per cent, however small; variations on the slower fall-off, also with some falling to 0% and others maintaining; and variations on these themes, showing rises and falls of varying degree. (See fig. 18).

The surprising truth of the matter is that none of the examples shown earlier, and none of the estimates shown, are

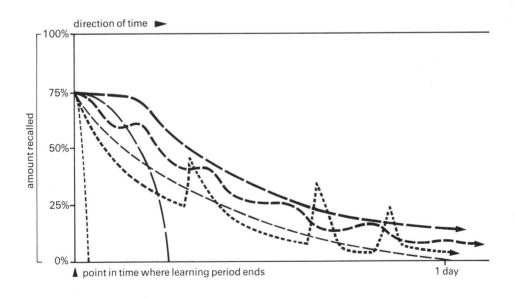

Fig. 18 *Recall after a learning period – people's estimates*
Graph showing the different kinds of answers people gave when asked to show how their recall functioned after a period of learning. See text this page.

Memory

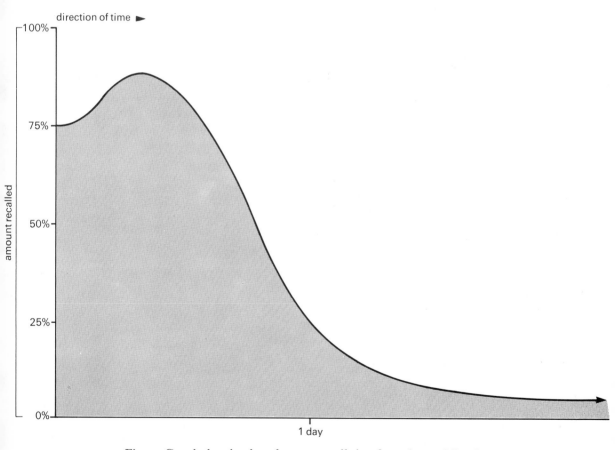

direction of time ▶

Fig. 19 Graph showing how human recall rises for a short while after learning, and then falls steeply (80% of detail forgotten within 24 hours). See text pp. 54/55.

correct. They have all neglected what is perhaps the most important point of all: recall after a learning period initially *rises*, and only then declines, following a steeply falling concave curve that levels off and never quite touches the bottom of the graph. (See fig. 19).

Once it is realised that this brief rise does take place, the reason for it can be understood: at the very moment when a learning period is finished, the mind has had little time to sort out all the new information it has been given, especially the last items. It needs a few minutes to complete and link firmly all the interconnections within the new material.

The decline that takes place after the small rise is a discouragingly steep one – within 24 hours of a one-hour learning period at least 80 per cent of detailed information is lost. This enormous drop in the amount remembered must be prevented, and can be by proper techniques of review.

Memory — review

If review is organised properly, the graph shown in fig. 19 can be changed to keep recall at the high point reached shortly after learning had been completed. In order to accomplish this, a programmed pattern of review must take place, each review being done at the time just before recall is about to drop. For example, the first review should take place about 10 minutes after a one-hour learning period and should itself take 10 minutes. This will keep the recall high for approximately one day, when the next review should take place, this time for a period of 2 to 4 minutes. After this, recall will probably be retained for approximately a week, when another 2 minute review can be completed followed by a further review after about one month. After this time the knowledge will be lodged in Long Term Memory. This means it will be familiar in the way a personal telephone number is familiar, needing only the most occasional nudge to maintain it. (See fig. 20).

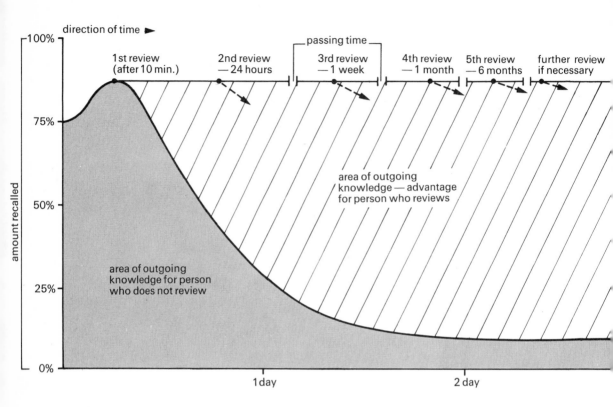

Fig. 20 Graph showing how properly spaced review can keep recall constantly high. See text p. 55.

The first review, especially if notes have been taken, should be a fairly complete note revision which may mean scrapping original notes and substituting for them revised and final copy. The second, third and fourth etc. review sessions should take the following form: without referring to final notes, jot down on a piece of paper everything that can be recalled. This should then be checked against the final notes and any corrections or additions to what has been recalled should be made. Both notes and jottings should be in the form of Recall-

Patterned-Note-Taking as explained on page 104.

One of the most significant aspects of proper review is the accumulative effect it has on all aspects of learning, thinking and remembering. The person who does not review is continually wasting the effort he does put in to any learning task, and putting himself at a serious disadvantage.

Each time he approaches a new learning situation his recall of previous knowledge gained will be at a very low ebb, and the connections which should be made automatically will be missed. This will mean that his understanding of the new material will not be as complete as it could be, and that his efficiency and speed through the new material will also be less. This continuingly negative process results in a downward spiral that ends in a general despair of ever being able to learn anything – each time new material is learned it is forgotten, and each time new material is approached it seems to become more oppressive. The result is that many people, after having finished their formal exams, seldom, if ever, approach text books again.

Failure to review is equally as bad for general memory. If each new piece of information is neglected, it will not remain at a conscious level, and will not be available to form new memory connections. As memory is a process which is based on linking and association, the fewer items there are in the recall store, the less the possibility for new items to be registered and connected.

On the opposite side of this coin, the advantage for the person who *does* review are enormous. The more he maintains his current body of knowledge, the more he will be able to absorb and handle. When he studies, the expanding amount of knowledge at his command will enable him to digest new knowledge far more easily, each new piece of information being absorbed in the context of his existing store of relevant information (see fig. 20). The process is much like that of the traditional snowball rolling, where the snowball gets rapidly bigger the more it rolls and eventually continues rolling under its own momentum.

to long term memory

57

Digression: review, mental ability and age

The way in which a person reviews has an interesting connection with popular ideas about the way human mental ability declines with age. It is normally assumed that I.Q. scores, recall ability, ability to see spacial relationships, perceptual speed, speed of judgement, induction, figural relations, associative memory, intellectual level, intellectual speed, semantic relations, formal reasoning and general reasoning etc., etc., etc., decline after reaching a peak at the age of 18 to 25 (see fig. 21a). Valid as the figures produced may be, two important factors must be noted:

   1 The decline over the life-time is little more than 5 to 10

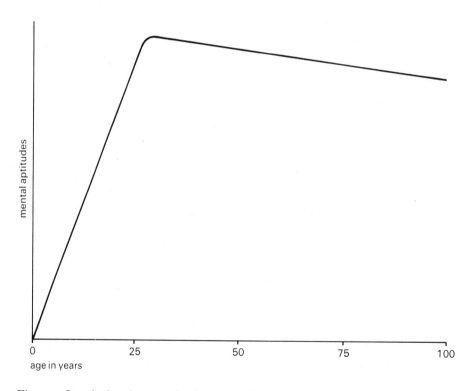

Fig. 21a Graph showing standard results of measuring mental aptitudes as a person gets older. It is assumed that after reaching a peak at approximately 18–25, decline is thereafter slow but steady. See text this page.

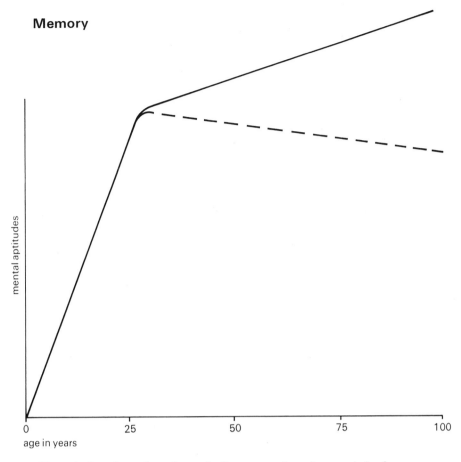

Memory

mental aptitudes

0   25   50   75   100

age in years

Fig. 21b Graphs such as shown in fig. 21a are based on statistics from people taught traditionally. A human being would naturally tend to improve these capacities with age if taught properly.

per cent. When considered in relation to the brain's enormous inherent capacity, this is insignificant.

2 The people who took part in the experiments which arrived at these discouraging figures had been educated traditionally, and therefore in most cases would not have been practising proper learning, reviewing and remembering techniques.

Looking at figure 21a it can be easily seen that such a person's mental 'conditioning' would have been at a very low level for an increasing number of years. In other words his real intellectual capacities would have been in 'cold storage'. It is not surprising that such an unused mind would do slightly worse after 20 to 40 years of mis- or no use – it is surprising that it still manages to do as well as it does!

59

If, on the other hand, the mind were continually used, and its capacities expanded, the effect on the graph for age would be dramatic. This can be seen by taking note of those older people who have remained active and explorative rather than assuming that they were going to get worse as the years passed. Very often their recall is almost total, and their ability to understand and learn new areas of knowledge far surpasses that of equally enthusiastic but younger and less experienced people.

In studying human mental performance it has been mistakenly assumed that the decline found with age is 'natural' and unavoidable. Instead a closer look should be taken at the people being studied, and then experiments should be performed to find out how abilities can be maximised rather than minimised.

Special memory systems—mnemonics (Test 4)

Since the time of the Greeks certain individuals have impressed their fellow men with the most amazing feats of memory. They have been able to remember: hundreds of items backwards and forwards and in any order; dates and numbers; names and faces; and have been able to perform special memory tricks such as memorising whole areas of knowledge perfectly, or remembering decks of cards in the order anyone chose to present them.

In most cases these individuals were using special memorising techniques known as mnemonics. Traditionally these techniques have been scorned as mere tricks, but recently the attitude towards them has begun to change. It has been realised that methods which initially enable minds to remember something more easily and quickly, and then to remember it for much longer afterwards, must be more than simple tricks.

Current knowledge about the ways in which our minds work shows that these techniques are indeed closely connected to the basic ways in which the mind functions. The use of mnemonic techniques has consequently gained respectability and popularity, and they are currently being taught in universities and schools as additional aids in the general learning process. The improvement of memory performances that can be achieved is quite remarkable, and the range of techniques is wide.

There is not enough space in the present chapter to give a complete coverage, but I shall introduce here the basic theory behind the systems, and a simple system for remembering up to ten items.

Let us assume that the items to be remembered are:

1 table
2 feather
3 cat
4 leaf
5 student
6 shoe
7 car
8 pencil
9 shirt
10 poker

In order to remember these it is necessary to have some system which enables us to use the associative and linking power of memory to connect them with their proper number.

The best system for this is the Number-Rhyme System, in which each number has a rhyming word connected to it.

The rhyming key words are:

1 **bun**
2 **shoe**
3 **tree**
4 **door**
5 **hive**
6 **sticks**
7 **heaven**
8 **gate**
9 **vine**
10 **hen**

Memory

In order to remember the first list of arbitary words it is necessary to link them in some strong manner with the rhyming words connected to the numbers. If this is done successfully, the answer to a question such as 'what word was connected to number 5?' will be easy: the rhyming word for 5, 'hive', will be recalled automatically and with it will come the connected image of the word that has to be remembered. The numbers, rhyming words, and items to be remembered can be thought of respectively as the clothes rail, the hangers, and the clothes in a clothes cupboard. (See fig. 22).

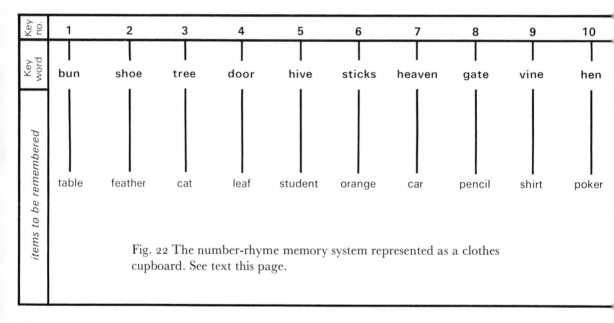

Key no.	1	2	3	4	5	6	7	8	9	10
Key word	bun	shoe	tree	door	hive	sticks	heaven	gate	vine	hen
items to be remembered	table	feather	cat	leaf	student	orange	car	pencil	shirt	poker

Fig. 22 The number-rhyme memory system represented as a clothes cupboard. See text this page.

The important thing in this and all other memory systems is to make sure that the rhyming word and the word to be remembered are totally and securely linked together. In order to do this, the connecting images must be one or many of the following:

exaggerated

The image must be made exceptionally or grotesquely large, or loud, etc.

absurd

Where possible the linked images should form a new image which is humorous or ridiculous.

sexual

If sex can be brought in in anyway, bring it in.

vulgar

Things which are obscene are recalled exceptionally well also!

sensual

As with sex, any of the basic bodily senses will help to form a memorable image.

moving

A moving image usually lasts longer than a static one.

coloured

Coloured as brightly and gaudily as possible.

imaginative

Imaginative in any other way not yet mentioned.

pure

The two items must be linked together with as few other items as possible. Linkages which are too witty, abstract or confused will not help.

It is important, when forming the images, to have a very clear mental picture in front of your inner eye. To achieve this it is often best to close your eyes and to project the image on to the inside of your eyelid.

To make all this clearer, let us try the ten items given.

1 bun   table

Imagine a giant bun on top of a fragile table which is in the process of crumbling from the weight.

2 shoe   feather

Imagine your favourite shoe with an enormous feather growing out of the inside, preventing you from putting your shoe on.

3 tree   cat

Imagine a large tree with either your own cat or a cat you know stuck in the very top branches frantically scrambling about and mewing loudly.

4 door   leaf

Imagine your bedroom door as one giant leaf.

5 hive   student

Imagine a student at his desk, and instead of a book in front of him, imagine an enormous bee hive with bees circling it and occasionally attacking him.

6 sticks   orange

Imagine large sticks puncturing the juicy surface of an orange that is as big as a beach ball.

7 heaven   car

Imagine all the angels sitting on cars rather than clouds.

8 gate   pencil

Imagine a gate made completely out of giant pencils rather than normal wood.

9 vine   shirt

Imagine a vine as large as Jack in the Bean Stalk's bean stalk, instead of leaves on the vine hang it all over with brightly coloured shirts blowing in the wind.

10 hen   poker

Be vulgar!

Now turn immediately to page 66 and fill in as many of the words as you can.

With a little practise it would be possible to remember ten out of ten each time, even though using the same system. The words to be remembered can, like the clothes they were com- ⌐ pared to, be taken off the hook and other clothes substituted. The words which must remain constant and which in any case are almost impossible to forget are the rhyming key words.

As mentioned earlier there are many other systems which are equally as easy to remember as this simple one. Ones which are particularly useful include the Major System, which enables recall of more than a thousand items in the manner of the Number-Rhyme System, as well as giving a key for memorising numbers and dates, and the Face-Name System which helps prevent the embarrassing and wide-spread habit of not being able to recall either the names or faces of people you have met.

Key words and concepts in remembering

As you will have gathered throughout the development of this chapter, memory is primarily an associative and linking process which depends in large part on key words and key concepts properly imagined.

Although the chapter entitled Memory is coming to an end the next three chapters on Key words and Creative pattern linkages are themselves very closely connected with remembering and recalling. The information in this chapter should be reconsidered after the following chapters have been completed.

In the spaces below write the rhyming key word for the Number-Rhyme System, and next to it the words used earlier in the chapter to illustrate the system.

	Rhyming key words	*Word connected*
1		
2		
3		
4		
5		
6		
7		
8		
9		
10		

Personal Notes

Key words – noting

Overview

- Exercise key words; standard responses
- Key words and concepts – creative and recall
- Memory – a comparison between standard note and key word noting
- Transition from advanced key word note taking to advanced creative pattern key word noting

Exercise and discussion

Imagine that your hobby is reading short stories, that you read at least five a day, and that you keep notes so that you will not forget any of them. Imagine also that in order to ensure a proper recall of each story you use a card filing system. For each story you have one card for the title and author, and a card for every paragraph. On each of these paragraph cards you enter a main and a secondary key word or phrase. The key words/phrases you take either directly from the story or make up yourself because they summarise particularly well.

Imagine further that your ten thousandth story is *Kusa-Hibari* by Lafcadio Hearne, and that you have prepared the title-and-author card.

Now read the story on page 69, and for the purpose of this exercise enter a key recall word or phrase for both the main and secondary idea for the first five paragraphs only, in the space provided in table 2, page 72.

68

Kusa-Hibari

His cage is exactly two Japanese inches high and one inch and a half wide: its tiny wooden door, turning upon a pivot, will scarcely admit the tip of my little finger. But he has plenty of room in that cage-room to walk, and jump, and fly, for he is so small that you must look very carefully through the brown-gauze sides of it in order to catch a glimpse of him. I have always to turn the cage round and round, several times, in a good light, before I can discover his whereabouts, and then I usually find him resting in one of the upper corners – clinging, upside down, to his ceiling of gauze.

Imagine a cricket about the size of an ordinary mosquito – with a pair of antennae much longer than his own body, and so fine that you can distinguish them only against the light. Kusa-Hibari, or 'Grass-Lark' is the Japanese name of him; and he is worth in the market exactly twelve cents: that is to say, very much more than his weight in gold. Twelve cents for such a gnat-like thing! . . . By day he sleeps or meditates, except while occupied with the slice of fresh egg-plant or cucumber which must be poked into his cage every morning . . . to keep him clean and well fed is somewhat troublesome: could you see him, you would think it absurd to take any pains for the sake of a creature so ridiculously small.

But always at sunset the infinitesimal soul of him awakens: then the room begins to fill with a delicate and ghostly music of indescribable sweetness – a thin, silvery rippling and trilling as of tiniest electric bells. As the darkness deepens, the sound becomes sweeter – sometimes swelling till the whole house seems to vibrate with the elfish resonance – sometimes thinning down into the faintest imaginable thread of a voice. But loud or low, it keeps a penetrating quality that is weird . . . . All night the atomy thus sings: he ceases only when the temple bell proclaims the hour of dawn.

Now this tiny song is a song of love – vague love of the unseen and unknown. It is quite impossible that he should ever have seen or known, in this present existence of his. Not even his ancestors, for many generations back, could have known anything of the night-life of the fields, or the amorous value of song.

They were born of eggs hatched in a jar of clay, in the shop of some insect-merchant: and they dwelt thereafter only in cages. But he sings the song of his race as it was sung a myriad years ago, and as faultlessly as if he understood the exact significant of every note. Of course he did not learn the song. It is a song of organic memory – deep, dim memory of other quintillions of lives, when the ghost of him shrilled at night from the dewy grasses of the hills. Then that song brought him love – and death. He has forgotten all about death: but he remembers the love. And therefore he sings now – for the bride that will never come.

So that his longing is unconsciously retrospective: he cries to the dust of the past – he calls to the silence and the gods for the return of time . . . . Human lovers do very much the same thing without knowing it. They call their illusion an Ideal: and their Ideal is, after all, a mere shadowing of race-experience, a phantom of organic memory. The living present has very little to do with it . . . . Perhaps this atom also has an ideal, or at least the rudiment of an ideal; but, in any event, the tiny desire must utter its plaint in vain.

The fault is not altogether mine. I had been warned that if the creature were mated, he would cease to sing and would speedily die. But, night after night, the plaintive, sweet, unanswered trilling touched me like a reproach – became at last an obsession, an afflication, a torment of conscience; and I tried to buy a female. It was too late in the season; there were no more kusa-hibari for sale, – either males or females. The insect-merchant laughed and said, 'He ought to have died about the twentieth day of the ninth month.' (It was already the second day of the tenth month.) But the insect-merchant did not know that I have a good stove in my study, and keep the temperature at above 75°F. Wherefore my grass-lark still

70

sings at the close of the eleventh month, and I hope to keep him alive until the Period of Greatest Cold. However, the rest of his generation are probably dead: neither for love nor money could I now find him a mate. And were I to set him free in order that he might make the search for himself, he could not possibly live through a single night, even if fortunate enough to escape by day the multitude of his natural enemies in the garden – ants, centipedes, and ghastly earth-spiders.

Last evening – the twenty-ninth of the eleventh month – an odd feeling came to me as I sat at my desk: a sense of emptiness in the room. Then I became aware that my grass-lark was silent, contrary to his wont. I went to the silent cage, and found him lying dead beside a dried-up lump of egg-plant as gray and hard as a stone. Evidently he had not been fed for three or four days; but only the night before his death he had been singing wonderfully – so that I foolishly imagined him to be more than usually contented. My student, Aki, who loves insects, used to feed him; but Aki had gone into the country for a week's holiday, and the duty of caring for the grass-lark had devolved upon Hana, the housemaid. She is not sympathetic, Hana the housemaid. She says that she did not forget the mite – but there was no more egg-plant. And she had never thought of substituting a slice of onion or of cucumber! . . . I spoke words of reproof to Hana the housemaid, and she dutifully expressed contrition. But the fairy-music had stopped; and the stillness reproaches; and the room is cold, in spite of the stove.

Absurd! . . . I have made a good girl unhappy because of an insect half the size of a barley-grain! The quenching of that infinitesimal life troubled me more than I could have believed possible . . . . Of course, the mere habit of thinking about a creature's wants – even the wants of a cricket – may create, by insensible degrees, an imaginative interest, an attachment of which one becomes conscious only when the relation is broken. Besides, I had felt so much, in the hush of the night, the charm of the delicate voice – telling of one minute existence dependent upon my will and selfish pleasure, as upon the favour of a god –

71

telling me also that the atom of ghost in the tiny cage, and the atom of ghost within myself, were forever but one and the same in the deeps of the Vast of being . . . . And then to think of the little creature hungering and thirsting, night after night and day after day, while the thoughts of his guardian deity were turned to the weaving of dreams! . . . How bravely, nevertheless, he sang on to the very end – an atrocious end, for he had eaten his own legs! . . . May the gods forgive us all – especially Hana the housemaid!

Yet, after all, to devour one's own legs for hunger is not the worst that can happen to a being cursed with the gift of song. There are human crickets who must eat their own hearts in order to sing.

TABLE 2   Key words or phrases for main and secondary ideas from Kusa-Hibari

	main	*secondary*
paragraph 1	_____	_____
paragraph 2	_____	_____
paragraph 3	_____	_____
paragraph 4	_____	_____
paragraph 5	_____	_____

Key words – noting

In table 3 you will find sample key words and phrases from the notes of students who have previously done this exercise. Briefly compare and contrast these with your own ideas.

TABLE 3   Students' suggested key words and phrases

	main	*secondary*
paragraph 1	his cage wooden door ceiling of gauze small insect	two Japanese inches wooden floor plenty of room discover whereabouts
paragraph 2	cricket weight in gold antennae Kusa-Hibari	Grass-Lark twelve cents market gnatlike
paragraph 3	sleep clean and well fed occupied absurd	fresh cucumber pains meditation small
paragraph 4	penetrating music electric bells soul	silvery rippling house vibrating penetrating hour of dawn
paragraph 5	Love amorous the hills Death	night life insect merchant significance love and death

Key words – noting

In the class situation instructors then circled one word from each section:

TABLE 4 *main* *secondary*

paragraph		main	secondary
	1	wooden door	discover whereabouts
	2	weight in gold	market
	3	occupied	pains
	4	penetrating	hour of dawn
	5	love	night-life

Students were then asked to explain why, in the context of the exercise, these words and phrases and not others had been selected. Answers usually included the following: 'good image words', 'imaginative', 'descriptive', 'appropriate', 'good for remembering', and 'evocative', etc.

Only one student in fifty realised why the instructors had chosen these words: in the context of the exercise the series chosen was disastrous.

To understand why, it is necessary to imagine a time some years after the story has been read when you are going to look at the notes again for recall purposes. Imagine that some friends have played a prank, taking out the title cards of some of your stories and challenging you to remember the titles and authors. You would have no idea to start with to which story your cards referred, and would have to rely solely on them to give you back the correct images.

With the key words from table 4 you would probably be forced to link them in the following way: 'wooden door', a general phrase, would gain a mystery-story air when you read 'discover whereabouts'. The next two keys 'weight in gold' and 'market' would confirm this, adding a further touch of intrigue suggesting a criminal activity. The next three key words, 'occupied' 'pains' and 'penetrating' might lead you to

74

assume that one of the characters, perhaps the hero, was personally in difficulty, adding further tension to the ongoing plot as
the 'hour of dawn', obviously an important and suspense-filled
moment in the story, approached. The final two keys, 'love'
and 'night-life' would add a romantic or risqué touch to the
whole affair, encouraging you to thumb quickly through the
remaining key words in search of further adventures and
climaxes! You would have created an interesting new story,
but would not remember the original one.

Words which seemed quite good at the time have not, for
some reason, proved adequate for recall. To explain why, it is
necessary to discuss the difference between key recall words
and key creative words, and the way in which they interact
after a period of time has passed.

A key recall word or phrase is one which funnels into itself
a wide range of special images, and which, when it is triggered,
funnels back the same images. It will tend to be a strong noun
or verb, on occasion being surrounded by additional key
adjectives or adverbs. (See fig. 23).

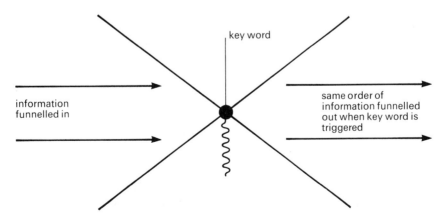

Fig. 23 Diagram representing key recall word. See text this page.

A key creative word is one which is particularly evocative and image-forming, but which is far more general than the more directed key word. Words like 'ooze' and 'bizarre' are especially evocative but do not bring back a specific image. (See fig. 24)

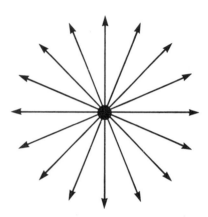

Fig. 24 A key creative word sprays out associations in all directions. See text this page.

Apart from understanding the difference between creative and recall words, it is also necessary to understand the nature of words themselves as well as the nature of the brain which uses them.

Every word is 'multi-ordinate', which simply means that each word is like a little centre on which there are many, many little hooks. Each hook can attach to other words to give both words in the new pair slightly different meanings. For example the word 'run' can be hooked quite differently in 'run like hell' and 'her stocking has a run in it'. (See fig. 25)

In addition to the multi-ordinate nature of words, each brain is also different from each other brain. As shown in the first chapter, the number of connections a brain can make within itself is almost limitless. Each individual also experiences a very different life from each other individual (even if two people are enjoying the 'same experience' together they are in

76

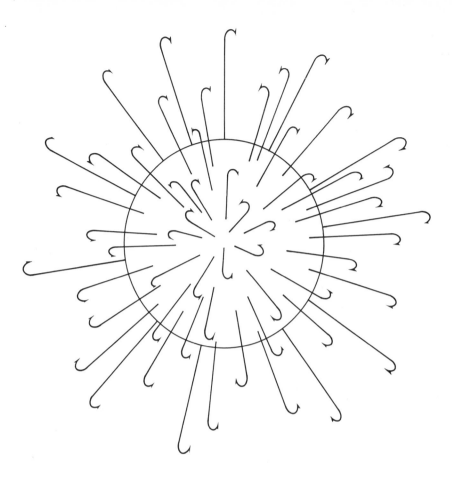

Fig. 25 Each word is multi-ordinate, meaning that it has a large number of 'hooks'. Each hook, when it attaches to another word, changes the meaning of the word. Think, for example, of how the word 'run' changes in different phrase contexts. See text p. 76.

very different worlds: A is enjoying the experience with B as a major part of it, and B is enjoying the experience with A as a major part of it). Similarly the associations that each person will have for any word will be different from everybody else's. Even a simple word like 'leaf' will produce a different series of images for each person who reads or hears it. A person whose favourite colour is green might imagine the general greenness of leaves; someone whose favourite colour is brown, the beauty of autumn; a person who had been injured falling out of a tree, the feeling of fear; a gardener, the different emotions connected with the pleasure of seeing leaves grow and the thought of having to rake them all up when they had fallen, etc. One could go on for ever and still not satisfy the range of associations that you who are reading this book might have when *you* think of leaves.

As well as the unique way in which the mind sees its personal images, each brain is also, by nature, both creative and sense-organising. It will tend to 'tell itself interesting and entertaining stories' as it does for example when we day- or night-dream.

The reason for the failure of the recall and creative words selected from *Kusa-Hibari* can now clearly be seen. When each of the multi-ordinate words or phrases was approached, the mind automatically picked the connecting hooks which were most obvious, most image-producing, or the most sense-making. The mind was consequently led down a path that was more creative than recall based, and a story was constructed that was interesting, but hardly useful for remembering. (See fig. 26).

Fig. 26 Showing how mind can follow the 'wrong connections' in a series of key words. See text this page.

Proper recall words would have forced the mind to make the proper links in the right direction, enabling it to recreate the story even if for all other intentional purposes it had been forgotten. (See fig. 27).

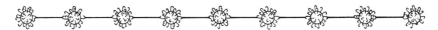

Fig. 27 Direction of correct associations when proper recall key words have been used. See text this page.

Key versus standard notes

The main body of a person's recalling is of this key concept nature. It is not, as is often assumed, a word-for-word verbatim process. When people describe books they have read or places they have been to, they do not start to 're-read' from memory. They give key concept overviews outlining the main characters, settings and events, adding descriptive detail. Similarly the single key word or phrase will bring back whole ranges of experience and sensation. Think for example of the range of images that enter your mind when you read the word 'child'.

How does acceptance of the facts about key recall affect our attitude toward the structure of note taking?

Because we have become so used to speaking and writing words, we have mistakenly assumed that normal sentence structure is the best way to remember verbal images and ideas. Thus the majority of students and even graduates have taken notes in a normal literary fashion similar to the example of a university student whose notes were rated 'good' by his professor. (See page 81).

Our new knowledge of key concepts and recall has shown that in this type of notes 90 per cent of the words are not necessary for recall purposes. This frighteningly high figure becomes even more frightening when a closer look is taken at what happens with standard sentence notes:

1 Time is wasted recording words which have no bearing on memory (estimated waste – 90%).

2 Time is wasted re-reading the same unnecessary words (estimated waste – 90%).

3 Time is wasted searching for the words which *are* key, for they are usually not distinguished by any marks and thus blend in with other non-recall words.

4 The connections between key words are interrupted by words that separate them. We know that memory works by

association and any interference by non recall words will make the connections less strong.

5 The key words are separated in time by intervening words: after one key word or phrase has been read it will take at least a few seconds to get to the next. The longer the time between connections, the less chance there will be of proper connection being made.

6 The key words are separated in space by their distance from each other on the page. As with the point made about time, the greater the distance between the words, the less chance of there being a proper connection.

You are advised to practise key word and phrase selection from any previous notes made during periods of study. It will also be helpful at this point for you to summarise this chapter in key note form.

In addition, reconsider key and creative words in the light of the information in the chapter on Memory, especially the section dealing with mnemonic techniques. Similarly the memory chapter itself can be reconsidered in the light of this chapter, with a similar emphasis on the relationship and similarities between mnemonic systems, key and creative concepts.

The review graph is another important consideration. Review is made much easier when notes are in key form, because less time is expended, and because the recall itself will be superior and more complete. Any weak linkages will also be cemented more firmly in the early stages.

Finally, linkages between key words and concepts should always be emphasised and where possible simple lists and lines of key words should be avoided. In the following chapter advanced methods of key word linking and patterning will be explained in full.

Fig. 28 An example of traditionally 'good' university student's notes. ⟶
See text p. 79.

July 3, 1962.   Psychology 205

Books   James Coleman   Personality Dynamics.
         Shaffer, Shoben   Psych. of Adjustment.

Course Outline
         I Biological Determinants of Behavior ... the genetic
              approach to behavior vs environmental.
I + II {
         II Normal and abnormal behavior.
- III {
         II Social Determinants of behavior ... class etc.
       *III Psychological determinants ... approaches to personality
              dynamics ① Psychoanalysis ... Freud, Jung, Adler.
                              "   in therapy.
                          ② Perceptual Cognitive approach and its
                              approach to psychotherapy and psych change.

BIOLOGICAL DET'S.
         Heredity produces a given organic structure — it is ... impos.
         to separate genetics from environment in analyzing behav.
         — even growth is not entirely genetic.
         there is no way of saying how much heredity or environment
         affects certain facet of the individual.
* Fuller + Thompson — Behav. Genetics.
         Research Methods for separating environ. from heredity.
              ① Study family lines to look for similarities — Family Biography
                 — disadv. ... may all have had same environment.
              ② Study of Twins ... so far the best method
                   (a) compare identical twins (monozygotic) vs fraternal
                       twins (dizygotic): non-similar heredity.
                   (b) co-twin control method — uses only identical twins,
                       having one set raised in same home, the other
                       set raised apart.
              ③ Hold environ. constant to see what will happen to
                 kids of diff. inheritance — Placing kids in foster-
                 homes, and comparing the diff. in its two homes.
INTELLIGENCE with growth and environ
         A. '37 — Newman — compared Binet I.Q. of identical twins in same home,
            with other ident. twins in separate homes. A correlation of
            .67 between separated pairs ∴ genet. influence strong;
            — the correlation was .91 ∴ diff was because of environment.

Personal Notes

Brain patterns for recall and creative thinking

Overview

- Exercise
- Linear history of speech and print
- Contrast: the structure of the brain
- Advanced note taking and patterning techniques

Exercise

In the space below, and starting immediately after having reached the end of this paragraph, prepare a half-hour speech on the topic of Space Travel. Allow no more than five minutes for the task, whether or not you have finished. This exercise will be referred to later in the chapter, before which time the problems experienced in performing the task should also be noted here.

- Space travel notes

Why — Adventure more basic needs)
Where : was in know of the universe
History of what has been done + is being done
Future of possibilities
Results — results — broadening etc

- Problems experienced

Deciding what to say
how to organize
arranging logically

83

Linear history of speech and print

For the last few hundred years it has been popularly thought that man's mind worked in a linear or list-like manner. This belief was held primarily because of the increasing reliance on our two main methods of communication, speech and print.

In speech we are restricted, by the nature of time and space, to speaking and hearing one word at a time. Speech was thus seen as a linear or line-like process between people. (See fig. 29).

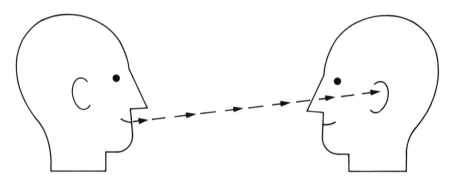

Fig. 29 Speech has traditionally been seen as a list-like affair. See text this page.

Print was seen as even more linear. Not only was the individual forced to take in units of print in consecutive order, but print was laid out on the page in a series of lines or rows.

This linear emphasis overflowed into normal writing or note-taking procedures. Virtually everyone was (and still is) trained in school to take notes in sentences or vertical lists. (Most readers will probably have prepared their half-hour speech in one of these two ways, as shown in fig. 30).

The acceptance of this way of thinking is so long-standing that little has been done to contradict it.

Recent evidence shows the brain to be far more multi-dimensional and pattern making, suggesting that in the speech/print arguments there must be fundamental flaws.

84

Fig. 30 Standard forms of 'good' or 'neat' notes.

       A. Normal line structure – sentenced-based
       B. Standard list structure – order-of-importance-based

See text p. 84.

The argument which says that the brain functions linearly because of the speech patterns it has evolved fails to consider, as do the supporters for the absolute nature of I.Q. tests, the nature of the organism. It is easy to point out that when words travel from one person to another they necessarily do so in a line, but this is not really the point. More to the point is, the question: 'How does the brain which is speaking, and the brain which is receiving the words, deal with them *internally*?'

The answer is that the brain is most certainly *not* dealing with them in simple lists and lines. You can verify this by thinking of the way in which your own thought processes work while you are speaking to someone else. You will observe that although a single line of words is coming out, a continuing and enormously complex process of sorting and selecting is taking place in your mind throughout the conversation. Whole networks of words and ideas are being juggled and interlinked in order to communicate a certain meaning to the listener.

Similarly the listener is not simply observing a long list of words like someone sucking up spaghetti. He is receiving each word in the context of the words that surround it. At the same time he is also giving the multi-ordinate nature of each word his own special interpretation as dictated by the structure of his personal information patterns and will be analysing, coding and criticising throughout the process. (See fig. 31).

You may have noticed people suddenly reacting to words you liked or thought were harmless. They react this way because the associations they have for these words are different from your own. Knowing this will help you to understand more clearly the nature of conversations, disagreements and misunderstandings.

The argument for print is also weak. Despite the fact that we are trained to read units of information one after each other, that these are presented in lines and that we therefore write and note in lines, such linear presentation is not necessary for understanding, and in many instances is a disadvantage.

The mind is perfectly capable of taking in information which

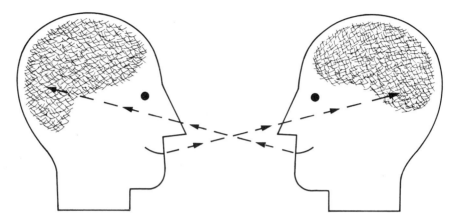

Fig. 31 It is the network inside the mind, and not the simple order of word presentation, which is more important to an understanding of the way we relate to words. See text p. 86.

is non-linear. In its day-to-day life it does this nearly all the time, observing all those things which surround it which include common *non*-linear forms of print: photographs, illustration, diagrams, etc. It is only our society's enormous reliance on linear information which has obscured the issue.

The brain's non-linear character is further confirmed by recent biochemical physiological and psychological research. Each area is discovering that the organism is not only non-linear but is so complex and interlaced as to defy description.

The brain and advanced noting

If the brain is to relate to information most efficiently the information must be structured in such a way as to 'slot in' as easily as possible. It follows that if the brain works primarily

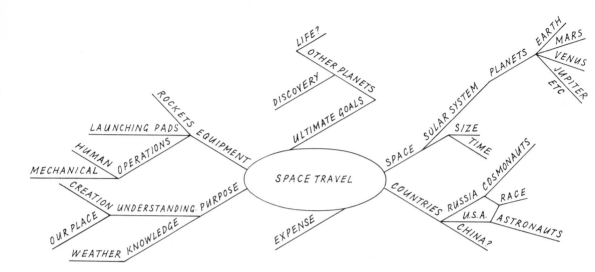

Fig. 32 Initial ideas jotted around a centre. See text pp. 87/8.

with key concepts in an interlinked and integrated manner, our notes and our word relations should in many instances be structured in this way rather than in traditional 'lines'.

Rather than starting from the top and working down in sentences or lists, one should start from the centre or main idea and branch out as dictated by the individual ideas and general form of the central theme. (See fig. 32).

A pattern such as that outlined in fig. 32 has a number of advantages over the linear form of note taking.

1 The centre or main idea is more clearly defined.

2 The relative importance of each idea is clearly indicated. More important ideas will be nearer the centre and less important ideas will be near the edge.

3 The links between the key concepts will be immediately recognizable because of their proximity and connection.

4 As a result of the above, recall and review will be both more effective and more rapid.

5 The nature of the structure allows for the easy addition of new information without messy scratching out or squeezing in, etc.

6 Each pattern made will look and be different from each other pattern. This will aid recall.

7 In the more creative areas of note making such as essay preparations etc., the open-ended nature of the pattern will enable the brain to make new connections far more readily.

In connection with these points, and especially with the last one, you should now do an exercise similar to your space travel speech notes at the beginning of this chapter, but this time using a creative pattern rather than the more linear methods.

In the space provided on page 91 branch out in the manner indicated in figure 32 in preparation for a speech on 'Environmental Problems'. While doing this exercise a number of things should be noted.

Brain patterns for recall and creative thinking

1 Words should be printed in capitals. For reading-back purposes a printed pattern gives a more photographic, more immediate, and more comprehensive feed-back. The little extra time that it takes to print is amply made up for in the time saved when reading back.

2 The printed words should be on lines, and each line should be connected to other lines. This is to guarantee that the pattern has basic structure.

3 In creative efforts of this nature the mind should be left as 'free' as possible. Any 'thinking' about where things should go or whether they should be included will simply slow down the process. The idea is to recall everything your mind thinks of around the central idea. As your mind will generate ideas faster than you can write, there should be almost no pause – if you do pause you will probably notice your pen or pencil dithering over the page. The moment you notice this get it back down and carry on. Do not worry about order or organisation as this will in many cases take care of itself. If it does not a final ordering can be completed at the end of the exercise.

Start the exercise now.

Although this first attempt at patterning may have been a little difficult, you will probably have noticed that the experience is quite different from that of the first exercise, and that the problems too may have been quite different.
Problems often noted in the first exercise include;

order	organisation
logical sequence	time distribution
beginning	emphasis of ideas
ending	mental blocking

ENVIRONMENTAL
PROBLEMS

These problems arise because people are attempting to select the main headings and ideas one after the other, and are attempting to put them into order as they go – they are trying to order a structure of speech without having considered all the information available. This will inevitably lead to confusion and the problems noted, for new information which turns up after the first few items might suddenly alter the whole outlook on the subject. With a linear approach this type of happening is disruptive, but with the pattern approach it is simply part of the overall process, and can be handled properly.

Another disadvantage of the list-like method is that it operates against the way in which the brain works. Each time an idea is thought of it is put on the list and forgotten while a new idea is searched for. This means that all the multi-ordinate and associative possibilities of each word are cut off and boxed away while the mind wanders around in search of another new idea.

With the pattern approach each idea is left as a totally open possibility, so that the pattern grows organically and increasingly, rather than being stifled.

You might find it interesting to compare your efforts so far with the efforts of three school children. (See figs. 33 to 35).

Figure 33 shows the normal writing of a fourteen-year-old boy who was described as reasonably bright, but messy, confused, and mentally disorganised. The example of his linear writing represents his 'best notes' and explains clearly why he was described as he was. The pattern of English which he completed in five minutes shows almost completely the reverse, suggesting that we can often misjudge a child by the method in which we require him to express himself.

7) SETTING   Time + places in which the novel is situated

8) IMAGERY   the kind of images the author uses to describe (usually by simile or metaphor)

9) SYMBOLISM   one thing stands for another
The witches in Macbeth signifying evil

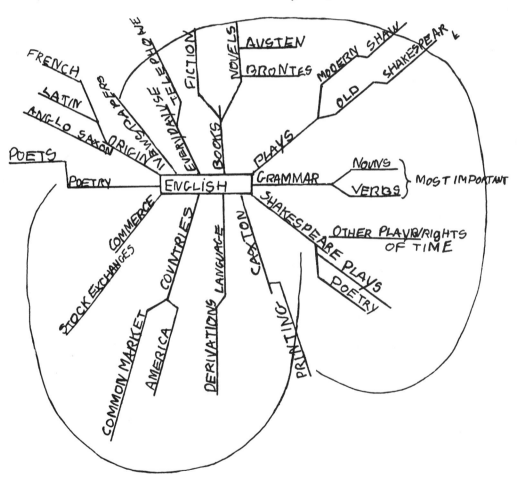

Fig. 33 The 'best notes' in linear writing of a 14 year-old boy, and his pattern notes on English. See text p. 92.

Figure 34 is the pattern of a boy who twice failed O level Economics and who was described by the teacher as having enormous thinking and learning problems combined with an almost total lack of knowledge of his subject. The pattern, which also was completed in five minutes, shows quite the reverse.

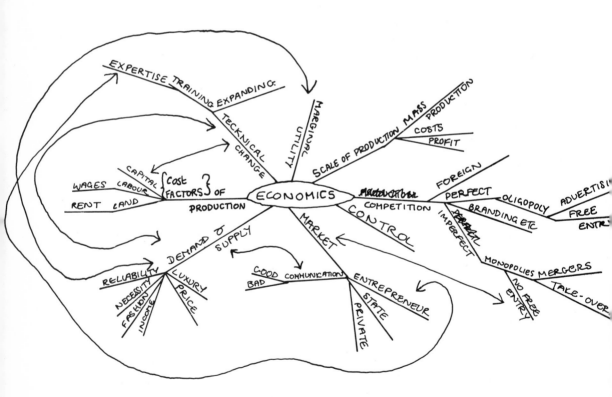

Fig. 34 Pattern by a boy who twice failed O level Economics. See text this page.

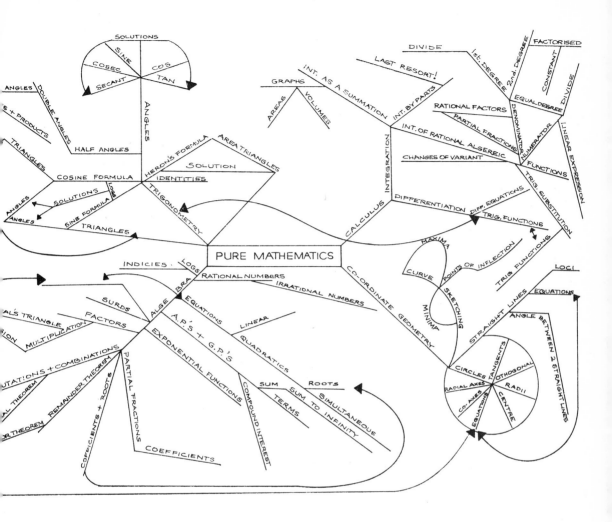

Fig. 35 Pattern by an A level grammar school girl on pure Mathematics. See text this page.

Figure 35 is a pattern done by an A Level grammar school girl on pure Mathematics. When this pattern was shown to a Professor of Mathematics he estimated that it was done by a University Honours student and that it probably took two days to complete. In fact it took the girl only twenty minutes. The pattern enabled her to display an extraordinary creativity in a subject which is normally considered dry, dull and oppressive. Her use of form and shape to augment the words will give an indication of the diversity possible in these structures. The following chapter extends this idea.

Personal Notes

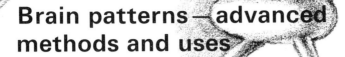

Brain patterns—advanced methods and uses

Overview

- Models for the brain
- Technology and new insights into ourselves
- Advanced brain patterning techniques
- Wider application of patterning techniques

Models of perception—brain—mind

As recently as the 1950s the camera provided the model for our perception and mental imaging: the lens of the camera corresponded to the lens of the eye, and the photographic plate to the brain itself (see fig. 36). This conception was held for some time but was very inadequate. You can confirm this inadequacy

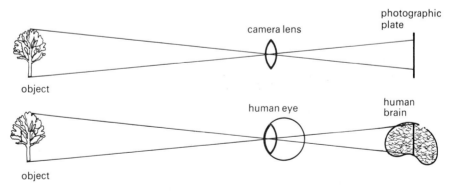

Fig. 36 As recently as 1950 it was thought that the brain operated in ways very similar in part to the camera. See text this page.

97

by doing the following exercises: in the way that one normally does when drowsily day-dreaming, close your eyes and imagine your favourite object. Having clearly registered the image on your inner eye, perform the following activities.

- Rotate it in front of you
- Look at it from the top
- Look at it from underneath
- Change its colour at least three times
- Move it away as if it were seen from a long distance
- Bring it close again
- Make it gigantic
- Make it tiny
- Totally change the shape of it
- Make it disappear
- Bring it back

These feats can be performed without much difficulty; the apparatus and machinery of a camera could not even begin to perform them.

Modern technology

Recent developments in more refined technology have fortunately given us a much better analogy: the hologram.

In this technique, an especially concentrated light or laser beam is split into two. One half of the ray is directed to the plate, while the other half is bounced off the image and then directed back to the other half of the ray. The special holographic plate records the millions of fragments into which the rays shatter when they collide. (See fig. 37) When this plate is

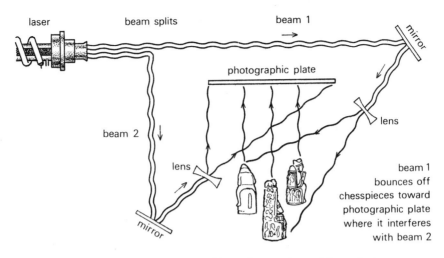

laser   beam splits   beam 1

mirror

photographic plate

beam 2

lens

beam 1
bounces off
chesspieces toward
photographic plate
where it interferes
with beam 2

lens

mirror

Fig. 37 Diagram showing the use of laser beams in making a holo-gram. See text pp. 98/9.

held up in front of laser beams directed at special angles towards it, the original image is recreated. Amazingly, it is not recreated as a flat picture on the plate, but is perfectly dupli-cated as a three-dimensional ghost object that hangs in space. If the object is looked at from above, below or the side, it is seen in exactly the same way as the original object would be seen. (See fig. 38)

Fig. 38 Two photographs of the same hologram. Each photograph has been taken from a different angle, proving the three-dimensional nature of this new and advanced form of photography. For com-parison of holograms with the brain's function, see text pp. 98/9.

Even more amazingly, if the original holographic plate is rotated through 90 degrees, as many as 90 images can be recorded on the same plate with no interference.

And to add still further to the extraordinary nature of this new development, if the plate is taken and smashed to smithereens with a hammer, each particle of the shattered plate will, when it is placed in front of the specially direct lasers, still produce the complete three-dimensional ghost.

The holograph thus becomes a far more reasonable model than the camera for the way in which our brain works, and begins to give us some idea of just how complex an organism it is that we carry about with us.

But even this extremely refined piece of technology falls far short of the unique capabilities of the brain. The holograph certainly approximates more closely the three-dimensional nature of our imaginations, but its storage capacity is puny compared to the millions of images that our brains can call up at an instant's notice, and randomly. The holograph is also static. It cannot perform any of the directional exercises of the kind described on page 98 which the brain finds so easy and yet which must involve the most unimaginably intricate machinery. And even if the holograph were able to accomplish all this, it would not be able to do what our minds can: to see its own self, with eyes closed, performing the operations!

The above gives considerable cause for thought, and even our most advanced sciences have as yet made little progress in this most interesting area of current research.

Advanced brain-pattern noting

Observing that the brain handles information better if the information is designed to 'slot in', and observing also the information from this chapter about the dimensional nature of the mind, it follows that notes which are themselves more 'holographic' and creative will be far more readily understood, appreciated and recalled. ━━━━━━━━━━━━━━━━━━━━━━━━

arrows

These can be used to show how concepts which appear on different parts of a pattern are connected. The arrow can be single or multi-headed and can show backward and forward directions.

codes

Asterisks, exclamation marks, crosses and question marks as well as many other indicators can be used next to words to show connections or other 'dimensions'.

geometrical shapes

Squares, oblongs, circles and ellipses etc. . . . can be used to mark areas or words which are similar in nature – for example triangles might be used to show areas of possible solution in a problem-solving pattern. Geometrical shapes can also be used to show order of importance. Some people, for example, prefer to use a square always for their main centre, oblongs for the ideas near the centre, triangles for ideas of next importance, and so on.

artistic three dimension

Each of the geometrical shapes mentioned, and many others, can be given perspective. For example, making a square into a cube. The ideas printed in these shapes will thus 'stand off' the page.

creativity

Creativity can be combined with the use of dimension by making aspects of the pattern fit the topic. One man, for example, when doing a pattern on atomic physics, used the nucleus of an atom and the electrons that surrounded it, as the centre for his pattern.

colour

Colour is particularly useful as a memory and creative aid. It can be used, like arrows, to show how concepts which appear on different parts of the pattern are connected. It can also be used to mark off the boundaries between major areas of a pattern.

There are many devices we can use to make such notes:

Patterns – use

The nature of patterns is intimately connected with the function
of the mind, and they can be used in nearly every
activity where thought, recall, planning or creativity are
involved. Figure 39 is a pattern of the use of patterns,
showing this wide variety of uses. Detailed explanation
of each of these aspects would of course take up a large
book, but in the remainder of this chapter I
shall explain the application of patterns to
the speech writing, essay writing, examination
type of task; to meetings and communications,
and to note taking.

MENTAL 'DOODLING'
OF MIND FIXATIONS
'GETTING OUT'
COURSE OUTLINE
BACKWARD CHILDREN
PARENT/CHILD
TEACHER/CHILD
RELATIONSHIPS
ALL CLASSROOMS
LECTURING
EXPLANATION

Transforming a pattern to a speech, article etc.

Many people, when first shown patterns, assume that they
cannot be used for any linear purpose, such as giving a talk or
writing an article. Nothing could be further from the truth. If
you refer to the pattern of this chapter (between pages 8/9),
you will find how such a transformation took place:

Once the pattern has been completed, the required information is readily available. All that is necessary is to decide the
final order in which to present the information. A good pattern
will offer a number of possibilities. When the choice is being
made, each area of the pattern can be encircled with a different colour, and numbered in the correct order. Putting this
into written or verbal form is simply a matter of outlining the
major areas to be covered, and then going through them point
by point, following the logic of the branched connections. In
this way the problem of redrafting and redrafting yet again is
eliminated – all the gathering and organising will have been
completed at the pattern stage. Using these techniques at
Oxford University, students were able to complete essays in one
third of the previous time while receiving higher marks.

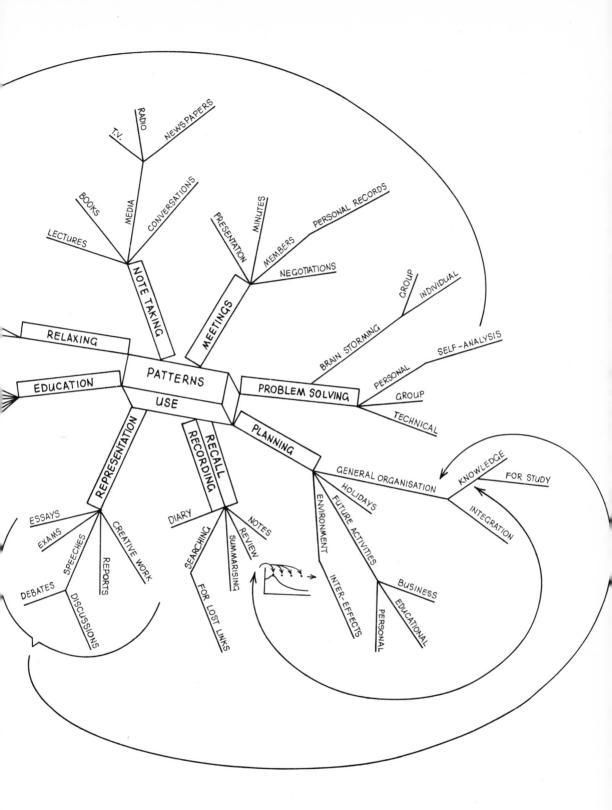

Fig. 39 A pattern on the use of patterns. See text p. 102.

103

Note taking

It is advisable, when taking notes, to have two blank pages ongoing at the same time. The left-hand page should be for patterned information and the right-hand page for more linear or graphic information such as formulas, special lists, and graphs etc. (See fig. 40).

When taking notes, especially from lectures, it is important to remember that key words and phrases are essentially all that is needed. It is also important to remember that the final structure will not become apparent till the end. Any notes made will therefore probably be semi-final rather than final copy. The first few words noted may be fairly disconnected until the theme of the lecture becomes apparent. It is necessary to understand clearly the value of so-called 'messy' as opposed to 'neat' notes, for many people feel apprehension at having a scrawly, arrowed, non-linear page of notes developing in front of them. 'Neat' notes are traditionally those which are organised in an orderly and linear manner. (See fig. 30 in the previous chapter.) 'Messy' notes are those which are 'untidy' and 'all over the page'. (See fig. 41). The word 'messy' used in this way refers to the *look* and not to the *content*.

In note taking and creative patterning it is primarily the content and not the look that is of importance. The notes which look 'neat' are, in informational terms, messy. As explained on page 92 the key information is disguised, disconnected, and cluttered with many informationally irrelevant words. The notes which look 'messy' are informationally far neater. They show immediately the important concepts, the connections, and even in some cases the crossing-outs and the objections.

Patterned notes in their final form are usually neat in any case and it seldom takes more than ten minutes to finalise an hour's notes on a fresh sheet of paper. This final pattern reconstructing is by no means a waste of time, and if the learning period has been organised properly will fit in perfectly as the first review. (See pages 55/6 and fig. 20).

104

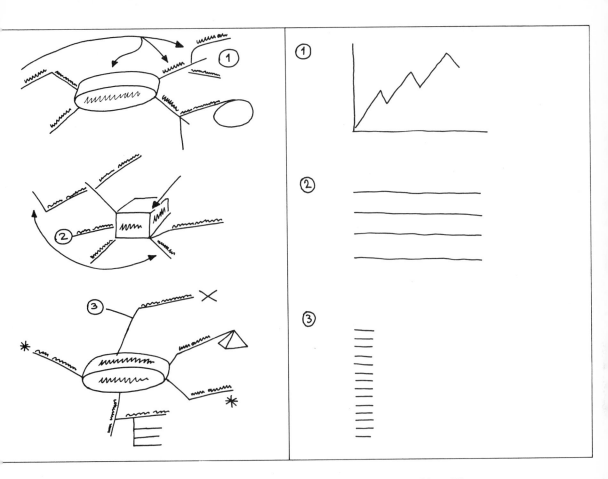

Fig. 40 Showing recommended general form for note taking. Two pages should be used concurrently, one for patterns, the other for graphic or more linear information. These notes may originally 'look messy' but they are in fact neater than traditionally 'neat' notes. See text p. 104.

Communications and meetings

Meetings, notably those for planning or problem solving, often degenerate into situations where each person listens to the others only in order to make his own point as soon as the previous speaker has finished. In such meetings many excellent points are passed over or forgotten, and much time is wasted. A further aggravation is that points which are finally accepted

105

are not necessarily the best, but are those made by the most vociferous or most important speakers.

These problems can be eliminated if the person who organises the meeting uses a creative pattern structure. On a board at the front of the room the central theme of the discussion together with a couple of the sub themes should be presented in basic pattern form. The members of the meeting will have pre-knowledge of what it is about, and will obviously have come prepared. As each member finishes the point he is making, he can be asked to summarise it in key form, and to indicate where on the overall pattern he thinks his point should be entered.

The following are the advantages of this approach:

1 The contribution of each person is registered and recorded properly.
2 No information is lost.
3 The importance given to ideas will pertain more to what was said than to who said it.
4 Digressions and long wafflings will be eliminated because people will be talking more to the point.
5 After the meeting each individual will have a patterned record and will therefore not have lost by the following morning most of what is said.

One further advantage of patterns, especially in note taking and communications, is that the individual is kept continually and actively involved in the complete structure of what is going on, rather than being concerned solely with 'getting down' the last point made. This more complete involvement will lead to a much greater critical and analytical facility, a much greater integration, a much greater ability to recall and a much greater overall understanding.

106

<u>Personal Notes</u>

The Organic Study Method: Introduction

The subject of Study is divided into three chapters: Introduction, Preparation, and Application.

Overview

- Problems of 'getting down' to study
- Reasons for the fear and reluctance many people feel when approaching study books
- Problems arising from the use of standard study techniques
- New study techniques

Approaching the study situation – a problem before you start

The Six-O'clock-In-The-Evening-Enthusiastic-Determined-And-Well-Intentioned-Studier-Until-Midnight is a person with whom you are probably already familiar. At 6 o'clock he approaches his desk, and carefully organises everything in preparation for the study period to follow. Having everything in place he next carefully adjusts each item again, giving him time to complete the first excuse: in the morning, he recalls, he did not have quite enough time to read all items of interest in the newspaper. He also realises that if he is going to study it is best to have such small items completely out of the way before settling down to the task at hand.

He therefore leaves his desk, browses through the newspaper and notices as he browses that there are more articles of interest than he had originally thought. He also notices, as he leafs through the pages. the entertainment section. At this point it will seem like a good idea to plan for the evening's first break – perhaps an interesting half-hour programme between 8 and 8.30 p.m.

108

He finds the programme, and it inevitably starts at about 7 p.m.

At this point, he thinks 'well, I've had a difficult day and it's not too long before the programme starts, and I need a rest anyway, and the relaxation will really help me to get down to studying . . . .' He returns to his desk at 7.45 p.m., because the beginning of the next programme was also a bit more interesting than he thought it would be.

At this stage, he still hovers over his desk tapping his book reassuringly as he remembers that phone call to a friend which, like the articles of interest in the newspapers, is best cleared out of the way before the serious studying begins.

The phone call, of course, is much more interesting and longer than originally planned, but eventually the intrepid studier finds himself back at his desk at about 8.30 p.m.

At this point in the proceedings he actually sits down at the desk, opens the book with a display of physical determination, and starts to read (usually page one) as he experiences the first pangs of hunger and thirst. This is disastrous because he realises that the longer he waits to satisfy the pangs, the worse they will get, and the more interrupted his study concentration will be.

The obvious and only solution is a light snack. This, in its preparation, grows like the associative structure of a creative pattern, as more and more tasty items are linked to the central core of hunger. The snack becomes a feast.

Having removed this final obstacle the desk is returned to with the certain knowledge that this time there is nothing that could possibly interfere with the dedication. The first couple of sentences on page one are looked at again . . . as the studier realises that his stomach is feeling decidedly heavy and a general drowsiness seems to have set in. Far better at this juncture to watch that other interesting half-hour programme at 10 o'clock, after which the digestion will be mostly completed and the rest will enable him to really, *really* get down to the task at hand.

At 12 o'clock we find him asleep in front of the T.V.

109

Even at this point, when he has been woken up by whoever comes into the room, he will think that things have not gone too badly, for after all he has had a good rest, a good meal, watched some interesting and relaxing programmes, fulfilled his social committments to his friends, digested the day's information, and got everything completely out of the way so that tomorrow, at 6 o'clock . . . .

The study book is a threat

The above episode is amusing, but the implications of it are significant and serious.

On one level the story is encouraging because, by the very fact that it is a problem experienced by everybody it confirms what has long been suspected: that everyone is basically both creative and inventive, and that the feelings that many have about being uncreative are not necessary. The creativity demonstrated in the example of the reluctant student is not applied very usefully. But the diversity and originality with which we all make up reasons for *not* doing things we should do suggests that each person has a wealth of talent which could be applied in more positive directions.

On another level the story is discouraging because it shows up the wide-spread and underlying fear that most of us experience when confronted with a study text.

This reluctance and fear arises from the examination-based school system in which the child is presented with books on the subjects he is 'taking' at school. He knows that text books are 'harder' than story books and novels; he also knows that they represent a lot of work; and he further knows that he will be tested on his knowledge of the information from the books.

The fact that the type of book is 'hard' is discouraging in itself. The fact that the book represents work is also discouraging, because the child instinctively knows that he is unable to read, note, and remember properly.

But the fact that he is going to be tested is often the most

110

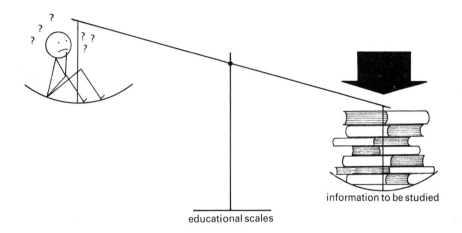

educational scales

information to be studied

Fig. 41 At the present time information is being given more importance and emphasis than the individual. As a result he is being mentally swamped and almost literally 'weighed down' by it all. Both the information and publication explosions are still continuing at staggering rates, while the ability of the individual to handle and study it all remains completely neglected. If he is ever to cope with the situation he must learn not more 'hard facts' but new ways of handling and studying the information—new ways of using his natural abilities to learn, think, recall, create, and solve problems. See also fig. 43 and text p. 115.

serious of the three difficulties. It is well known that this threat can completely disrupt the brain's ability to work in certain situations. The number of cases are enormous of people who literally cannot write anything in an exam situation despite the fact that they know their subject thoroughly – as are the number of cases of people who, even though they are able to write some form of answer, have gigantic mental blocks where whole areas of knowledge are completely forgotten during an exam period. And in even more extreme cases many people have been known to spend a whole two hour period writing frantically, assuming that they were answering the question, but in fact repeating over and over again either their own name or one word.

Faced with this kind of threat, which for many is truly

terrifying, the child has one of two choices: he can either study and face one set of consequences, or not study and face a different set of consequences. If he studies and does badly, then he has proven himself 'incapable', 'unintelligent', 'stupid', a 'dunce' or whatever the appropriate negative expression is at the time. Of course this is not really the case, but he has no way of knowing that in fact it is the system which is not testing him properly.

If he does *not* study, the situation is quite different. Confronted with having failed a test or exam, he can immediately say that of course he failed it because he 'didn't study and wasn't interested in that kind of stuff anyway'.

By doing this, he solves the problem in a number of ways:
1. He avoids both the test and the threat to his self-esteem that studying would involve;
2. He has a perfect excuse for failing;
3. He gets respect from the other children because he is daring to attack a situation which is frightening to them. It is interesting to note that such a child will often find himself in the position of a leader.

It is also interesting to note that even those who do make the decision to study will still reserve a little part of themselves for behaving like the non-studier. The person who gets scores as high as 80 or 90 per cent will also be found using exactly the same excuses for not getting 100 per cent, as the non-studier uses for failing.

Old and new study approaches

The situations described above are unsatisfactory for everyone concerned, and have arisen for various reasons, many of them outlined in earlier parts of this book. One further and major reason for poor study results lies in the way we have approached both study techniques and the information we wanted people to study.

We have surrounded the person with a confusing mass of

different subjects or 'disciplines' demanding that he learn, remember and understand a frightening array under headings such as Mathematics, Physics, Chemistry, Biology, Zoology, Botany, Anatomy, Physiology, Sociology, Psychology, Anthropology, Philosophy, History, Geography, Trigonometry, Paleontology, etc., etc., etc. In each of these subject areas the individual has been and is still presented with series of dates, theories, facts, names, general ideas and so on. (See fig. 42) What this really means is that we have been taking a totally lopsided approach to study and to the way in which a person deals with and relates to the information and knowledge that surrounds him. (See figs. 42 and 43).

As can be seen from the figures we are concentrating far too much on information about the 'separate' areas of knowledge. We are also laying too much stress on asking the individual to feed back facts in pre-digested order or in pre-set forms such as standard examination papers or formal essays

This approach has also been reflected in the standard study techniques recommended in Schools, Universities, Institutes of Further Education and text books. These techniques have been 'grid' approaches in which it is recommended that a series of steps always be worked through on any book being studied. One common suggestion is that any reasonably difficult study book should always be read through three times in order to ensure a complete understanding. This is obviously a very simple example, but even the many more developed approaches tend to be comparatively rigid and inflexible – simply standard systems to be repeated on each studying occasion.

It is obvious that methods such as these cannot be applied with success to every study book. There is an enormous difference between studying a text on Literary Criticism and studying a text on Higher Mathematics. In order to study properly, a technique is needed which does not force the same approach to such different materials.

First, it is necessary to start working from the individual outwards. Rather than bombarding him with books, formulas

113

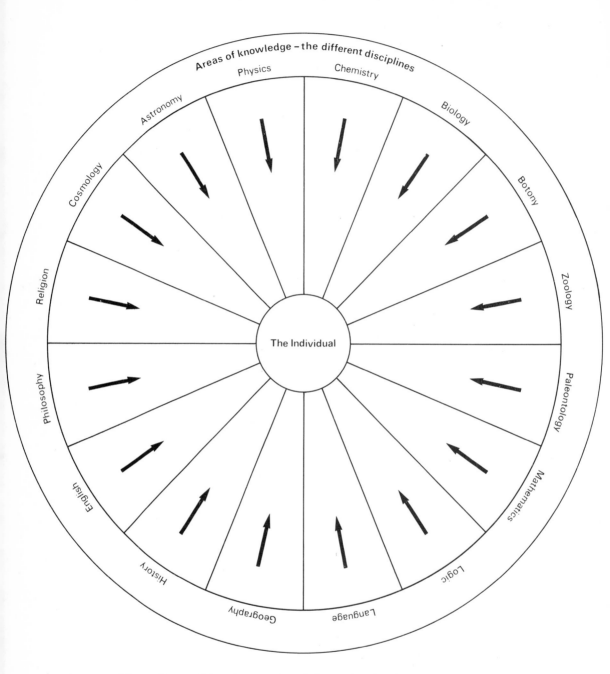

Fig. 42 In traditional education information is given or 'taught' about the different areas of knowledge that surround the individual. The direction and flow is *from* the subject *to* the individual – he is simply given the information, and is expected to absorb, learn and remember as much as he possibly can. See also fig. 41 and text pp. 110/113.

and examinations we must begin to concentrate on teaching each person how he or she *can* study most efficiently. We must teach ourselves how our eyes work when we read, how we remember, how we think, how we can learn more effectively, how we can solve problems and in general how we can best use our abilities, whatever the subject matter.

One is tempted to note here that in our society we have Instruction Manuals and 'How To Do It' booklets on nearly everything, including the simplest of machines. But when it comes to the most complicated, complex, and important organism of all, ourselves, we offer practically no help.

Most of the problems outlined in the first chapter will be eliminated when we finally do change the emphasis away from the subject and information toward the individual and how he can select and understand any information he wants to. People will be equipped to study and remember whatever area of knowledge is interesting or necessary. Things will not have to be 'taught to' or 'crammed in'. Each person will be able to range subjects at his own pace, going for help and personal supervision only when he realises it is necessary. (See fig. 43).

Yet another advantage of this approach is that it will make both teaching and learning much easier, more enjoyable and more productive. By concentrating on the individual and his abilities we will finally and sensibly have placed the learning situation in its proper perspective.

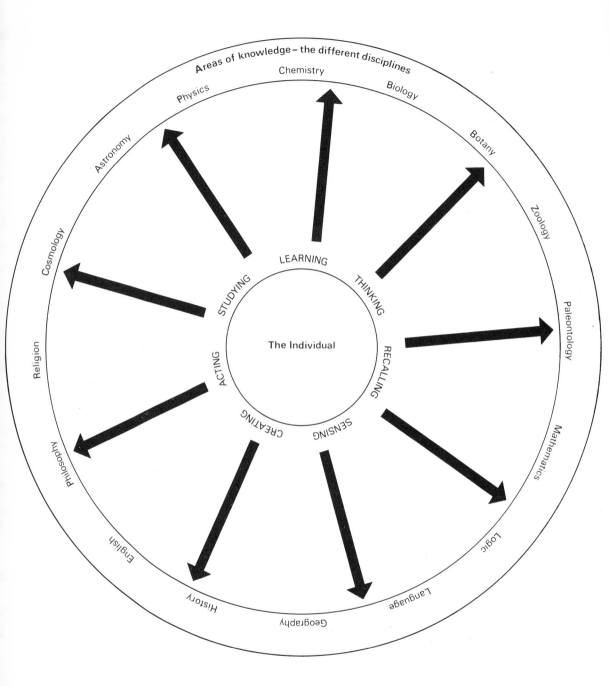

Fig. 43 In the new forms of education, the previous emphases must be reversed. Instead of first teaching the individual facts about other things, we must first teach him facts about himself – facts about how he *can* learn, think, recall, create, and solve problems etc. See text p. 115.

Personal Notes

Personal Notes

The Organic Study Method: Preparation

The Organic Study Method is divided into two main sections: Preparation and Application. Each of these sections is divided into four sub sections:

Preparation   Time
                     Amount
                     Knowledge
                     Questions

Application   Overview
                     Preview
                     Inview
                     Review

It is important to note at the outset that although the main steps are presented in a certain order, this order is by no means essential and can be changed, subtracted from and added to as the study texts warrant.

This chapter will deal with the Preparation section:

Overview

- Deciding on the best use of time
- Defining the areas of study (amount)
- Gathering all the information the reader currently has about the subject
- Defining goals and reasons for studying in the first place

Time and amount

These two aspects can be dealt with together because the theory behind them both is very similar.

The first thing to do when sitting down to study a text book is to decide on the period of time to be devoted to it. Having done this, decide what amount to cover in the time allocated.

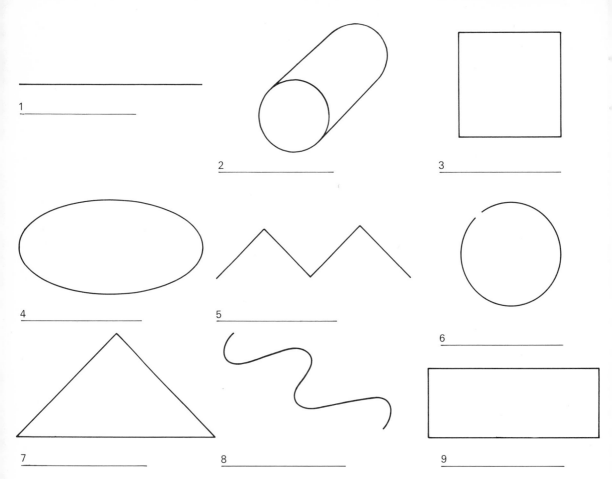

1 _____

2 _____

3 _____

4 _____

5 _____

6 _____

7 _____

8 _____

9 _____

Fig. 44 *Shape recognition*
Enter the name of the shape of each of the items above next to the
appropriate number. See text this page *after* completion.

The reason for insisting on these two initial steps is not
arbitrary, and is supported by the findings of the Gestalt
Psychologists, and some of the most recent findings in Systems
Theory (before reading on, look at figure 44).

The Gestalt Psychologists discovered that the human brain
has a very strong tendency to complete things – thus most
readers will find that they labelled the shapes in figure 44
straight line, cylinder, square, elipse or oval, zig-zag line, circle,
triangle, wavy or curved line, rectangle. In fact the 'circle' is
not a circle but a 'broken circle.' Many actually see this
broken circle as a circle. Others see it as a broken circle but
assume that the artist intended to complete it!

120

A more abstract example of our general desire to complete things is our universal tendency as children to build up a language that helps us to make sense of and form completed ideas of our surroundings.

In study, making a decision about Time and Amount gives us immediate knowledge of the entire terrain, as well as the end point or goal. This has the added advantage of enabling the proper linkages to be made rather than encouraging a wandering off in more disconnected ways.

An excellent comparison is that of listening to a lecturer. A good lecturer who is attempting to expound a lot of difficult material will usually explain his starting and his ending points and will often indicate the amount of time he intends to spend on each area of his presentation. The audience will automatically find his lecture easier to follow because they have guide-lines within which to work.

It is advisable to define the amount to be read by placing reasonably large paper markers at the beginnings and ends. This enables the reader to refer back and forward to the information in the amount chosen.

A further advantage of making these decisions at the outset is that the underlying fear of the unknown is avoided. If a large study book is plunged into with no planning, the reader will be continually oppressed by the number of pages he eventually has to complete. Each time he sits down he will be aware that he still has 'a few hundred pages to go' and will be studying with this as a constant and real background threat. If, on the other hand he has selected a reasonable number of pages for the time he is going to study, he will be reading with the knowledge that the task he has set himself is easy and can certainly be completed. The difference in attitude and performance will be marked.

There are still further reasons for making these time and amount decisions which are concerned with the distribution of the reader's effort as time goes on.

Imagine that you have decided to study for two hours and

that the first half-an-hour has been pretty difficult, although you have been making some progress. At this point in time you find that understanding begins to improve and that your progress seems to be getting better and faster.

Would you pat yourself on the back and take a break?

Or would you decide to keep the new and better rhythm going by studying on for a while until you began to lose the new impetus?

Ninty per cent of people asked those questions would carry on. Of those who would take a break, only a few would recommend the same thing to anyone else!

And yet surprisingly the best answer is to take a break. The reason for this can be seen by referring back to the discussion in the chapter on Memory and the amount that is recalled from a period of learning. Despite the fact that understanding may be continually high, the recall of that understanding will be getting worse if the mind is not given a break, thus the graph, fig. 16, is particularly relevant in the study situation. It is essential that any time period for studying be broken down into 20–40 minute sections with small rests in between. (See fig. 17). The common student practice of swotting five hours at a stretch for examination purposes should become a thing of the past, for understanding is *not* the same as remembering, as all too many failed examination papers give witness.

The breaks themselves are also important for a number of reasons.

1 They give the body a physical rest and a chance to relax. This is always useful in a learning situation, and releases the build-up of tension.

2 They enable recall and understanding to 'work together' to the best advantage.

3 They allow a brief period of time for the just-studied information completely to relate each part of itself to the other part, or to intra-integrate. (See fig. 19).

122

This last point also refers to the Memory chapter and the graph on forgetting as time progresses. During each break the amount of knowledge that can immediately be recalled from the section just studied will increase and will be at a peak as the next section is commenced. This means that not only will more be recalled because the time period itself is best, but also that even more will be recalled because of the rest period.

To assist this even further, do a quick review of what you have read and a preview of what you are about to read at the beginning and end of each study period.

It has taken a number of pages to explain the necessity of deciding on a period of time and on an amount to be covered, but remember that the decisions themselves are extremely brief and will seldom take more than a couple of minutes. When these decisions have been made the next step can be taken:

Noting of knowledge on the subject

Having decided on the amounts to be covered, next jot down as much as you know on the subject as fast as you can. No more than two minutes should be devoted to the exercise. Notes should be in key words and in creative pattern form.

The purpose of this exercise is to improve concentration, to eliminate wandering, and to establish a good mental 'set'. This last term refers to getting the conscious mind filled with important rather than unimportant information. If you have spent two minutes searching your memory banks for pertinent information, you will be far more attuned to the text material, and will be far less likely to continue thinking about the strawberries and cream you are going to have after.

From the time limit of two minutes on this exercise it is obvious that a person's entire knowledge is not required on the pattern – the two minute exercise is intended purely to activate the storage system and to set the mind off in the right direction.

123

One question which will arise is 'what about the difference if I know almost nothing on the subject or if I know an enormous amount?' If knowledge in the area is great, the two minutes should be spent forming a pattern of the major divisions, theories and names etc. connected with the subject. As the mind can flash through information much faster than the hand can write it, all the minor associations will still be mentally 'seen' and the proper mental set and direction will be established. (See fig. 45).

If the knowledge of the subject is almost nothing, the two minutes should be spent patterning those few items which are known, as well as any other information which seems in any way at all to be connected. This will enable the reader to get as close as he possibly can to the new subject, and will prevent him from feeling totally lost as so many do in this situation. (See fig. 46).

Apart from being immediately useful in study, a continued practice with patterning information gives a number of more general advantages. First, the individual gains by gathering together his immediate and current state of knowledge on areas of his interest. In this way he will be able to keep much more up to date with himself and will actually know what he knows, rather than being in a continually embarrassing position of not knowing what he knows – the 'I've got it on the tip of my tongue', 'if only I could make sense of what I know' pattern of behaviour.

In addition this continued practice of recalling and integrating ideas gives enormous advantage in situations where such abilities are essential: examination, impromptu speeches and answering on the spot questions, to name but a few.

Once the two-minute period is up, the next stage should be moved to immediately.

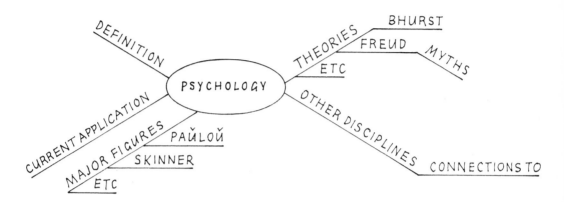

Fig. 45 Knowledge pattern in preparation for study. The studier has some knowledge of the subject before starting. See text p. 124.

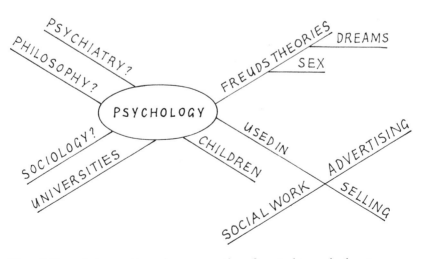

Fig. 46 Knowledge pattern in preparation for study made by a studier with no knowledge of the subject. See text p. 124.

Asking questions—defining goals

Having established the current state of knowledge on the subject, it is next advisable to decide what you want from the book. This involves defining the questions you want answered during the reading. The questions should be asked in the context of goals aimed for and should, like the noting of knowledge, be done in key word and pattern form. Many prefer to use a different coloured pen for this section, and rather than starting a new pattern they add their questions to the already existing pattern on knowledge.

This exercise, again like that for noting knowledge, is based on the principle of establishing proper mental sets. It should also take not much more than two minutes at the outset, as questions can be redefined and added as the reading progresses.

A standard experiment to confirm this approach takes two groups of people who are generally equal in terms of age, education, aptitude etc. Each group is given the same study text and is given enough time to complete either a major section or the whole book.

Group A is told that they are going to be given a completely comprehensive test on everything in the book and that they must study accordingly.

Group B is told that they will be tested on two or three major themes which run through the book, and that they also must study accordingly.

Both groups are in fact tested on the entire text, a situation which one would immediately think unfair to the group that had been told they would be tested only on the main themes.

One might also think that in this situation the second group would do better on questions about the themes they had been given, the first group better on other questions and that both groups might have a similar final score.

To the surprise of many, the second group not only does better on questions about the themes, but they achieve higher total scores which include better marks on all parts of the test.

126

The reason for this is that the main themes act like great grappling hooks through the information, attaching everything else to them. In other words the main questions and goals acted as associative and linking centres to which all other information became easily attached.

The group instructed to get everything had no centres at all to connect new information to, and because of this were groping through the information with no foundations. It is much like a situation where a person is given so much choice that he ends up making no decision; the paradox where attempting to get everything gains nothing.

Asking questions and establishing goals can be seen, like the section preceding it, to become more and more important as the theory behind becomes better understood. It should be emphasised that the more accurately these questions and goals are established, the more able the reader will be to perform well in the Application section of the Organic Study Method.

Personal Notes

Personal Notes

The Organic Study Method: Application

Overview

- Study Overview
- Preview
- Inview
- Review
  a Memory b Note taking c Visual aiding
  d Continuing review techniques

Study Overview

One of the interesting facts about people using study books
is that most, when given a new text, start reading on page one.
It is *not* advisable to start reading a new study text on the first
page. The following situation is a parallel illustration of this
point:

Imagine that you are a leader of a search party which has
been landed in unknown territory in order to search for a
group of friends who are lost somewhere in the wilderness, and
who have had all radio and other communications cut off.
Upon gathering your forces together you find that all maps,
compasses and other materials for locating yourselves have been
lost. All that is known about the surrounding territory is that
it is very rough terrain, being generally forested, and containing hills, mountains, swamps, rivers, a few paths and some
slightly more open areas.

In this situation, and assuming that you were still intent on
locating your friends, what would you do to carry out the task
as easily and efficiently as possible?

The inevitable answer, after having rejected such possibilities
as 'give up' and 'hand over command'! is to send out a few

130

Fig. 47 In the figure above, the patrol group is searching for the lost friends. If it is imagined that the patrol group have just been dropped in the terrain, and have themselves lost all maps and compasses etc., what must their leader first do in order to carry out the mission most effectively and easily? The answer is connected to the reason given for *not* starting to read a study text on the first page (Why not?). See text pp. 130, 132.

reconnaissance scouts. Their function being to provide the rescue patrol with all information necessary for overcoming difficulties and finding the most accessible path to your friends.

It should now be clearer why it is not advisable to commence studying on page one, which would be similar to leading all your troops in what seemed to be the best initial direction, with the chance of them all ending up in the swamp.

The difficult study situation can be likened to this example and should be approached similarly: the patrols can be seen as your brain with its varying skills; the lost friends as your studying goals; the mountains and hills as especially difficult areas of text; the swamps as bad literary style; the open spaces as easier passages; and the rivers and paths, as the more direct ways of getting the special information you want.

This illustrates that the most reasonable approach for study texts, especially difficult ones, is to get a good idea of what's in them before charging head-first into a learning catastrophe.

The overview is designed to perform this task. It may be likened to having a helicopter's eye-view of the terrain you are about to cover. It is a reasonably comprehensive covering of the outline of a book. This means that all material not in the regular body of the print should be covered and includes:

back cover   tables   table of contents

marginal notes   illustrations   capitalised words

photographs   subheadings   dates

italics   graphs   footnotes   statistics

The function of this is to provide you with a good knowledge of the graphic sections of the book, not skimming the whole thing, but selecting specific areas for relatively comprehensive coverage. (See fig. 48).

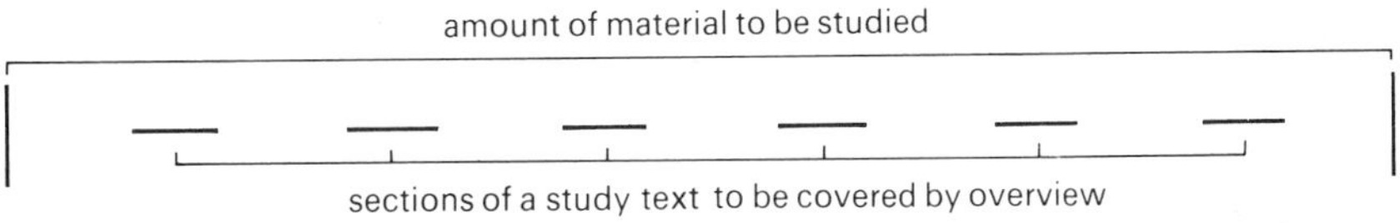

amount of material to be studied

sections of a study text to be covered by overview

Fig. 48 Sections of a study text to be covered by overview. See text p. 132.

It is extremely important to note that throughout the overview a pen, pencil, or other form of visual guide should always be used.

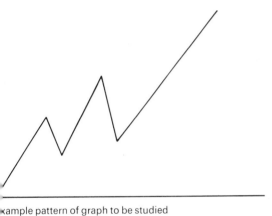

xample pattern of graph to be studied

The reason for this can best be explained by reference to a graph. If the eye is unaided, it will simply fixate briefly on general areas of the graph, then move off, leaving only a vague visual memory and an interference to that memory because the eye movement will not have 'registered' the same pattern as the graph.

If a visual aid is used, the eye will more nearly approximate the flow of the graph and the memory will be strengthened by each of the following inputs:

1 The visual memory itself.
2 The remembered eye movement approximating the graph shape.
3 The memory of the movement of the arm or hand in tracing the graph (Kinaesthetic memory).
4 The visual memory of the rhythm and movement of the tracer.

standard pattern of unguided eye movement on graph causing conflicting memory of shape of graph

Fig 49

133

The overall recall resulting from this practice is far superior to that of a person who reads without any visual guide. It is interesting to note that top accountants often use their pens to guide their eyes across and down columns and rows of figures. They do this naturally because any very rigid linear eye movement is difficult to maintain with the unaided eye.

Preview

The second part of study reconnaissance is the preview – covering all that material not covered in the overview. In other words the paragraphed, language content of the book.

During the preview, concentration should be directed to the beginnings and ends of paragraphs, sections, chapters, and even whole texts, because information tends to be concentrated at the beginnings and ends of written material.

If you are studying a short academic paper or a complex study book, the Summary Results and Conclusion sections should always be read first. These sections often include exactly those essences of information that you are searching for, enabling you to grasp that essence without having to wade through a lot of time-wasting material.

Having gained the essence from these sections, simply check that they do indeed summarise the main body of the text.

In the preview, as with the overview, you are not fully reading all the material, but simply concentrating once again on special areas. (See fig. 50)

The value of this section cannot be overemphasised. A case in point is that of a student taught at Oxford who had spent

amount of material to be studied

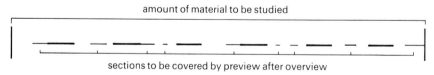

sections to be covered by preview after overview

Fig. 50 Sections to be covered by preview after overview. See text this page.

four months struggling through a 500-page tome on psychology. By the time he had reached page 450 he was beginning to despair because the amount of information he was 'holding on to' as he tried to get to the end was becoming too much – he was literally beginning to drown in the information just before reaching his goal.

It transpired that he had been reading straight through the book, and even though he was nearing the end, did not know what the last chapter was about. It was a complete summary of the book! He read the section and estimated that had he done so at the beginning he would have saved himself approximately 70 hours in reading time, 20 hours in note-taking time and a few hundred hours of worrying.

In both the overview and preview you should very actively select and reject. Many people still feel obliged to read everything in a book even though they know it is not necessarily relevant to them. It is far better to treat a book in the way most people treat lecturers. In other words if the man is boring skip what he says, and if he is giving too many examples, is missing the point or is making errors, select, criticise, correct, and disregard as appropriate.

Inview

After the overview and preview, and providing that still more information is required, inview the material. This involves 'filling in' those areas still left. It is *not* necessarily the major reading, as in some cases most of the important material will have been covered in the previous stages. (See fig. 51).

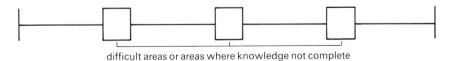
difficult areas or areas where knowledge not complete

Fig. 51 Sections covered after inview has been completed. See text this page.

It should be noted from fig. 51 that there are still certain sections which have been left incomplete even at the inview stage. This is because it is far better to move *over* particularly difficult points than to batter away at them immediately from one side only. They are seldom essential to that which follows them, and the advantages of leaving them are manifold:

1 If they are not immediately struggled with, the brain is given that most important brief period in which it can work on them subconsciously. (Most readers will have experienced the examination question which they 'can't possibly answer' only to find on returning to the question later that the answer pops out and often seems ridiculously simple.)

2 If the difficult areas are returned to later, they can be approached from both sides. Apart from its obvious advantages, considering the difficult area in context also enables the brain's automatic tendency to fill in gaps to work to greater advantage.

3 Moving on from a difficult area releases the tension and mental floundering that often accompanies the traditional approach. (See fig. 52)

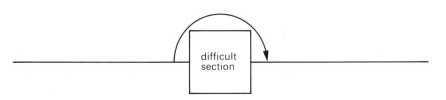

Fig. 52 'Jumping over' a stumbling block usually enables the reader to go back to it later on with more information from 'the other side'. The block itself is seldom essential for the understanding of that which follows it. See text this page.

An adjunct to this last point is that it tends to make studying a more creative process:

Looking at the normal historical development of any discipline, it is found that a fairly regular series of small and logically connected steps are interrupted by great leaps forward.

The propounders of these giant new steps have in many cases 'intuited' them, and afterwards been met with scorn. Galileo and Einstein are examples. As they then explained their ideas step by step, others gradually and progressively understood, some early in the explanation, and others as the innovator neared his conclusion.

In the same manner in which the innovator jumps over an enormous number of sequential steps, and in the same manner in which those who first realised his conclusions did so, the studier who leaves out small sections of study will be giving a greater range to his natural creative and understanding abilities. (See fig. 53)

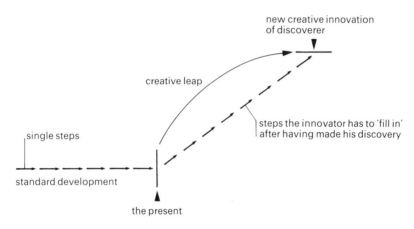

Fig. 53 Historical development of ideas and creative innovations. See text this page.

During the inview initial preparations for note taking should be made. These should include a marking of the previously mentioned difficult areas, as well as areas which the reader considers might be worthy of note.

The marking can be made with a very soft pencil in the margin of the text, and should be in the form of a straight line

137

next to noteworthy material, and a
curving line next to material to be
reconsidered etc. If the pencil is soft
enough, and if a very soft rubber is
used, the damage to the book will be
less than caused by the average
thumb. (See fig. 54).

Fig. 54 Marking text

straight line
mark for
important or
noteworthy
material

curved line
mark for
difficult or
unclear
material

Review

Having completed the overview, preview and inview, and if
further information is still required, a review stage is necessary.

In this stage simply fill in all those areas as yet incomplete,
and reconsider those sections marked as noteworthy. In most
cases it will be found that not much more than 70 per cent of
that initially considered relevant will finally be used.

This percentage figure indicates why note taking is left to
the last stage: it is difficult to take notes on something one does
not know about, and one cannot have knowledge of a section or
chapter until it has been completed.

Taking notes at the end of study also avoids those inherent
dangers encountered by the person who takes notes as he goes
along. For example, you may confront a note from the author
explaining that everything up to page 50 in his book can be
summarised 'in the following few sentences' after ten or so
pages of notes have been taken!

The note taking should be a structure in the form explained
on page 104. In study it is especially advisable to keep a large
central pattern of the subject area growing in conjunction
with the new and smaller patterns from various readings.

This central pattern will obviously be relatively general, but
will serve a number of functions:

1 It will give you an immediate, up to date and comprehensive overview of your current knowledge.

138

2 It will enable you after a reasonable amount of basic study, to see just where the areas of confusion in your subject are, and to see also where your subject connects with other subjects. As such it will place you in the creative situation of of being able to: integrate the known; realise the relevance to other areas; and to make appropriate comment where confusion and debate still exist.

Apart from the immediate review a continuing review programme is essential, and should be constructed in the light of the knowledge we have concerning memory as discussed in the chapter on Memory.

It was seen then that memory did not decline immediately after a learning situation, but actually rose before levelling off and then plummetting. (See fig. 55)

This graph can be warped to your advantage by reviewing just at that point where the memory starts to fall. A review here, at the point of highest memory and integration, will keep the high point up for another one or two days and so on as explained on page 55, see also fig. 56.

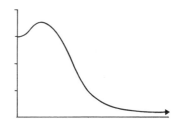

Fig. 55 Graph showing that memory actually rises after learning, before declining sharply.

Fig. 56 This graph shows how quickly forgetting takes place after something has been learned. It also shows how review can 'warp' this graph to enormous advantage. See text this page.

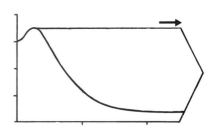

The Organic Study Method:
summary

The entire Organic Study Method must be seen not as a step by step progression, but as a series of inter-related aspects of approaching study material. It is quite possible to switch and change the order from the one given here. The amount to be covered may be decided upon before the period of time; the subject matter may be known before the time and amount are decided upon and consequently the knowledge spray pattern could be completed first; the questions can be asked at the preparation stage or after any one of the latter stages; the overview can be eliminated in books where it is inappropriate, or repeated a number of times if the subjects were mathematics or physics. (One student found that it was easier to read four chapters of post-degree mathematics 100 times quickly using the survey technique, than to struggle through one formula at a time. He was of course applying to its extreme, but very effectively, the point made about skipping over difficult areas); a preview can be eliminated or broken down into separate sections; and the inview and review can be variously extended or eliminated.

In other words each subject, and each book of each subject, can be confidently approached in the manner best suited to it. To each book you will bring the knowledge that whatever the difficulties, you possess the fundamental understanding to choose the appropriate and necessarily unique approach.

Study is consequently made a personal, interactive, continually changing and stimulating experience, rather than a rigid, impersonal and tiresomely onerous task.

It should also be noted that despite the apparently greater number of 'times the book is being read', this is *not* the case. By using the Organic Study Method you will be on average reading most sections once only and will then be effectively reviewing those sections considered important. A pictorial representation can be seen in fig. 57.

Fig. 57 'Number of times' book is covered using Organic Study Method. See text p. 140.

Fig. 58 'Number of times' book is covered using traditional 'once through' reading techniques. See text pp. 140/1.

By contrast, the 'once through' reader is *not* reading it once through but is reading it an enormous number of times. He thinks he is reading it through once only because he takes in one piece of information after another. He does not realise that his regressions, back-skipping, re-reading of difficult sentences, general disorganisation and forgetting because of inadequate review, result in an actual reading of the book or chapter as many as ten times. (See fig. 58)

As you approach the end of *Use both sides of your brain* you will be realising that it is not the end, but the real beginning. By now you will have built up a basic structure of the book from which you can construct a pattern of the new information you have acquired. Review this from time to time relating it to aspects of your study and personal life.

141

Bibliography

Adams, J. A. *Human Memory*. McGraw-Hill, 1967.

Alexander, F. M. *The Resurrection of the Body,* selected by E. Maisel. Delta Books, 1971.

Alexander, F. M. *The Use of the Self*. Methuen, 1920 (o.p.).

Bergamini, D. *The Universe*. Time-Life Books, 1968.

Bono, E. de. *Children Solve Problems*. Harper & Row, 1974.

Brown, G. S. *Laws of Form*. Julian Press, 1972.

Buzan, A. *Speed Reading*. Warner Books, 1972.

Cohen, D. *The Learning Child*. Wildwood House, 1973 (paperback).

D'Arcy, P. *Reading for Meaning*. 2 vols. Hutchinson Educational, 1973.

Einstein, A. *Relativity*. Crown Publishers, 1961 (paper edition, Peter Smith).

Encyclopaedia Britannica, 24 volumes E. B., latest edition 1973.

Eyken, W. van der. *The Pre-School Years*. 2nd rev. edn. Penguin Books, 1969.

Farb, P. *Ecology*. Time-Life Books, 1970.

Freire, P. *Pedagogy of the Oppressed*. Seabury, 1971 (paperback).

Gattegno, C. *What We Owe Children*. Avon Books, 1971.

Hall, J. F. *The Psychology of Learning*. J. B. Lippincott, 1966.

Harris, E. E. *Hypothesis and Perception*. Humanities Press, 1970.

Henry, J. *Essays on Education*. Random House, 1972.

Hoggart, R. *The Uses of Literacy*. Oxford University Press, 1970 (paperback).

Holt, J. *How Children Fail*. Pitman, 1964.

Huxley, A. *The Doors of Perception*. Harper & Row, 1964.

Illich, I. D. *Deschooling Society*. Harper & Row, 1971.

———. *Celebration of Awareness*. Calder and Boyars, 1971.

Julesz, B. *Foundations of Cyclopean Perception*. University of Chicago Press, 1971.

Klee, P. *The Thinking Eye*. Wittenborn, 1973.

Lapp, R. E. *Matter*. Time-Life Books, 1969.

Luria, A. R. *The Man with a Shattered World*. Basic Books, 1972.

Maslow, A. H. *Towards a Psychology of Being*. Van Nostrand Reinhold, 1968.

———, ed. *Motivation and Personality*. 2nd edn. Harper & Row, 1970.

McCulloch, W. S. *Embodiments of Mind*. M.I.T. Press, 1965.

Moore, R. *Evolution*. Time-Life Books, 1969.

Neill, A. S. *Summerhill*. Hart, 1960.

Neumann, J. von. *The Computer and the Brain*. Yale University Press, 1958.

Newson, J. and E. *Infant Care in an Urban Community*. Aldine House, 1963.

Nourse, A. E. *The Body*. Time-Life Books, 1966 (n.e. paperback, 1969).

Pfeiffer, J. *The Cell*. Time-Life Books, 1965 (n.e. paperback, 1970).

Postman, N. and Weingartner, C. *Teaching as a Subversive Activity*. Delacorte, 1969 (Dell paperback).

Razzell, A. G. *Juniors: Postscript to Plowden*. Penguin Books, 1968.

Reimer, E. *School Is Dead*. Doubleday, 1972.

Rudolph, M. and Mueller, C. *Light and Vision*. Time-Life Books, 1972.

Saint-Exupery, A., de. *The Little Prince*. Harcourt Brace Jovanovich, 1968 (paperback).

Sandstrom, C. I. *The Psychology of Childhood and Adolescence*. Penguin, 1975.

Sawyer, W. W. *Introducing Mathematics*, vol. 1, *Vision in Elementary Mathematics*. Penguin Books, 1964.

Schaff, A. *Introduction to Semantics*. Pergamon Press, 1962.

Starling, E. H. and Evans, Sir Charles. *Principles of Human Physiology*, edited by H. Davson and M. G. Eggleton. 13th edition. Churchill, 1962.

Suzuki, S. *Nurtured by Love*. Exposition, 1969.

Tanner, J. M. and Taylor, G. R. *Growth*. Time-Life Books, 1967.

Tolansky, S. *Revolution in Optics*. Penguin Books, 1968.

Vaizey, J. *Education for Tomorrow*. Penguin Books, n.e. 1970.

Wilson, J. R. *The Mind*. Time-Life Books, 1969.

Wilson, M. *Energy*. Time-Life Books, 1965 (paperback, 1969).

Winnicott, D. W. *The Child, the Family and the Outside World*. Penguin Books, 1964 (paperback, 1975).

Yates, F. A. *The Art of Memory*. University of Chicago Press, 1966.

Dutton Paperbacks of Related Interest

SELF-HYPNOSIS IN TWO DAYS, Freda Morris
CREATIVE ANALYSIS, Richard Samson and Albert Upton
STATES OF CONSCIOUSNESS, Charles Tart

144

PENGUIN BOOKS

Portraits of the RIVIERA

New Zealander Carolyn McKenzie was first drawn to Italy in the 1970s. She has lived in the regions of Calabria and Piemonte, and moved to her present home in Ventimiglia Alta, on the coast, in Liguria's extreme west, in 1997.

Thanks to an enthusiastic team of builders, renovating her new home perched in the town's medieval ramparts was great fun. Teaching English part-time left Carolyn free to explore her slice of the Riviera, and her fascination with the Roman and medieval periods, with the quirky and the eerie, and her love of train travel have taken her to many of the Riviera's more out-of-the-way destinations. When she isn't teaching, travelling or writing, Carolyn enjoys pottering in her miniature garden in the ramparts, and welcoming guests from all around the world.

Portraits
of the
RIVIERA

Carolyn McKenzie

PENGUIN BOOKS

PENGUIN BOOKS

Published by the Penguin Group

Penguin Books (NZ) Ltd, cnr Airborne and Rosedale Roads, Albany,
Auckland 1310, New Zealand

Penguin Books Ltd, 80 Strand, London, WC2R 0RL, England

Penguin Group (USA) Inc., 375 Hudson Street, New York, NY 10014,
United States

Penguin Books Australia Ltd, 250 Camberwell Road, Camberwell,
Victoria 3124, Australia

Penguin Books Canada Ltd, 10 Alcorn Avenue, Toronto,
Ontario, Canada M4V 3B2

Penguin Books (South Africa) (Pty) Ltd, 24 Sturdee Avenue, Rosebank,
Johannesburg 2196, South Africa

Penguin Books India (P) Ltd, 11, Community Centre, Panchsheel Park,
New Delhi 110 017, India

Penguin Books Ltd, Registered Offices: 80 Strand, London, WC2R 0RL,
England

First published by Penguin Books (NZ) Ltd, 2004

1 3 5 7 9 10 8 6 4 2

Copyright © Carolyn McKenzie, 2004
Copyright © photographs Carolyn McKenzie, 2004

Designed by Mary Egan
Typeset by www.eganreid.com
Printed in Australia by McPherson's Printing Group

ISBN 0 14 301911 2

A catalogue record for this book is available
from the National Library of New Zealand.

www.penguin.co.nz

Contents

Maps   7

Acknowledgements   9

Introduction   11

PART ONE: But why Ventimiglia?

1 Darkness and light   23

2 So why not Ventimiglia?   33

3 Just a little bit more   45

4 Good omens and a trip to Sainte-Agnès   57

5 Renovations begin   71

6 Tiles unlimited   81

PART TWO: On and beyond the Riviera

7 The citrus fruit festival in Menton   87

8 The pine cone villages of the Nervia valley   96

9 Cervo – gateway to the Riviera of Flowers   106

10 Green vegetable pie   113

11 Perinaldo – reaching for the stars   119

12 Triora – in memory of witches past   124

13 Spring in the hanging gardens   131

14 The Battle of the Flowers and the Hanbury
Botanic Gardens   141

15 A walk around Ventimiglia Alta   148

16 Sospel – on the salt route   155

17 The Valley of Wonders and the Valley
of Fontanalba   164

18 Places in the sun   181

19 Taking the train   192

20 A long way from St Petersburg   210

21 The Route Napoleon – the return of an emperor   217

22 The Massif de l'Esterel – bandit country   232

23 Odd jobs   240

Postscript   244

Practicalities   246

References   251

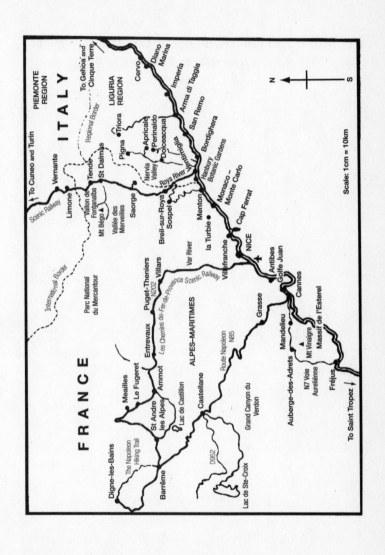

This book is dedicated to GD and M
with love and thanks

Acknowledgements

THANK YOU VERY MUCH – *GRAZIE MILLE* – *Merci beaucoup* – to all the friends and people met along the way, who have helped and encouraged me in so many different ways during the researching and writing of this book.

From my old life in Alba, many thanks Piera, Ipi and Riccardo, Nadia, Alison, Annamaria, Marisa, and Brian for their input in choosing and help in actually buying the new house.

From my new life in Ventimiglia, many thanks to the people who welcomed me here: to Rosella, to Michele and all his team, to Marianne, to Mariella who has so patiently put up with me as a neighbour; to Marco and Chiara; to my new friends who have all in their own ways contributed something to this book: to Michele, Yvonne, Barbara, Cristina and Delia; and to all my students who have taken an active interest in this project.

On the other side of the world, in Auckland, a big thank you to my dear Dad for his patience and encouragement and to Raewyn too; to my Aunt Laura for first introducing me to Italy; to Sharon who, as a psychic, *saw* me *surrounded by writing*; and to my agent Ray Richards and his team, to Bernice Beachman and all at Penguin New Zealand, and to Tessa Duder – you have all kept me focused and on course.

In the course of doing my research I have met some lovely people and would especially like to thank them for sharing their enthusiasm for their work, and for their patience: especially Melanie at the Tourist Information Office in Sospel; Franco Ferrero at the Ethnographic Museum in Cervo; Luc Fioretti, excursion guide in the Vallée des Merveilles, and a young lass in La Clappe who made sure my welcome there was much warmer than Napoleon's had been, and all those other people who, even fleetingly, answered my questions and pointed me in the right direction.

As almost all the outings have been researched with the use of public transport, a very big thanks also goes to local bus and train services on the Italian and French Rivieras and hinterland, and in particular to the PACA SNCF and the Chemins de Fer de Provence rail services and to Riviera Trasporti western Ligurian bus company.

Finally, a big thanks to all the people who in the course of the thousands of years of the Riviera's history, whether through art or architecture or simply being *who* they were, have left behind that tantalising, lingering *something special* that makes the Riviera the fascinating place it is today.

Introduction

Which Riviera – and why?

IN THAT PART OF THE NORTHERN MEDITER-
ranean known as the Ligurian Sea, almost 400 kilometres of
coastline separate Saint Tropez in the west from Marinella
di Sarzana in the east. So many kilometres that it seems
improbable that these two coastal towns – the one world-
famous and the other rarely spoken of – can have anything in
common: except that those 400 kilometres curve around in a
wide arc of coastline referred to as 'The Riviera'.

But how can one highly evocative name embrace such a
wide area? Just as all the pieces in a jig-saw puzzle interlock
to make up the complete picture, or as all the colours in the
rainbow merge to give us every hue and tone which an artist's
palette can create, so there are many Rivieras that, piece by
piece, or splash of colour by splash of colour come together
to be *the* Riviera.

True, there is an Italian Riviera and a French Riviera, but geography is only one measure of distinction. In Italy and France alike, there are salty, suntan-oil scented Rivieras for sun and sea holidays. You can choose from long sandy beaches like Laiguelia or Villefranche-sur-Mer; or tiny hidden ones you can reach only on foot or by boat, such as San Fruttuoso or Le Calandre. For those who like pebbly or rocky beaches, and find sand gritty and invasive, there are sandless beaches and coves like the Balzi Rossi and the Calanques of the Corniche de l'Esterel, where you can snorkel about among the rocks.

There are stretches of beach that are free for all, and others where private concession-holders colour the beaches with sun umbrellas and deck-chairs which are hired out by the day or half-day.

In summer the Riviera's public beaches are often so crowded by mid-morning that you have to queue for space just to spread your towel out. The Blue Flag beaches are the ones deemed free of pollution. Even so, when hundreds of people are bathing close together, some of that carefully applied sunscreen washes off and an unappealing oily sheen rises to the surface.

Early in the morning, though, when the sand is still criss-crossed with the webbed prints of seabirds, the sea is clear and clean, and you can swim blissfully with the little fish. By late afternoon too, the beaches are less crowded, even though the sea, the sand and the rocks hold their warmth long into the evening. It's daylight until around 9 p.m., and as the seabirds gather on the beach for the night and the prevailing current carries away any impurities on the surface of the sea, it's a perfect time to take a picnic supper and watch spell-bound as the moon rises over the sea: it's a magical moment when the moon is full. For *après-plage* relaxation, many of the beaches back onto pleasant waterfront promenades where you can stroll or loll at a pavement café or gelateria; in some places you can dine on the pavement overlooking the beach, or even on a restaurant terrace built on stilts above the beach. When the sea is stormy, the waves break right under your feet.

Out of season, from late September to early May, many locals still consider it unwise – dangerous for your health, even – to go swimming. This attitude is gradually being questioned, but for now, those autumn and spring swims and days spent on the beach are the most pleasant of all. In the truly suntrap bays, an invigorating mid-winter dip is a real treat.

But maybe your Riviera isn't just swimming and sunbathing. What about a star-studded Riviera to view from pavement cafés, and from places so fashionable that, to truly savour and dress the part, you need to travel about with a change of clothes for every morning, afternoon and evening of your holiday? This is a Riviera of glitter and glamour, sparkling with names such as St Tropez, Cannes and Portofino. It's a carefully airbrushed Riviera, which earns enough to keep every attractive money-spinner spic-and-span, and any undesirable blemish swept out of sight. Even so, from St Tropez's Vieux Port to Portofino's tiny harbour, it is fun to sit and watch glitz and glamour, trends and tastes – good, bad and absolutely mind-boggling – saunter by. From the Café de Paris facing the Monte Carlo Casino, and from outside the Palais des Festivals in Cannes, the view is just as enticing. During the Cannes Film Festival or the Monaco Grand Prix it isn't all that difficult to meet, and maybe even speak to, someone famous. In Nice, why not treat yourself to afternoon tea at the Negresco Hotel? This pink-domed, *belle époque* beauty is one of Nice's waterfront landmarks. Nowadays its main entrance is from the shoreline Boulevard des Anglais, but when it was built in the very early 1900s, sun and sea weren't considered major attractions and the hotel's main entrance was at what is now the back of the hotel, in the mundane little street behind it. The spacious and elegant lobby opens into the oval Salon Royal: a hotel fitting in every way to the illustrious guests who have graced it over the years. Don't miss the collage of famous faces and the list of famous names that reads like a *Who's Who* of the jetset, politicians, singers, actors and writers, and crowned heads. Everyone is here, from Edith Piaf to Elton John; from Sir Winston Churchill to President Jacques Chirac; from Charlie Chaplin to Omar Sharif.

Further away at the French Riviera's western end lies St Tropez. The road hugs the coastline from St-Raphaël to Ste Maxime. From here it's less than half an hour to St Tropez by boat (or ninety minutes from Cannes in the summer season) and this is perhaps the best way to approach St Tropez. Coming into the tiny harbour, maybe for a moment you can envisage yourself on board one of those jetset yachts. If you must approach St Tropez by road, be prepared during high season to be stuck in a traffic jam as you near the town. Between Ste Maxime and St Tropez lies the Venice-on-the-Riviera-like marina at Port Grimaud. Take the boat trip around the canals and admire the pastel-painted apartments, each with private moorings. It's an entirely man-made marina, the dream of architect and sailor François Spoerry. In 1960 he bought a worthless swampland and turned it into an attractive Provençal leisure port. Complete with walkways and humped bridges, cafés and restaurants, souvenir and craft shops, it's a pleasant and different place to spend a few hours. For an overall view, climb the church tower. Port Grimaud is at the inner end of the Gulf of St Tropez, a narrow tongue of water which St Tropez guards on the southern, seaward end. Because of this unique position, it is the only town on the Riviera that faces north towards the mountains rather than south to the open sea. Its harbour quay is a colourful open-air gallery for local artists, while nearby, housed in a de-consecrated chapel, the Musée de l'Annonciade has a fine collection of modern art, including paintings by Signac (who lived in St Tropez), Mattise, Bonnard and Dufy. Place des Lices hosts a fine Provençal street market on Tuesdays (the only day l'Annonciade is closed) and behind it is a maze of narrow lanes. They end here in a tiny quay where the sea almost laps at the foot of the houses, here in a shady pictur-esque square, or there where the paths lead off uphill to the citadel that overlooks the town, or around the cliffs on the Sentier Littoral to rocky coves and beaches.

Italy's Riviera glamour port is Portofino, a short distance east of Genova. Like St Tropez, it is a frustrating bottleneck for traffic during the summer, so why not take the boat from Rapello or Santa Margherita? It's a short but pleasant trip, and the town is very photogenic as you approach from the sea. The ferry's next stop on from Portofino is San Fruttuoso: this secluded cove can be reached only by boat or on foot; and only by boat if the sea is calm enough for the ferry to approach the jetty. As well as the ferries from Portofino, there is a service from Camogli, around the cliffs to the west, and walks through scented pine woods lead to San Fruttuoso from both these places too. The forest comes down to the backs of the cluster of houses and simple fish restaurants that stand at either end of the Abbey of San Fruttuoso, which strides across the width of the bay. This black-and-white marble Benedictine Abbey was built in AD 984 on the site of an earlier one which had been destroyed by marauding Saracens. Snorkelling and diving is great here too, or if you prefer a more sedate approach, take a trip in a glass-bottomed boat.

There is a Riviera of magnificent museums and art galleries, and the famous names that go with the art. In some villages like St Paul de Vence, Eze, Castillon or Bussana Vecchia, arts and crafts vie for your attention in intriguing little shops that are so small that the goods spill out enticingly onto the pavements. Shopping or just looking, there is a Riviera for you too. For local flavour, where better than the traditional street markets such as in Ventimiglia, Nice or Antibes? You can find seasonal vegetables and fruit, local honeys, cheeses, salamis and olives, herbs and spices galore, or bags and shoes, clothes and tablecloths, Provençal fabrics and household gadgets. In the villages you will find shops selling local products; in the towns and cities, designer boutiques and department stores.

Then, because of the diverse and abundant vegetation, there is a Riviera of Olives, one of Flowers, and another of Palms. There are walking trails between coastal villages along the shorelines, and inland hikes through the woods. The Riviera has all of this to offer.

In fact, the Riviera that is famous worldwide is all of these Rivieras and more. And because they are an attraction in themselves, for the shortest and fleetingest of visits, there is yet another Riviera: one to flit through in a day or two – a 'been there done that' kind of Riviera. Most of all, there are too many Rivieras for just one holiday, unless it's going to last a lifetime and then some, and too many for just one book.

The Riviera of this book is deliberately one to linger over

and to wander through rather than rush. It is a Riviera to reach slowly, on foot or by narrow-gauge or regular train; by village bus, or cruising quietly along narrow roads. A Riviera to savour, spread out below you from a ridge or perched village, or wrapped cloak-like around you, so that you are immersed in the culture and history of its narrow, cobbled alleys and in its scented fields and woods and ancient byways.

It is a Riviera that isn't entirely on the main tourist circuits – you need to make a little effort to reach it. It is yet another Riviera that will welcome you with intriguing history and beguiling legends.

There is a non-riviera Riviera in this book too – a hinterland (*entroterra* in Italian, *arrière-pays* in French) that none the less has its links to the coast; and a non-sparkling Riviera that is, however, far from dull – a mysterious, bewitching place to venture into with eyes wide open. This book's Riviera is largely un-airbrushed; an unashamedly everyday one where what you see today is the way things are today. Delve down into its yesterdays though and perhaps you will find traces of a very different reality.

And because all the Rivieras are embraced by *two* interlocking Rivieras – an Italian one and a French one – most of all this is a book that fans out from the coastal border crossing between Italian Ventimiglia and French Menton, and encompasses destinations that are seldom more than seventy or eighty kilometres away from these two border towns. This book's Riviera is a bi-national, trans-frontier one, a Riviera experience that crosses at will from one country to the other – and back again.

But it isn't a guidebook. It doesn't even attempt to cover all the destinations and tell you a little about each of them in a superficial or telegraphic way. And it doesn't aim to rehash what you already know about the most famous or most well publicised destinations, precisely because you do already know. It is a selection of destinations that can be easily reached in a day – a long and leisurely day – or even from your armchair or a deck-chair in your own garden. It draws you into the heart and origins of the Riviera, to follow in the footsteps of Bronze Age people and Roman colonisers, emperors, bandits and star-gazers, and then leads you – contented, challenged, invigorated: perhaps all three and more – back to the twenty-first century.

So where does this book's Riviera begin or end?

On a clear day the humps of Mont Vinaigre and Pic de l'Ours in the Massif de l'Esterel stand out on the western horizon of the French Riviera as seen from the Franco-Italian border: they are the red-rocked, cork oak-forested western boundary posts of this book. Italy's western-most Riviera is the Riviera dei Fiori, lying within Imperia Province. The enticing medieval coastal village of Cervo, surrounded by pine woods and olive groves, is the eastern limit of the Riviera of Flowers, and this book's eastern boundary post. To the north of Ventimiglia, the 2873-metre Bronze Age sacred mountain peak of Mont Bégo stands out on a clear day as you cross the Roya river. In altitude and latitude it is this book's highest point and northern-most destination.

Living year-round in a medieval border town in Italy, within sight of the skyscrapers of Monte Carlo and within an hour by train of Nice-Côte-d'Azur Airport, is in itself a multi-cultural experience. Days out can be either purely Italian or entirely French-flavoured. Heading north along the international border, they can just as easily be Italian *and* French. Such is the joy of life in a border town. But a foreigner in a medieval Italian town is always being bombarded with FAQs.

To answer them, the first part of this book is threaded through with the replies to 'How did you end up here? But why Ventimiglia? How did you find this house? What was it like when you bought it? What about the renovations? Was it difficult? Was it stressful? How did you find the builder?' The questions roll on and the answers are, I hope, both informative and entertaining. Having read of my experience, if you decide to venture into buying a place in the sun of your own, then I wish you the same good fortune as I had – and a sound roof, because it does rain here sometimes.

If you decide just to read, to visit and to enjoy, then I wish you *Buon Viaggio* and *Bon Voyage*, even if it's simply armchair – or deck-chair – travel.

But why
Ventimiglia?

CHAPTER 1

Darkness and light

BEYOND THE LANDING ON THE FIRST FLOOR, it was dark: pitch-black on black slate stairs. On the first visit to the flat, Angelo from the real estate agency had lit the way with his cigarette lighter. Now there wasn't even that glimmer of flame to guide me. I felt every step forward with the toes of my shoes, my hand groping along the cold stone wall. On each floor, raucous television programmes, audible in spite of sturdy front doors, told me that the neighbours were in. I wished that someone would open their front door or at least turn on their stairwell lighting. And I prayed that no one would open their door and scream with fright when they saw me prowling there.

Angelo had shown me the fourth-floor flat three months before. Since then he had taken me over it several more times. I had also been back alone, like today, to snoop around, standing outside and wondering: to buy or not to buy? A wise purchase, or sheer folly? Some lucky people fall in love at first

23

sight with their place in the sun and buy it in the time that it takes to count the banknotes. Others search and search for that dream home and then know instantly when they've found it. Four months and several visits later, I was still dithering.

The flat's boundary is actually halfway up the stairs between the third and the fourth floors. A dark brown wooden gate opens onto the turn in the stairs, with the front door immediately at the top of the stairs. The fourth floor landing has been incorporated into the flat as its hallway. I had almost reached this gate now, without stumbling, or clattering into a neighbour's umbrella stand. I still had to negotiate the broken fridge which the family on the third floor was using as a storage cupboard. As the fourth floor had been unoccupied for so long, they had taken over the landing. I thought of how to tackle changing that if I did buy the flat. Not only the fridge, full of discarded shoes, but also a clutter of toys, wine flagons, gas cylinders, withered pot plants . . .

High up in the wall on the outside of the stairwell, a tiny, narrow, dusty window let in a pale ray of light. I gazed up through the stair railing and the locked gate at what could become my front door: not a very inspiring sight in the almost-darkness, made even less inviting by the dull brown door itself. No wonder it hadn't been love at first sight. In my mind I tried to see how I could flood this gloomy space with lightness and airiness if I bought the flat: and it was still a very big if.

I turned to considering the neighbours. So far I hadn't met any of them. What about these people on the third floor? Would they mind, after so many years, having someone living above them again, and would they mind having to move that fridge? Earlier in the week Angelo, urging me to come to a decision, had mentioned another tentative buyer, whether real or invented I would never know. It didn't really matter. My summer holiday ended the following Monday. I was just as anxious to decide before then as Angelo was either to get rid of me or to see some of my money.

Maybe I hadn't climbed the stairs so quietly after all. Suddenly the door on the third floor was flung open behind me and a woman about my own age strode out onto the landing. Who was I? What was I doing, hanging about on the stairs?

I spluttered that I was thinking of buying the flat. With a haughty laugh she began haranguing me. If I did buy the flat, she stormed, I could start by repairing the damage to her ceiling. Rain water infiltrated from above!

'Could you show me?' I asked timidly.

'Yes, of course I'll show you,' she snorted. I ventured into a dim, narrow passageway. The walls were papered and the ceiling lined with dark, varnished wood. Two or three very small stains showed at the top of the papering. Bruna, my perhaps-soon-to-be neighbour, said that the water even seeped through to the flat on the floor below her corridor and bathroom. If I didn't believe her, I could go and ring the doorbell downstairs – the doorbell of the woman I had heard referred to as 'the Swiss woman'. Thoughtfully, I retreated to the landing.

With that, Bruna slammed her front door shut and the lock clunked dismissively into place. The problem of shifting the fridge would have to be tackled another day.

Serious doubts began to whirl round in my head. Did water really percolate through from above? How could it? Why hadn't Angelo mentioned it? Could there really be seepage through to the second floor as well? Hardly – but then . . . Maybe I should toss in this crazy dream and go back to living in an anonymous rented flat in a modern part of a town I liked less and less every week.

The medieval town of Ventimiglia Alta held a strategic position in the Genovese Republic. In 1529, to improve the defences of the town, the republic started the construction of the fortified wall that still flanks the western boundary of the town. The main entry and exit to the town, through the western part of the wall, was by way of Porta Nizza, which opened onto Piazza Funtanin and the main road towards the nearest large town of Nice – *Nizza* in Italian. At that time they were separated by olive groves and fishing villages.

Mine is one of the last houses in the Via before you pass under the archway of Porta Nizza. There's a small storage room on the ground floor, with stairs starting up alongside it, snug against the inside of the town wall. The first-floor flat opens off the right of the landing. A small, tatty, old door on the left opens into a long storage space hollowed out of the fortification wall itself. Not so long ago, before everyone had an indoor toilet, the communal loo was in this passage. The second-floor flat also opens off to the right of the landing, while on the left there's a newish wooden door. It opens as a back entrance into a narrow passage that leads into another flat, which is normally reached from the square outside Porta Nizza. This is 'the Swiss woman's' flat: its main area is part of the adjoining building. Bruna's front door, on the third floor, opens on the left of the landing, with her front door immediately above the Swiss woman's back door. Unlike the first two flats, Bruna's is U-shaped, around three sides of the stairwell.

Until the early 1900s the building had only three storeys. The old roofline can still be seen where the tiles jut out between the third and fourth floors, just below the level of the ramparts. In 1908 permission was granted to build on a fourth floor.

This extra storey brought the height of the building up above the ramparts of the fortification wall, with windows facing out to sea over the parapet. The entrance to the new flat was originally off the right of the landing, as on the first and second floors. Later, a tiny narrow bathroom was added, built right in the ramparts themselves and occupying roughly two-thirds of their meagre width. This bathroom, tapering from 120cm at its widest to a metre at its narrowest, was reached by crossing the landing. More recently, the landing was walled in, in a rather makeshift way, using the cheapest possible materials, and a flimsy door was hung at the top of the stairs, so that the landing became part of the flat itself. The remaining third of the width of the ramparts, little more than 50cm wide, serves as a kind of gutter on the outside of the building. Rainwater off the roof of the adjoining house, where the Swiss woman has her flat, flows down this gutter, along the top of the ramparts, and eventually reaches a downpipe further along. The living-room, which faces onto the town's main Via, opens into a long narrow kitchen. End-on to the bathroom, the kitchen continues along the ramparts, fanning out to a width that is just right for a small table on one side of the broad French doors that open onto the ramparts, and a small washing machine on the other side, again with the gutter space behind.

I knew from the times that Angelo had taken me to inspect the flat that the guttering had been lined not so long ago with a tarred sealant, so I was fairly sceptical about there being any sort of seepage through to the third floor. With certain misgivings, though, I rang the back-door bell on the second floor and identified myself as best I could, not even sure if the occupant spoke English or Italian. My reply resulted in mysterious scraping and grunting, after which the lock turned once, twice, three, four times, and then a smiling face peered around the door to greet me. This put Bruna's welcome in the shade. Marianne was squeezed into the corridor, between the half-opened door and the small wardrobe that she'd had to shove aside in order to open the door. Laughing and explaining in a mixture of English, Italian and, to me, incomprehensible Swiss-German, that they didn't normally use that door, she led me into the main part of the house. I told her why I was there and Marianne threw her hands in the air and tossed back her head. 'Oh, là, là!' She had dealt with Angelo too, and there wasn't a more honest real estate agent in all of Ventimiglia. What a relief.

And as for Bruna! Water didn't seep down into Marianne's flat – it poured down, to be caught in a bucket or two, every time Bruna used the bath or the washing machine. Worse still, she had the most intriguing range of delaying tactics to prevent the plumber being let in, at Marianne's expense, to fix the broken pipe. I'd stepped into a battle that had been raging for nearly a year, and remained unsolved in spite of the intervention of lawyers, the fire brigade, the insurance company, the plumber and the builder.

I was lucky to have met Marianne. She and Willy were down from Switzerland for only a few days. She wanted to show me the room that was being inundated. We made our way back along the little passageway and wriggled past the wardrobe and into a slightly widened continuation of the passage. This would eventually be a pleasant sunny reading room, Marianne hoped, but at the moment it was dank and musty, with bowls and buckets strategically placed to catch the water that periodically poured down from Bruna's bathroom directly overhead. The vaulted stone ceiling, as old as the fortifications themselves, glistened with moisture. Marianne was at a loss as to how to solve the problem – owning a holiday home abroad wasn't meant to be this stressful. From the end of this room we went outside through another narrow door onto a sort of walkway over the archway of Porta Nizza, and directly under what would perhaps become my terrace. Solid stone wall on the outer side, a hip-high parapet on the inner side, looking down into the Via. At the far end of the walkway a steep flight of high steps, little more than a handspan wide, took us onto the terrace. A terrace in the ramparts. Another hip-high parapet and some rusty chicken wire netting prevented us from falling into the Via, while a higher parapet formed the outer side of the fortifications. We peered through the loopholes, as the soldiers would have done hundreds of years before. Beyond Piazza Funtanin, directly below us, we admired glimpses of the sparkling blue Mediterranean.

We shouldn't even have been there, on private property. However, the French doors that led from the kitchen to the terrace were securely shuttered and fastened on the inside: we couldn't possibly get into the flat.

I had thought we were alone up there, and turned guiltily as a youngish man appeared at the top of the steps behind us. Mid-thirties, nearly two metres tall; warm, green eyes; a wide, friendly smile; a firm, confident handshake; and a green flannel tartan shirt. Marianne's enthusiastic greeting and introductions followed. So this was Michele. She had already spoken of him in glowing terms. Her builder. He was soon telling me that he could see the terrace in the future, with flowering plants and a desk or two for my students to have their summer lessons outdoors. His vision then inspired me, even though I knew a lot of traffic would pass through Porta Nizza before it became anything like a reality.

Cautiously we made our way back down the steps, along the walkway and through the reading room. Marianne let me out her front door. It was mid-afternoon on Saturday, and Angelo would have left his office for the weekend. I knew that on Monday I would start definite negotiations to buy the flat in the ramparts above Porta Nizza.

I'm an Aucklander, and the sea has nearly always been present in my life. In January 1988, I arrived in Alba, some seventy kilometres south of Turin in land-locked Piedmont. I was starting my new career, teaching English in a private language school. I hadn't expected my stay in Alba to be a long one. I thought I was on my way to China. Three and a half months in China as a tourist in 1987 had enchanted me, and I was keen to return to work there as a teacher. First, though, I had to get some experience. A position came up in Alba, and I arrived there on a freezing cold, foggy day, just three days into the New Year. In the late 1970s I'd lived in a coastal town in Calabria in southern Italy. There the winters are short and mild, and now I was startled in those early days by how quiet Alba was. I hadn't expected anywhere in Italy to be like this. The bitter cold and clinging, damp fog meant that people stayed indoors as much as possible.

Here there was none of the southern Italian street life that I fondly remembered from before, nor the colour of outdoor activity and evergreen vegetation. The washing was hung out of sight indoors to dry. Window boxes and balcony planters were empty and even the houses seemed colourless. Beyond the fog, the hillsides, fields and vineyards were bare and brown, ploughed up ready for the snow that might fall, and the trees were stark with leafless branches. Thankfully this drabness, all surrounding grey and earthy brown, burst open dramatically with the spring, into a landscape of enormous beauty.

For the first few years in Alba, the cycle of a teacher's life passed pleasantly enough: it is a small prosperous market town in the heart of the Piedmontese wine-producing area and I decided to stay on for a while. Until, that is, nearly two years before my forty-fifth birthday. I began to understand that my future wouldn't be in Alba. I had never taken to the hills and mountains the way some people do in Piedmont: they didn't appeal to me so much, either for walking in the spring and summer or for skiing in the winter. My job would never be anything more than it already was. Those long, dreary winters began to dishearten me too. When friends and colleagues wished me 'many happy returns' for my forty-fourth birthday in October, I thought, but said aloud only to my three very closest friends, 'Thanks, but not in Alba!'

To those in the know outside Alba, excitement at the prospect of my leaving there had been catching. A friend in England sent me some money to buy something for the new home that I had yet to find, and on New Year's Day when my Finnish friend Ipi, her husband Riccardo and I drank champagne we toasted the new house, 'wherever it may be'.

If not in Alba, then where? A little at a time I hatched the idea of setting up home where I could offer accommodation to fellow Kiwis on their OE. I would look for my new home somewhere that would appeal to weary travellers and could be easily reached by public transport. A place in the sun.

Over the following months, I mulled over the idea of moving to one of several other towns in Piedmont that I liked far more than Alba. I scrutinised Saluzzo, Pinerolo and Mondovì, ran them through my 'want and don't want' check-list, and rejected all of them.

I widened my search area. One particularly grey February weekend in 1996, I travelled to Ventimiglia and on to Menton, to the annual Fête du Citron, the citrus fair. Luxuriant ever-green foliage and early spring flowers – just imagine, cherry blossoms and daffodils in February – gleamed in the warm sunshine. A bright blue sky set off the stark Maritime Alps. Best of all, the sea looked warm and inviting; a handful of hearty souls were swimming at Menton's Sablette Plage. Piedmont and Alba were suddenly a whole season away. By travelling 172 kilometres south-west, winter had become spring. Before taking the train back to Piedmont, I strolled up to Ventimiglia Alta. Although it was Sunday, Rosella's florist's shop was open. San Valentino was just around the corner. A barrow of rainbow-bright primulas was too beauti-ful to resist.

I returned to Alba clutching two potted primulas in a plastic bag, never imagining that one day Rosella and her sister would be among my students and friends, but knowing for sure that I would leave Piedmont for the western Italian Riviera.

CHAPTER 2

So why not Ventimiglia?

THE THIN CRESCENT OF LAND KNOWN AS Liguria is Italy's north-western coastal region. For roughly 250 kilometres, rugged cliffs alternate with wide-open bays and sandy or pebbly beaches; behind this, terraced hills are backed by the Maritime Alps. Towns are established on strategic outcrops and on those precious patches of flat land where rivers run down to the sea. Ventimiglia is the last town of all before crossing into France. Medieval Ventimiglia Alta clings to a spur above the river delta where Ventimiglia Bassa was established in the late nineteeth century.

I had decided to move to Liguria. Now to find the right spot for me on that 250-kilometre coastline. The big cities and towns were easily crossed off my list, as were the smaller towns where the trains didn't always stop. And as I didn't want to live in the modern part of a town, I was looking for somewhere distinctive, interesting, unusual. A place steeped in history but still humming with life all year round.

Somewhere medieval and yet unashamedly working class. Did it exist?

In a certain major seaside town one sun-drenched Sunday morning in mid-winter, four Yorkshire terriers tugged on their leashes and trotted along the waterfront promenade, four matching doggie jackets and colour-coordinated bows between their ears. Their henna-rinsed signora trotted past me in a fur coat. Faded peeling posters advertising long-forgotten summer fun flapped in the breeze. Beach cafés were boarded up; the few bravely open restaurants were deserted. A winter ghost town. It wasn't cold or stormy – just out of season. Not for me.

Sifting through the remaining coastal towns, I considered my other criteria: economic factors, maintaining contact with my friends in Piedmont, being able to live in Italy and yet have a toe in France. Above all, I longed for somewhere that was distinctive in itself and was set in attractive and interesting surroundings. It isn't difficult to understand why Ventimiglia stood out so clearly as the right choice.

The name 'Ventimiglia' has its origins over 2000 years ago. Then the hillside at the mouth of the Nervia river, the eastern boundary of present-day Ventimiglia, was occupied by the Intemeli, one of the strongest of the ancient Ligurian tribes. Forging their way westwards, the Romans sought to establish an outpost for their empire on the plain at the base of the Intemeli stronghold.

From 180 BC onwards the Intemeli people were absorbed into the Roman settlement, which took its name from them and was known in Latin as Albium Intemelium, 'albi' meaning a settlement on raised ground.

This name, mutating in time to Albintimilium and then to Vintimilium, eventually became modern Ventimiglia. The

Roman settlement, still partially visible in segments beside the railway line, the gas works, and the hospital, was an important one: the last town of the empire proper. Beyond Albium Intemelium, the border was marked by the River Var, near the present-day Nice-Côte d'Azur airport; across the river were 'the provinces', now the French region of Provence. With the decline of the empire, Albintimilium lost its importance. Those few straggling habitants who hadn't set off back to Rome drifted about a kilometre westwards to the bluff above the western banks of the Roya River. A fortified medieval town grew and flourished here, dominating the valley and the mouth of the Roya, facing out to sea like the prow of a great ship. On the south-western sun-drenched flank, the homes of the nobility had fine views down the coast towards Cap Ferrat, Cap d'Antibes and the Massif de l'Esterel.

The steep, north-eastern side of medieval Ventimiglia Alta, being less exposed to the sun, remained down the centuries the working-class side of the town. When the railway arrived in the 1870s, the coastal Nice-Ventimiglia line passed at the foot of Ventimiglia Alta on the northern side. In the 1920s the completion of the Cuneo-Ventimiglia line brought more rail traffic, and again this line curved around towards Ventimiglia station below the northern face of the old town. Later still the motorway crossed the Roya valley – bursting out of one tunnel and then hurtling into another – close to the railway line. That vast, almost sheer wall of workaday medieval housing, drab and grey from so long in the shade, draped with washing flapping from windows and tiny balconies, has become for many travellers their most lasting impression of Ventimiglia.

The transformation from fishing village to tourist resort made the neighbouring towns of Bordighera, San Remo and

Menton first popular wintering places for the well-to-do of northern Europe, and then bustling summer resorts. Ventimiglia attracted its share of holidaymakers and tourists too, but remained relatively unscathed by the demands of mass tourism. By the mid-1900s Ventimiglia Alta had fallen into disrepair, and had then been resettled by Calabrians and Sicilians seeking work in the post-war building boom in southern France. Family disputes, shady dealings in goods with dubious origins, poor sanitation and a disregard for education gave it a bad reputation. Never mind that the next generation managed to claw its way out of poverty and lawlessness, the reputation stuck. The length of Liguria and in the well-to-do towns of Piemonte and Lombardy the reaction was the same: avoid Ventimiglia Alta! Don't go there! None of these people bothered to venture up the hill to check things out. Few tourists dared to either. They'd been warned.

So, although steeped in history and incredibly picturesque, Ventimiglia Alta has miraculously escaped the invasion of a tourism that could have prettied it up to become an attraction. Nor, in favour of modern housing in Ventimiglia's new town, has it fallen completely into decay and abandon. A happy balance has been maintained. The permanent residents go about their everyday lives as they have done for generations, except now they're more law-abiding. Other residents are newcomers: a few are foreigners like myself, others have moved here from other parts of Italy, and even from Ventimiglia itself. Ventimiglia Alta caters for the people who live here: schools and kindergartens, grocery shops and hairdressers, post office, chemist and police station. Holiday-makers and tourists are welcome, and postcards abound, but at the same time discerning visitors will soon realise that they are in a real town with a medieval backdrop, not one that has been spruced up just for their benefit.

I began to make the three-and-a-half-hour train journey through the mountains from Alba to Ventimiglia practically every weekend. Now that my mind was made up I felt optimistic again for the first time in several years. My forthcoming departure from Alba was still top secret. My colleagues sensed the change, noted the frequent trips away to Liguria, and thought I was in love.

One June morning, after a particularly harrowing week at work, I walked into a real estate agency in Ventimiglia. I had arrived in the middle of a power failure, and Teresa was standing out on the footpath, waiting for the office lighting to come back on. She took me to see a house in Ventimiglia Alta. It had only just come onto the market. Perhaps it would have been the last one I looked at, if I had known that it was only the first of twenty or so houses I would see in the months to come. Although I liked this flat's rooftop terrace very much, there were several more practical aspects that were definitely off-putting. Many of the windows were too high up in the walls to see out of, so although the rooms were light and airy, there was no view, and instead, a feeling of being closed in and isolated from the outside. The main bathroom was up a narrow staircase and across the terrace: okay in fine weather, not so good if it was cold or raining. The wet-weather loo was under the stairs, in a cubbyhole opening off the kitchen. Worse still, the house was opposite a bar and very near the cathedral: I imagined disturbed nights from revelry in the bar, early wakenings from the bells. The vendor and her sons, and Teresa and her colleague, seemed anxious to make a sale, but I realised that my funds didn't stretch to buying the place and doing necessary alterations such as relocating the bathroom. And I was keen to have a view. Teresa's comment that I could see the sea by standing on the edge of the bidet wasn't helpful.

Several other agencies didn't have anything to show me at all. I was feeling quite downcast when an ad in the window of Angelo's agency caught my eye. He didn't usually open the office on Saturday: that was his day for working on the Côte d'Azur, selling holiday flats to clients from the landlocked regions of northern Italy. However, he agreed to meet me the following weekend. He said he had a couple of places to show me.

My friend Piera wasn't going to miss this trip to the seaside and we set off from Alba at daybreak. Our appointment was for three o'clock and Angelo arrived punctually: a charming, nattily dressed, ex-army man in his mid-fifties. Pince-nez, stylishly folded cravat and a neat goatee completed his image.

Finding the first property seemed like going through a three-dimensional maze: up a narrow, steep stairway, across a landing, around a corner, up some more, another landing and another corner, some more steps, and all in semi- or total darkness lit by Angelo's cigarette lighter. Why hadn't he brought a torch? So many of the slate steps had semicircular chips out of them. I later learned that these were caused by bumps from the gas cylinders which have to be delivered regularly for cooking and heating if the household hasn't converted to town gas.

The flat was awful, with a pokey, impractical room layout. Milk rotted in a long-abandoned fridge. A small terrace overlooked an alleyway and a school, and was overlooked in turn by the neighbours upstairs.

The second place was the exact opposite. It had an attractively lit stairwell, and had been recently renovated. Our spirits rose at the sea view, although there was no balcony or terrace. It was too expensive, though: I couldn't seriously consider it.

Angelo shrugged resignedly. He'd been working in France since early that morning and it was now going on for 4.30 p.m. He was probably ready to get home and Piera wanted to go back to the beach before we got the train back to Alba. Out in the carpark once more, looking up to a gable end just peeping over the top of the parapet above Porta Nizza, Angelo's disparaging comment was that of course there was always 'that place', but he didn't suppose I'd like it. Why not? As he'd just shown me what I imagined were the two extremes of Ventimigliese real estate, I said I would like to see it. Angelo and Piera exchanged despairing glances, eyes raised towards heaven. Even so, Angelo returned to his office to get the key.

I curiously scanned the building while we waited, and felt quietly excited. Its façade, especially on the lower floors, was in a pretty grim state, with the once-golden plaster flaking off in large chunks, and strung untidily with wires for the electricity, telephone, television aerials, and washing. But at least the flat I was going to see was on the top floor: my days wouldn't be darkened by an upstairs neighbour's sheets, pegged so low on the washing line that they flapped across my windows. I noticed too that the top flat still caught the afternoon sun, while the lower flats were already in the shadow.

With Angelo's return, we started up the stairs in total darkness. His cigarette lighter gleamed fitfully, and sinister shadows leaped around the stairwell. Luckily the steps were in good condition, with newish marble treads to the second floor, and then fine black slate ones. At last we reached Bruna's fridge-cum-cupboard and the brown wooden gate. This feature intrigued me: I'd already seen an indoor gate at the place Teresa had shown me, and I liked the idea of having one of my own.

Angelo wrestled for an age with the ingenious system of handles, clasps and latches to open the gate. Eventually, taking the three of us by surprise, it opened. We were in the turn in the stairs between the third and fourth floors. Then through a flimsy compressed cardboard door, held closed with a latch but no lock: this was the front door. It opened into total darkness once again. We came to a locked door now: in the past this had been the front door, opening off the top of the landing, on the right-hand side. In a bedroom off the passage enormous, elaborately carved wooden beds were flanked by marble-topped bedside cupboards, and an ornate wardrobe loomed out of the shadow of the far corner. It wasn't quite high enough to conceal the stains on the ceiling and on the wall where the roof evidently leaked quite badly. Angelo said he couldn't open the shutters as they were broken and might fall into the street far below.

The living-room, painted pale green, was dominated by a large, black, keyboardless piano: the vendor had been a music teacher. Here Angelo did reluctantly open the shutters: we looked out into the Via, and across the terrace in the ramparts out to sea. Some forlorn, long-forgotten plants struggled to stay alive in pots along the edge of the parapet.

Letting in some light should have created a better impression, but in fact with the shutters open I was even more dismayed by the all-pervading neglect. Loose floor tiles under foot, shabby walls and cracked ceilings, windows and shutters all jammed shut with disuse, and their paint flaking off to the touch. Tatty wire-mesh mosquito nets covered the windows, so full of holes that they wouldn't have kept out a bat, let alone a mosquito.

Worst of all, though, was the electrical system. Clearly it had been installed long ago, before there were stringent safety regulations. Almost all the wiring was external, with the wires tacked onto the walls, or floating free where the tacks had come away. No wonder Angelo hadn't wanted to turn the power on – you don't want your client to get electrocuted on the first visit.

From the living-room we continued into the kitchen. An old enamelled, ceramic double sink, with work surfaces on either side: 1.5 metres long, and the kitchen was just over three metres long in all. Being built right on the ramparts, the kitchen wasn't very wide. At its narrow end it was 1.2 metres, and at the wider end, where French doors opened onto the terrace, 1.7 metres.

Angelo protested against opening the French doors as they were tightly stuck with disuse and salt spray, and shuttered on the outside. In any case I was so shocked by what I'd already seen that I couldn't wait to get out – and I hadn't seen the bathroom yet. Where was it? Maybe there wasn't one. Surely it wasn't out on the terrace too?

Back out on the landing we saw that an ancient door to the left opened into a tiny bathroom, tiled with bright pink walls and a black floor, barely two paces long by less than an arm-span at its wide end where it backed onto the kitchen, and just four-and-a-half 20cm tiles wide at its narrow end. In this confined space there was a dilapidated toilet, a grubby handbasin and a miniature hip-bath in a low-ceilinged alcove. One very small window, which obviously wasn't going to be opened just then, completed the scene.

Stunned by the gloominess of the rooms and the overall state of abandon and disrepair, I scuttled down the stairs and out into sunshine. Angelo seemed despondent as we thanked him for his time and said goodbye. I don't imagine that he ever expected to see me again.

On the beach, Piera and I took stock. The first place we'd seen was awful and expensive; the second was desirable and even more expensive; the last one was awful and cheaper, but would surely need a fortune to renovate. We put all three of them from our minds, and went off to buy an ice-cream.

July and August passed busily in Alba with some summer teaching. I didn't return to Ventimiglia: the sultry heat of a Ligurian summer hardly seemed the best time for choosing my new home. By September I had a week's holiday coming up and I decided to revisit Ventimiglia Alta. I discarded the first two places which Angelo had shown me and drew up a list of pros and cons for reconsideration of the one I'd seen with Teresa. When it came to the third place Angelo had shown me and Piera, I realised I didn't really remember it clearly. It occurred to me now that with some loving attention maybe . . . I couldn't picture the layout of the rooms, and asked Piera what she remembered. She remembered even less than I did, just those scary dark stairs, the green living-room and the sad, neglected plants on the terrace. Were there two bed-rooms or only one very big one? Was the bathroom just across the landing or down some steps as well? We simply couldn't remember.

A friend was over from England and keen to see what I was up to, so I made another appointment with Angelo. The days were cooler now and he didn't seem so weary when we

met him. He'd brought a torch too. Having Marisa with me
was fortunate: I was still prejudiced by my grim memories
from the previous visit, whereas she was seeing the place in a
far more open frame of mind.

As soon as we were inside and Angelo began opening
shutters, we saw that there were two bedrooms: the big one
that I remembered would be ideal for the friends and relatives
who would surely flock to stay with me, and a smaller one
next to it and facing south into Via Garibaldi with a glimpse
of the sea behind: it would suit me fine. Knowing what I was
looking for, Marisa murmured, 'You could do something with
this.' As Angelo finally butted those stubborn full-length
shutters open onto the terrace and we stepped out of the
kitchen onto the ramparts, I felt sure that Marisa was right.
We saw that the bathroom was on the same level as the rest
of the flat: there'd be no tumbling down steps in the night.

But, oh, such a tiny, pokey bathroom, and overall so much
work to do! Could I face it? Angelo made a quick estimate of
how much (or, in real-estate agent speak, how little) I would
need to spend to do basic renovations. I was already thinking
ahead and doubled his conservative estimate – correctly as it
turned out. Angelo's basic scheme didn't, for example, include
completely retiling the floors and putting in central heating
and a totally remodelled bathroom, while mine did. There
were still a lot of fors and againsts to weigh up, but as we said
goodbye to Angelo that evening we were both optimistic. He
showed us a second flat nearby but it only served to highlight
the good points in the place I'd just seen for the second time.
I decided that later in the week I would spend the last few
days of my holiday in Ventimiglia and talk things over very
carefully with Angelo at leisure in his office. Then I'd snoop
about a bit near the house, in the early morning and at night

to get the feel of the environment. Decision time was fast approaching.

CHAPTER 3

Just a little bit more

AS SOON AS HE SAW THAT I REALLY WAS interested, Angelo did everything he could to help me reach a decision. I liked his style: helpful but casual. If he had tried to convince me to buy the flat I would have balked and been suspicious. Instead, he talked about the overall property market, the advantages and drawbacks of buying in the medieval quarter of any town. Above all, he cautioned me that this would be a long-term investment. 'Don't even think of re-selling for at least ten years,' he advised.

Marisa and I had agreed that as far as real estate agents went, he seemed a fairly genuine and trustworthy person. I know Marisa's assessments of human nature: spot on every time. And in fact Angelo would shortly prove himself to be worth his weight in millions of Italian lire.

Provided the purchase didn't require a new roof or a repainted façade just yet, the advantages of buying in the old town seemed to outweigh the drawbacks. Climbing four flights of stairs in a stairwell too old and narrow ever to accommodate a lift didn't deter me. I haven't got a car, so having to park in Piazza Funtanin wasn't a problem either. The national heritage people dictate the colour of window shutters and forbid new windows to be opened in the old façades, but the flat was already well supplied with windows, and what's wrong with flag- and forest-green shutters? In the old town the houses are close together, and the community more close-knit. I could live alone without feeling isolated. Best of all, one storey higher than all the surrounding houses, it would be a treat to have a bird's-eye view of activity in the Via: my own little niche in the fabric of Ventimiglia Alta. I'd be close enough to the new town to walk to the bank and the supermarket and yet almost in the country, with the mountains climbing up behind Piazza Funtanin. A neighbour kept goats on a little plot of land off the lane that led off one side of the Piazza – the country was that close.

During that last week of my summer holiday either Angelo or Fabio, his young offsider, showed me over the flat several more times. It rained and some funny little weeds in a tub on the terrace became a mass of pretty purple flowers. At the same time I was thankful that I'd decided against the place Teresa had shown me months before: dashing across the terrace in a downpour to have a bath wouldn't have been much fun as summer turned to autumn. Fabio even managed to leave me entirely alone in the flat for about half an hour one day, so that I could get the feel of it without distractions. I liked what I felt.

After my encounter with Bruna, Angelo explained that he had personally investigated the water seepage problem in Marianne's flat, and that it was in no way connected with the guttering in the ramparts. He showed me again that the guttering was sealed with tarred building paper, and assured me that it was impossible for water to seep through. He also showed me how the roof had been repaired over the big bedroom, so that even though the wall and ceiling were badly stained, the roof no longer leaked. Finally he backed up his estimate of renovation costs by getting a builder to make out an itemised quote for basic work. All told, looking beyond the makeshift front door, the gloomy entrance way, the loose floor tiles, stained walls and the grime and dust of years of neglect, and stoically doubling the builder's very conservative quote for renovations, I knew that I'd found my new home.

Just four months after the search began, I offered the vendor fifteen per cent less than the asking price and began to dream of renovating, furnishing and redecorating. Negotiations began between the vendor and me, with Angelo as middleman, and the price was agreed to verbally, midway between what I'd offered and what the vendor had originally asked. At this point the standard procedure required me to meet the vendor in Angelo's presence, and hand my cheque for the deposit over to her personally. Before this meeting, Angelo faxed me a copy of the purchase document. I took a real-estate agent friend in Alba into my confidence, and went over the legal jargon with her. Everything was clear enough but, intrigued by what I was doing, Nadia said she'd come with me on the day that I went to pay the deposit.

I was delighted to accept her offer, as I still wasn't a hundred per cent sure about Angelo's impartiality: maybe he was more anxious to make a sale than to protect my interests. So Nadia would be there to keep an eye on him and protect me from any tricks.

I could hardly contain my excitement now. The evening before the big day Angelo phoned me to say that he'd just spoken to the vendor. She was happy about the price, couldn't wait to have finally sold the place. Everything would go really well the next day, he assured me. We would meet at the flat to show Nadia over it and then meet the vendor in Angelo's office at 3.30 p.m.

Back in the flat for the last time before it became mine, Nadia bravely told me she wouldn't buy it even if I paid her to do so – a courageous unbiased opinion that I've never regretted totally disregarding. I didn't even want to know her reasons.

While we waited in his office, Angelo went over the purchase document with us again and impressed upon me not to be persuaded by the vendor to pay any more than what we had already agreed to over the phone. I figured that as a foreigner, and as a single woman, I was probably already paying slightly more than an Italian man would have paid, so I was also determined not to pay anything more than we had agreed.

Angelo does most of his work outside his tiny office so it was a bit of a squeeze around the desk, and anxiety mounted when the vendor didn't arrive punctually. About four o'clock her daughter and son-in-law turned up, apologising for the delay. Her mother was still at home, Franca said. Angelo seemed put out and asked Franca if she had authority to sign on her mother's behalf. No, came the reply. She wouldn't be signing anything as they had talked it over and decided that they wanted more money.

Without looking at me, Franca confidently asked Angelo if, in order to finalise the sale, I would like to put in a little bit more.

My quiet, dismayed 'No' was drowned by Angelo's holler of disbelief as he leaped to his feet, brushing Franca's husband aside, and shouted, 'No!' He filled the mini-office now as he berated Franca, telling her this was no way to treat a customer and that the property was neglected and rundown. Where did they think the flat was? On the Croisette in Cannes? They were lucky to have found a buyer at last. Why, only last night her mother had said . . .

Franca and her husband neither flinched nor protested at Angelo's rage. They remained stone-faced, but bright-eyed with defiance. Eventually, at a pause in Angelo's tirade, Franca admitted that they should have notified me the day before, but in fact they were happy to sell the flat if only I would put in a little bit more. Angelo glared at me. 'Don't you dare,' his eyes said, while tucked away beside me, almost out of sight in the corner, Nadia muttered the same words. For twenty dramatic minutes or so Angelo went on pleading, cajoling, almost begging Franca to accept my offer and to go and get her mother. She kept quietly insisting that all I needed to do was put in a little bit more.

Surely mother wasn't at home, but waiting calmly outside in the car, I thought. I watched and listened, fascinated, and grudgingly even admired Franca: I would have crumpled in the face of Angelo's indignation, but she remained undaunted. Her husband stood quietly to one side. He had no doubt seen Franca do battle before, and probably admired her for it.

Although Angelo and Franca were largely locked into a one-to-one duel, every few minutes I was consulted, only to repeat that I wasn't going to put in any more, as I already believed I was putting in plenty. Finally, I decided to enquire just how much, in Franca's opinion, this 'little bit more' was. Maybe she meant some insignificant token amount that I would gladly throw in to get this ridiculous episode over with. Angelo and Nadia sucked in their breaths. Had I gone completely crazy? 'No!' Nadia moaned in the corner, and Angelo shot me another scathing glare. So much for an agent's impartiality. He'd come down firmly on my side. I hoped Franca and her husband weren't too aware of it. In fact, Franca's 'little bit more' was eight times more than what I'd just been contemplating adding as a gesture of goodwill, so there was no danger of my putting in anything. It seemed that they wanted me to pay some taxes that her mother, the vendor, was required to pay.

'That's illegal! Don't even suggest it in this office!' Angelo stormed. Realising that she was defeated, but still insisting that she hoped there were no hard feelings, Franca scuttled out of the office with her husband in tow before Angelo could physically put them out. Even then I still believed that it was just part of an elaborate charade, and that in a minute mother would come in and say she'd accept my offer.

Angelo knew better. He was almost in tears of rage and frustration at having let me down, and at not having made a sale, and he feared it would be a long time before they came round to accepting my offer, if ever. I was very disappointed, but more than that, angry at what I saw as shoddy treatment on the part of the vendor and her family. In spite of what Angelo said as he locked the office and we went to drown our sorrows at the bar next door, I still thought it was only a matter of waiting a few days for the vendor to have a change of heart in my favour. Anyway, as I had found this flat reasonably easily, if the sale did fall through I would surely find something else.

Luckily my anger and indignation, and conviction that a change of heart was at hand, carried me through the next few days so that I didn't get too despondent. I thought of the sale only as being postponed. As the scene in Angelo's office had been so dramatic and totally unexpected, I also had an entertaining tale to relay to the few friends who were in the know.

Even though Angelo and Fabio and I remained in regular contact with each other, and Angelo contacted the vendor again from time to time, as Christmas approached my optimism began to fade. I had decided to resume the search and in the last weekends of 1996 I scoured the real-estate agencies and ads in the local paper, and saw fifteen or sixteen other properties. From places in dark, damp alleys and places larger and more expensive than I either wanted or could afford, to a gutted shell where an elderly gent had, until his recent death, kept his hunting dogs and ammunition, fishing nets and rabbits in their hutches: from attics, cold in winter and stifling in summer, to ground floor or semi-underground cellars and basements, some still awaiting council permission to be converted into habitations, cool in summer and freezing cold and damp in winter: from urgent or not-so-urgent private sales, including one that jumped fifteen per cent in price as soon as the vendor realised I was a foreign woman on her own, to places that had pride of place on an agency's books. None of them had that key 'everything I want and then something else' that had finally swayed me in favour of that funny little house with its kitchen in the ramparts.

Just before Christmas Fabio showed me a couple of unlikely places which surely neither he nor Angelo can have really thought were what I was looking for. As we came away from the second place I admitted to Fabio that it was really Franca's mother's place that I'd set my heart on. I expected sympathy, or at least an offer to try to contact the vendor yet again and convince her to accept my offer. Instead his terse reply jolted me into reality: 'If you don't offer them more money, somebody else will. I'll let you know the day I see the shutters are open and new curtains in the windows. Then you'll know that someone has bought it!' I decided that that wasn't going to happen. Over the Christmas break I would get down off my high horse, and reconcile myself to 'putting in a little bit more'.

Back on the search in January, Angelo told me that he had had a fairly abrasive encounter with the vendor and she had withdrawn the house from the market and taken away her keys. He no longer knew what her intentions were, and couldn't contact her now that they weren't on speaking terms.

I renewed my contacts with all the other agencies, but there didn't seem to be very much available just then. It seemed I'd already seen all the possibilities before Christmas.

There is an agency down an alley-way in Ventimiglia Bassa and I'd only been there once before Christmas. One Saturday morning in January I called there for the second time. I went over my requirements again and the agent listened carefully. He didn't have anything suitable but perhaps his friend in another agency, right at the eastern end of Ventimiglia, did.

Although I only heard one side of the phone conversation that followed I knew from the details that were repeated for my benefit that I had not only found my dream home, but that it was in fact *my place* back on the market again. My erstwhile vendor had taken her business to the far end of Ventimiglia, as far away from Angelo's agency as possible. I hadn't even visited this agency, as I was sure it wouldn't have anything in Ventimiglia Alta: it was just too far away.

Flavio, from this agency, had valued the property slightly higher than Angelo had, but when I explained what had happened before, he began to negotiate a price with the vendor that was slightly lower than what I had originally

52

agreed to pay several months before. These negotiations went ahead with the discretion of a secret-service operation. Flavio didn't tell her that it was me again: 'a buyer from near Turin' was how he truthfully described me. I stipulated that my final offer really was my final offer this time. I was prepared to meet her midway between Flavio's valuation and my second offer, but not a lira more. In this way I would be paying three million lire more than what I had agreed to pay in November.

While the vendor was making up her mind I saw Michele, who asked me how things were going. I was anxious by now that the vendor might decide that if someone could offer more than I had offered before, then maybe another someone else would offer even more. Or perhaps when she found out that this 'buyer from near Turin' was in fact me, maybe she would expect me to 'put in a little bit more'.

Michele asked me if this was the house I really wanted, and when I nodded, he said that, in that case, it would be worth paying the vendor's price. It was either that, or go through life regretting that I hadn't, and maybe I'd never find another place that was even a poor second-best. Buying a home is too important for compromising, he said. No one else had had the courage to put it into words, but I knew he was right.

During the coming week I was on the phone to Flavio nearly every day to find out if the vendor had accepted my offer. Like me, he was getting quite exasperated with her indecision. It was obvious to him, as it had been to Angelo, that while the vendor, a woman in her seventies, was willing to sell the property, it wasn't easy for her to make the final decision to part with the flat for sentimental reasons. Fair enough. It had been built by her grandfather and, like her parents before her, she had always lived there until ten or so years ago. I understood this, but at the same time, the flat *was* on the market, and presumably a buyer wasn't expected to pay for sentimental value. At the same time, Franca and her husband were clearly holding out for the highest possible price – a large part of the money would go towards a new house they were building. Experts at stalling tactics, they found another hitch: that black, broken piano, trapped in the house because it was too big to go down the stairs. They wondered if the buyer would be prepared to keep the piano in the flat, even after the settlement date, until they could arrange to get a crane to take it out the window. I relayed my reply back through Flavio: if the wretched piano was still darkening my living-room on settlement day I would personally dismantle it, with the aid of an axe rather than a screwdriver, and take it downstairs to the rubbish bins.

A friend from London was visiting me in Alba and I told him in a fit of rage on the Thursday afternoon that I felt like phoning Flavio and withdrawing my still anonymous offer.

'Do it,' he said, and I did.

Well, almost.

I told Flavio that I would withdraw my offer twenty-four hours later if it hadn't been accepted. He backed me up one hundred per cent. 'It's the only way to deal with these people,' he muttered.

Twenty-three hours later the vendor had agreed to accept my final offer. We would meet a week later, in the last weekend in February, to sign the documents and I would pay the deposit. My spirits soared as I went to the bank and ordered the bank cheque.

Finally at 11 a.m. we were all seated in Flavio's office. The great day had arrived. Flavio as middleman was charged with keeping the action moving between myself and my friend Riccardo on one hand, and the vendor, her husband, Franca and her husband on the other. Initially the atmosphere was polite but strained. During the week I had provided Flavio with all the personal details that were needed for preparing the purchase document, including my date of birth, and now he had the document on his desk. Completely unexpectedly, Franca turned to me and smiled. She said that they had just discovered an astonishing fact that surely changed everything. She asked shyly if she might be allowed to mention it.

'We saw the documents, complete with your date of birth,' she explained, 'and guess what? You were born on the very same day, in the very same year, that my parents were married!'

Destiny had surely brought me to that very house. The ice thawed. Even Franca's mother, while understandably a little sad about the sale, managed a wan smile, and the proceedings continued. There was only one small hitch. I had insisted that the document must stipulate that I accepted no responsibility for water damage to Bruna's flat. The vendor and her family threw up their hands in protest! What water? What damage? That woman downstairs!

'We'll have to call the fire brigade, and ask them to investigate,' Franca's husband said.

Flavio suggested that it would be easier to call on Bruna and ask to see the damage. We piled into a couple of cars, drove up to Ventimiglia Alta and rang the doorbell. Bruna was so surprised to see us that she let us into the passageway without any sort of protest. The tiny stains were still there at the edge of the ceiling, no bigger than all those months before, in spite of the winter rains.

Franca's father, by far the most diplomatic of all of us, told Bruna that if she had any complaints to make, she was to make them to him within the next three months, the time it would take to reach settlement date. That was the last any of us heard of the matter. Trooping down the stairs he told us we'd been lucky that Bruna had been so obliging.

All that remained now was to sign the documents and hand over the money. This was quickly done and we were out in the sunshine, the old lady misty-eyed but brave.

We had to wait for the bureaucratic wheels to turn, as foreigners have to be thoroughly vetted before they can own property in a border town in case they are political undesirables or known terrorists – a law hanging over from fascist times. The *nulla osta*, a certificate of no impediment, would take three months to trickle down, by registered mail, from military headquarters 120 kilometres away in Turin, and would cost me a further 200,000 lire. Settlement date had been set for three months hence: 31 May.

CHAPTER 4

Good omens and a trip
to Sainte-Agnès

WITH LITTLE MORE THAN A CENTIMETRE OR two to spare top and bottom, but without breaking the fragile, century-old panes of glass, the piano had been eased out the window and lowered to the ground in a sling. Angelo had intervened to give his ex-colleagues a nudge in military offices in Turin and my *nulla osta* had arrived in late May. For my part, I'd spent the last three months in furniture shops gleaning all the inspiration I could from home-decorating and renovating magazines. Scale plans of the rooms littered my desk and fell out of my bag at odd moments. I experimented with positioning the furniture that I'd like. That miniature bathroom niggled away in my brain, day and night, as I weighed up various space-saving solutions. Best of all, considering what lay ahead, slightly more than expected had come through from the sale of some property I had in Auckland: Dad had proved himself a very determined negotiator on my behalf.

A week before settlement date I ordered the bank cheques and the cash needed for the final payment. At the same time I started packing my bag for my first weekend in my new home. Camping gear it would have to be – sleeping bag and camp mattress, and a little gas cooker. The vendor kindly agreed to leave me a kitchen cupboard and six dining-room chairs: otherwise the flat was bare.

While I was quietly preparing lessons at school on Friday, 30 May, my boss, normally a very reserved individual, put a photo of an old farmhouse on my desk and announced that this was what he was going to buy in a village near Alba the next morning. As casually as possible, I said that his house looked about the same age as the one I was going to buy in the morning. I'm not sure who was more surprised. When he asked me where, I said, 'Top secret!' What a strange working environment we had: with our desks less than a metre apart, for months we had both been pursuing a similar goal in total secrecy. And somehow fate had contrived to bring us both to settlement date at 9.30 a.m. the next day.

A shooting star zipped across the pre-dawn skyline as I was leaving Alba the next morning. A good omen, surely.

The final legal procedure had to take place in a notary's office, and once again we were all there, this time in an office which my whole flat would have fitted into: the vendor and her husband, Franca and her husband, Flavio and me, and the distinguished notary himself. Plush leather chairs seated us around his imposing desk, although I was so excited that I perched on the edge of mine for the whole reading of the deeds. Without any preamble, the notary began to read the document, glancing at me occasionally over his glasses to make sure I was following, and to elaborate on any particular points. A considerable taxation penalty would be levied if I sold the flat within five years and didn't buy another property in Italy. It was all straightforward and finally he put down the document and asked the vendor if she had given me the key yet.

'Not yet. I'm still waiting for the money.'

I was wondering when the signal would come to pay. Flavio scowled at me. Afterwards I realised that I'd probably been expected to start handing out my cheques while we were still in the notary's waiting room. The notary asked me if I had the money and when I indicated that I had, he told us to get on with it then. In the time that it took to countersign my handful of low-denomination cheques and for Franca and her mother to count the cash, the saga was over. As we left his office the notary put his arm around the vendor's shoulder, two old-timers together, and asked her what was for lunch. It was a kind gesture that warded off any pending sadness.

The key for the front gate, nearly 12cm long and almost as old as the flat itself, was finally mine. I'd been up since 5 a.m. and it was lunchtime already – and there was so much to do. At first I was so excited that I couldn't do very much at all. It was a treat just to throw open the shutters and the windows, and let in fresh air and sunshine. With light and warmth flooding in, and the sea sparkling just beyond the parapet, each room was transformed. What a pity Angelo hadn't shown it to Piera and me like this a year before. Now it was mine: shabby and neglected as it was, I would care for it, tidy it up, and coax it back to life. Stepping out onto my terrace I wondered at the history that was right under my feet, and marvelled at my luck in finding my new home on such an historical site.

For the first time ever I found pleasure in sweeping,

scrubbing, cleaning windows. Each window was dim with salt spray, but pane by pane they glistened again. Until the renovations were complete there wasn't much I could do just yet but clean windows, and crisp new curtains made a big difference. Camping conditions reigned in the kitchen where I made do with a little gas cooker. Years before, the electricity had been disconnected in the kitchen, so I had my fridge in the spare bedroom, and supper by candlelight – perfect! The sound of the sea was all the background music I needed. There were plenty of other background noises too, and they took me by surprise the first day. The Via curves around almost in a right angle below my window so all the street sounds are perfectly amplified. That child laughing as it plays on its doorstep, those people gossiping, that motorbike revving up – in the days when the flat was almost empty, the rooms echoed and all those street sounds seemed to be up there in the flat with me.

Each weekend I carried a few more things down by train: plates, more bedding, a solar shower, a few pots and pans, and friends who came down by car brought bulkier items. What a treat it was the weekend a little folding plastic table arrived. We sat around it on the terrace, eating and drinking, chatting and listening to the sea. The sun set behind the Maritime Alps, and much later, several doors away, the baker began his night shift, baking in a wood-fired oven. The delicious aroma wafted up to us. Fishing boats left the tiny port and their lights and buoys bobbed brightly on a calm sea. Towards the horizon, a cruiser headed for more glamorous ports of call. I didn't envy the passengers. Somewhere I'd read that shifting home was like a bereavement, and I waited anxiously to feel grief at leaving Alba. Instead I felt reborn, and revelled in it.

The men who delivered the new fridge had taken away

Bruna's old one from on the landing. I marvelled at how they manoeuvred my fridge up the stairs and around the landings, seemingly without any great physical effort. Bruna was pleased to see the old one go, and had welcomed me to my new home. Provided I didn't clomp about in the night she said she was glad to have someone living upstairs after all these years. She said she felt safer, less alone. I discovered that she was a solo mother, and she welcomed a neighbour of her own age. For my part I was willing to be cautiously neighbourly.

As soon as possible I had to find a builder. I met Michele where he was working nearby, and told him the flat was finally mine. He downed tools and gave me a big hug and a kiss on each cheek. 'Welcome to Ventimiglia,' he said. He came to look over the flat and prepare a quote; the builder Angelo had recommended came too. I'd been advised to get three quotes but Michele's quiet, confident way inspired me. He lives just a few doors away and took me to see how he had restored his own home from a burnt-out shell.

His quote was slightly beyond my budget, and he saw how disappointed I was. 'Think it over for a few days,' he said, 'and if you can possibly afford not to, don't sacrifice the details. Now's the time, while the place is in an upheaval, to do everything, once and for ever.' That evening, I walked the full length of the waterfront, thinking over what he had said and doing my sums over and over again. By the next morning, having slept very little, I accepted. After all, he would supervise the entire task, find a plumber, an electrician, a plasterer and a tile-layer, and ferry me around to the carpenter's and to choose tiles, bathroom fittings, a door, whatever. He was already consulting me about what I wanted, discussing the merits and drawbacks of some of my ideas, without trying to dissuade me from any of them. I realised that we would work together in harmony and mutual respect: he wouldn't intimidate me or try to override my wishes, while I trusted him and would accept his advice. 'Can you start straight away and be finished by the beginning of September?' I asked.

'Actually, I can't start until the middle of September at the earliest.' At least his reply was honest. This was a major setback. I had imagined that when I left Alba at the end of August I'd be moving straight into a newly renovated flat. If not, I couldn't face lugging all my furniture up to the flat and then shifting it out again when Michele started work. He saw my dismay and came to the rescue with the offer to store my things downstairs in his own basement. Not just a builder but a complete removal package.

I had already given my landlord in Alba six months' notice. The Monday after the purchase I handed in three months' notice at the school. No more bridges left to burn. Sorting and packing, I flipped through some papers relating to a short marketing course that I'd done almost ten years before. At the time I was in New Zealand, having left Alba temporarily. Knowing that I'd be there for about six months, I'd taken a job with a vacuum-cleaner sales company. I was among a handful of new sales recruits who would be doing a pre-sales demonstration in private homes, and earning on a commission basis. The sales manager had given us a few hints about getting ahead in our new job: 'Set realistic goals and write them down. Don't write them in the future tense: write in the present, as though you're already there, ten years on.' He stressed the need to take immediate action: in my notes I underlined that three times. How many vacuum cleaners would I have to sell, I wondered.

Not to be put off by what might be considered realistic, I wrote that I was sitting on the terrace of my medieval, pastel-coloured apartment, sipping a glass of wine and looking out to sea as the sun set behind the Alps. Not far away I smelled the aroma of fresh pizza baking in a wood-fired oven. With a jolt, reading this nine years later, I realised that I'd made only one mistake: the sun set further round to the west, while the Alps were directly behind me. Now, I mused, destiny had guided me to Ventimiglia Alta. And out of that wide range of properties for sale, something had led me to the right house.

Finding that scrap of paper, and telling friends about it, intrigued us all. No one who came to inspect my new home could deny that ten years before I even knew it existed or had even considered leaving Alba, I had described its position perfectly.

At the end of August I shifted to Ventimiglia. Carton upon carton went into Michele's basement as promised; bare essentials were hauled upstairs. Imagining that the renovations would be finished by September, I had looked forward to a visit from Dad and his friend Raewyn in October. Now I was mortified that they were going to have to 'camp' too, and it would be much less fun as winter drew in. Faced with putting off their trip or camping on the fourth floor, they bravely decided to come anyway. No matter how spartan the conditions, it was nothing a glass of wine (or two) and a steaming hot plate of pasta wouldn't cure.

Being in the medieval town means that the town council has to keep an eye on renovations and the exterior of the building can't be altered in any way. I was replacing the glass in one window and renewing the shutter, so Vito, the architect who was supervising the renovations, applied for a permit from the council at the end of October. At the same time, seven weeks after I'd left Alba, I celebrated my forty-fifth birthday.

'What do you want to do for the day?' Dad and Raewyn wanted to know. I decided we would start the day by taking the bus to the French border at Ponte San Luigi. The bus ride itself is spectacular as it follows the old main road to the border, about ten kilometres from Ventimiglia Alta. After the village of Latte the road starts to climb, winding up beyond the cluster of houses that are La Mortola Inferiore and the turnoff to the upper hamlet of La Mortola Superiore, before swooping down to the Customs offices. In 1997 these offices were still manned, although crossing the border was only a formality.

Ponte San Luigi crosses a ravine in the rocky mountain-side that is just a few metres away from the sea. In the past the border was a colourful place with a bustling café and stallholders selling souvenirs of the Riviera and the Côte d'Azur, while Customs officers checked the documents of everyone who passed and flirted with the local women. Today the café remains, although the border offices were closed early in 1998; the souvenir kiosk has moved to the lower border crossing on the new coastal road at Ponte San Ludovico. Passing motorists frequently stop at Ponte San Luigi to admire and photograph the breathtaking view of Menton. In the foreground at Garavan, the port for pleasure craft stretches along the waterfront that was built under Napoleon's orders, with the backdrop of Old Menton, pretty and picturesque in its pastel colours, the stark white monuments of the international cemetery on the hillside above, and close behind the soaring heights of the rugged Alpes Maritimes. A short walk down from the bridge, you reach the waterfront at Menton Garavan. Looking back up the hill from the waterfront, up beyond the Customs offices, a large grey stone mansion perches on the hillside. Above it is a square tower, topped off-centre by a small round dome. Until the early 1800s this property belonged to the Grimaldi family of Monaco, while the tower is much older. It dates back, as a lookout, to the times when the Saracens terrorised Liguria in the ninth and tenth centuries. The Grimaldi family sold the property, with its 26,000 square metres of park, to the English doctor, John Henry Bennet. Over the next thirty years Dr Bennet dedicated himself to caring for those of the British community who had chosen to winter on the Riviera for health reasons. Queen Victoria was among his private guests: he put the gardens at her disposal while he was treating Prince Leopold in the early 1880s. The doctor was a keen gardener, and marvelled at the rampant growth of almost everything he planted: only his attempts to coax snowdrops into flower failed. When he sold the property, the mansion was built on the site, and this in turn was sold to a Swiss family. In 1921 the Appenzeller family put the mansion and surrounding property up for auction and this was bought by the Russian scientist, Serge Voronoff, in 1921. More recently, the mansion has been converted into a number of flats, and the gardens that enhance it are no longer open to the public.

The New Zealand writer Katherine Mansfield, ill with tuberculosis, lived in Menton Garavan from autumn 1920 to spring 1921. It was here, in the house called 'Isola Bella' that she found contentment for a few months, and wrote to Middleton Murry, 'You will find Isola Bella in poker work on my heart.' In a setting that she found so conducive to writing, she produced such fine works as 'The Daughters of the Late Colonel', 'The Stranger', and 'The Life of Ma Parker'. The little house is a simple one-room studio, with the airy terrace above where Katherine enjoyed writing so much still used as a writing room by distinguished New Zealand writers during their sojourn in Menton as winners of the Katherine Mansfield Fellowship. Just a few metres back from the waterfront, beyond the railway bridge, on the corner of a lane off what is now Avenue Katherine Mansfield, the little house is a popular destination, almost a pilgrimage, for many of my visitors from New Zealand. Directly across and below the road on the seaward side, trains rattle past on the main east-west line, more frequently than they did in Mansfield's time, but between trains there is still a certain sense of calm and tranquillity, of being just that precious one step removed from the distracting bustle of modern Menton.

Along the waterfront to Menton itself, the pedestrian precinct hums with the tourist trade of colourful Provençal design fabrics, ceramics and perfumes, and the footpath is busy with outdoor cafès and restaurants. While we ate traditional Mentonese *pan bagnet* filled rolls in a sunny square, a pigeon shat on me: surely a good omen on my birthday!

We stopped for coffee where my Canadian friend Petra and her French husband Jean-Philipe have a street kiosk. J-P was preparing a sign for tourists. 'We speak French, German, English, American, Canadian, Australian and . . . How do you say "New Zealand English"?'

'Try Kiwi,' we said and went laughingly on our way to his protests of 'But it's a bird, a fruit . . . I can't say that!'

We told them we were heading for the village of Sainte-Agnès. 'Sit in the front of the bus if you suffer from travel sickness,' Petra warned.

Several times a day the bus wends its way up into the mountains to the highest coastal village in Europe. At 780 metres above sea level, Sainte-Agnès straddles a ridge only three kilometres from the coast, although by winding, narrow road it is nine kilometres away from Menton. The position is spectacular – a bird's-eye view that extends from Menton eastwards towards Bordighera, and westwards as far as the cliffs above Monaco. Distant hang-gliders float down towards the beach. Well over 100 kilometres out to sea, the island of Corsica dominates the horizon on a clear day. To the north, in the circle of mountains that are so close behind the village, the highest peak at 1378 metres is Mt Grammondo, back over the border into Italy.

Legend claims that a Roman Princess, Agnès, and her escorts found shelter in a cave here during a violent thunder-storm. Afterwards, she built a little shrine in thanksgiving, dedicated to her patron saint, and it was close by that the castle was built and a village sprang up in the twelfth century. The castle is in ruins now: a short steep climb up to the orientation table within its former tower affords the widest view, and interest is added here with the reconstruction of a small medieval garden. The essence of the garden is in the creation of a refined, almost sacred place, where it is a pleasure to walk, meditate or write. The Fountain of Life and the Tree of Knowledge are essential focal points in the garden, emphasising the sacred and scholarly importance of the landscaping; the layout of the flower beds is symbolic, rather than the garden being simply a conservatory of medieval plants.

I had chosen Sainte-Agnès as my birthday destination, expecting to find, as indeed we did, a pretty medieval village and panoramic outlook. What I hadn't expected to find was a military fort on the Maginot Line. This massive concrete structure, for the most part concealed underground, was part of a series of similar forts in strategic positions along France's eastern border, built between 1932 and 1938. We decided to take the guided tour but the English-speaking guide wasn't there. The ticket seller seemed to indicate that the French guide spoke a little English, so we strode after him into the first of the fort's tunnels. In fact the guide didn't speak any English at all, but the general concept of gun emplacements, lookout turrets, chutes for tossing grenades out of, air-circulation fans, operations rooms, dormitories, an infirmary and so on, was clear enough. The fort is a multi-storeyed warren of bare, echoing passageways with massive armoured doors opening into various operational areas. How strange to step outside again into the wan autumn sunshine and the cobbled streets of the village.

The following week Dad and Raewyn wondered why the florists were all selling chrysanthemums. It was the last week of October: on November the first and second, Italians honour their dead with potted plants and cut flowers, in particular yellow, white or mauve chrysanthemums. These are taken to the freshly spruced-up family plot or vault in the cemetery. Relatives may come from all over Italy to honour their parents or grandparents. 'We only see our relatives at weddings, funerals and on All Souls' Day,' friends sometimes complain. At this time of year the cemeteries are beautiful by day, glowing with fresh flowers, and enchanting by night too, as hundreds of newly lit votive candles glimmer inside their red plastic holders.

Dad and Raewyn left from Rome on 3 November. Michele was ready to start work once the town council gave the go-ahead. Marianne had offered to help out in two invaluable ways. First, the furniture that I had temporarily moved into the flat could be stored in her would-be reading room two floors below where, covered in plastic, it would be safe from the water that still poured down from above. Secondly, I could stay for a nominal charge in a small flat that she owns in an alleyway off Via Garibaldi. I would be on hand to see how the work was going and saved the expense and inconvenience of staying in a hotel or moving back to stay with friends over the mountains in Piedmont.

Autumn couldn't be ignored now – cooler mornings, clear, brilliantly sunny days and chilly nights. An ancient electric heater was ineffectual, and I went out for brisk walks along the waterfront after dinner. The moon shone on a pounding, forbidding sea. In the very early mornings, hunters and their dogs left the reluctantly waking town to roam the hills in search of game birds or wild boar.

The newspapers talked of a hunt of a different sort: the search for the 'monkey-man' of Grimaldi Superiore. Even today old-timers in the nearby village of Grimaldi Superiore remember Serge Woronoff, the monkeys that he kept in cages in the gardens of the Villa Grimaldi and the experiments that he did, transplanting monkey testicles into elderly men: not all his patients had lasting success from the operation. Now the newspapers revived the excitement surrounding the sightings of several months before. A student and a policeman had each seen the creature at dusk, in the countryside outside the village. Two metres tall, covered with hair, furtive behaviour. Could this be an off-spring of one of the men who had had Woronoff's operation? The villagers were sceptical but one of them was thinking of opening 'Bar Yeti'. Someone thought a monkey had escaped from a passing circus. Religious rumblings about tampering with reproduction vied with opinions about protecting the creature's privacy. Viagra was still a year away. The local paper sold well, but the creature had disappeared into the mist.

With every breath of wind, leaves fell, rustling stealthily, spookily.

I decided not to explore Grimaldi Superiore just yet.

Sainte-Agnès

Getting there: suggested transport in **bold**
9km from Menton, narrow and winding.
Bus several times/day from Menton

Eating and staying overnight:
Hotel/Restaurant, Le Saint Yves tel 0493 35 91 45

Maps for walking:
IGN 3742 OT 1cm = 250m

Alpes Ligures – itineraires transfrontaliers 1cm = 500m

IGC 14 San Remo-Monte Carlo 1cm = 500m

Info and website:
www.sainteagnes06.fr

e-mail mairiesainteagnes@wanadoo.fr

Mairie: 0493 35 84 58

Espace Culture et Tradition 0493 35 87 35

Climate and when to go:
The Maginot Fort is open every weekend afternoon, and every afternoon during summer. Guided tours.

Castle ruins and Medieval Garden: every day except Monday, guided tours 2–5 p.m.

Foliage and vegetation are best in spring and autumn; it can be cold and bleak in winter or clear and crisp. Heat haze in summer makes the view less spectacular than at other times.

CHAPTER 5

Renovations begin

MICHELE'S MESSAGE WAS ON MY ANSWER-phone one Thursday morning in late November. 'Oh, Carolyn. We're starting at your place on Monday. Um . . . be ready!'

After all these months he seemed to be as surprised as I was that work could finally get under way.

After months of waiting and planning, suddenly I didn't want to leave my sunny flat with its awful green living-room, its ghastly pink and black bathroom, its unliveable bedroom, and non-existent front door: I had grown so fond of it, defects and shabbiness and all.

Dutifully I told Michele I would shift over the weekend: the flat would be his on Monday morning. Although I did shift my belongings I couldn't bear to sleep in Marianne's flat on the Sunday night, so I was up at dawn to enjoy one last sunrise and to pack away my bedding.

Michele and his cousin Salvatore arrived at nine o'clock armed with metal buckets, sledgehammers and chisels, and the makings of a hoist to bring material up from the street and take away rubble. This obviously wasn't a social call. Even then I didn't want to go: the coffee-making gear was still in the kitchen, so I offered them coffee. Salvatore opened his mouth to accept, but Michele firmly and politely said, 'No, thank you. Neither of us wants coffee. We're here to work.' He propelled me gently out of the house, and before I had reached the street the sledgehammers were striking ringing blows to the chisels – the characteristic sound of *un muratore* hard at work.

Marianne had lent me a ground-floor flat – three steps down from street level, and straight into the living/dining-room-kitchen. The adjoining bedroom and bathroom were one floor above the next parallel alley, and a steep pedestrian 'tunnel' connected the two alleys under the bathroom. Directly across both alleys, other houses (including my own outside the kitchen window) loomed three or four storeys high, blotting out the sun. These little basement flats are ideal summer lets, prized refuges from the shimmering heat of July and August. They offer all the advantages of troglodyte dwellings. In winter, though, they are hard to heat, and dark all day long. It is much warmer outside than in. At 11 a.m. the only sliver of sunlight to enter the flat all day long fell across the washing machine in the bathroom. By 11.10 it had moved off again. The flat was in the shade all day.

Michele had undertaken to finish the renovations by the end of January: I pinned a photo of my old pink and black bathroom on the kitchen wall – a talisman to help me be patient about staying away from my bright, sunny eyrie until then. At the same time I really appreciated being able to stay almost 'on site' in these early, critical days of the renovations. Michele and Vito had both confided that they feared that Bruna might contrive to stop or delay the work if she found the noise too disturbing, or if even the tiniest crack appeared in any part of her ceiling. In fact, in the week just before the work started, I had accepted her offer of a morning coffee in order to take in the overall condition of her ceilings and try to memorise it. If any problems emerged, I was grateful to Marianne that I would be right there to help Michele and Vito deal with it. Luckily during the day I would have to go out and choose floor and wall tiles, kitchen and bathroom fittings, a front door, a bathroom door, and every few days I would have to meet Michele or the plumber or the electrician or the architect to make decisions in the flat and approve their progress. A translation job in Alba was still going on too, so I would be there for some of the time.

Michele and Salvatore, with Enzo their teenage nephew, had to remove all the floor tiles and break up the concrete floor, and remove the wall tiles, too, in the kitchen and bathroom. In the bathroom they would take the tile base back as far as they could on the walls, in order to gain just that centimetre or two in the size of the room.

Work started noisily at eight every morning, as sledge-hammers drove chisels into tile and concrete. All the rubble had to be barrowed into the kitchen, dumped there and then relayed out onto the terrace. From there it was lowered slowly in buckets to the street and transferred to the back of the truck. Teamwork kept Enzo filling alternate barrows and huge buckets, Salvatore manning the electric hoist and Michele emptying the barrows. I watched them from the street – it all seemed so slow. Could they really finish in nine weeks' time? Being a Kiwi, I wanted to help. Knowing Italy, I accepted that this was not a woman's job.

One morning I woke up later than usual, surprised that I hadn't been disturbed at five o'clock by someone going off to work on a motorbike. In fact I hadn't been awakened by anything. What was wrong? Why were the sledgehammers silent? Something terrible had happened, I thought as I dressed quickly. Hurrying outside, I realised it was Sunday.

If I'd woken to the vibrations of shattering tiles and disintegrating concrete for the last five mornings, two doors away around the corner, I imagined that all my neighbours were thrilled that the men didn't work on Sunday. Bruna certainly was. On the second day she had tried to stop work while she had a rest in the afternoon. Salvatore had negotiated a compromise: he'd take an hour and a half for lunch instead of an hour. 'The fewer interruptions you cause us, the sooner we'll be finished,' he persuaded her. Nonetheless I didn't want to be ambushed on the stairs so I waited until lunchtime until I crept upstairs.

'*Permesso*! Can I come in?' I whispered out of habit as I negotiated tools and extension leads and rubble in the hallway. It certainly didn't feel very much like my home anymore. The bathroom had been gutted: pink and black had given way to the cold, uncompromising grey of jagged cement. A hole where the toilet had been, no sign of the handbasin, and a pile of rocks where the seat of the hip-bath had been. The toilet had formerly been visible from the passage and the handbasin just out of sight. They were going to change places, and a 70cm x 70cm shower with one rounded corner would, I insisted, replace the bath. Michele was already telling me to put in a full rectangle shower base, 90cm x 70cm. I'd regret anything else, he claimed, and the curved doors were much more expensive. He'd made the same mistake in his own home, and never enjoyed his shower; this tall, robust man cramped into little more than a 70cm-sided triangle. I wanted the base hard up into the outside corner, leaving about 40cm outside the shower for a stool or a small cupboard.

Very downcast by the state of the bathroom, I picked my way into the main part of the flat. The toilet bowl and hand-basin had found an incongruous temporary home in the middle of the big bedroom. Maybe they were going to be recycled somewhere.

Most of the floor was down to bare planking – not floor boards, just a rough base for concreting over – and Salvatore had already started to sand off some of the green paint in the living-room. That at least was an improvement.

I tiptoed from room to room. More rubble in the kitchen. A heap of multi-coloured tiles – pink, black, tan from the living-room, dark green from the big bedroom, tawny from the little bedroom, fawn from the passage, white from the kitchen walls. I wanted to keep, but reposition, the original sink. 'We'll never get it detached from the wall without cracking it,' Michele and Salvatore had chorused.

'I trust you both to handle this with the greatest of care and to keep it safe until it's time to re-install it,' I replied. '*Coraggio*! I know you can do it!' Now the sink was resting on its end against one wall, intact except for one insignificant chip. I'd been given the chipped-off piece for safekeeping. Later on I'd glue it back again.

I basked in the sunshine next to the hoist: dismayed and depressed by the debris and chaos, encouraged by the speed with which the team had progressed so far. The plumbing and wiring would be channelled down the walls and across the floor, under the new tiles. Once the floor was laid bare completely it would be levelled to take out the characteristic inward slope which a lot of older floors have here, with the new concrete going down on a reinforced wire-mesh base.

Marco the electrician and Piero the plumber could start on Monday. I'd already met Marco: just before Dad and Raewyn arrived he'd rigged up a temporary light in the kitchen. I knew he wasn't a relative of Michele's and as far as I knew, neither was the plumber.

The plumber had sent me his quote in August and I'd accepted it straight away: there didn't seem to be any point in bartering over the amount, as the quote itself was very reasonable. Since then, though, I'd decided to put a hand-basin in the guestroom. The plumber said I would have to pay more, because three months had passed, prices had gone up and now I was adding things. 'Foreign women!' I could hear him grumbling.

Michele sided with me, pointing out that I'd accepted his original quote without any quibbling – he would come now and do the work for the original amount, or Michele would find another plumber.

He did find another plumber, who at the last minute had an accident and couldn't start when he was needed. Never dismayed for long, Michele had now found a third solution – a plumber willing to do the job for marginally less than the original quote, including the extra handbasin. A bargain!

I looked forward to my tour of inspection on Monday.

There was a tremendous buzz of activity – men and tools everywhere. Someone was squatting in the bathroom, his hand down the hole where the toilet had been. A small, compact man, with dark hair and moustache, and piercing, mischievous, black eyes. Wriggling his hand free from the hole, he held it out to me and grinned through a haze of cigarette smoke. *'Salve! Sono Piero. Piacere!'* As I introduced myself in return he was already back at work and Michele had appeared. 'Have you met my brother?' he asked. Piero grunted down his hole, pulling some tubes into position. I marvelled at how unalike they were, and wondered if any more of the family were in the team.

Marco the electrician and I drew light-switch and power-point positions on the wall, and Marco casually asked if black switches would be okay. I was shocked: surely no one wanted black light switches. 'You'll never find white ones in the dark, and they'll show every little finger mark,' Marco argued.

'Nothing that normal cleaning products can't handle,' I countered, 'and light-switch positions are easily learned.'

Marco shrugged in good-natured acceptance, and made a note – white light-switches for the foreign lady. I supposed then that black ones were on special at the supplier's, or maybe he had some left over from a previous job. Now I know better: black light-switches are standard fare in Italian homes.

Piero called us back into the bathroom. The pile of rock in the corner where the seat part of the hip-bath had been was still there, exactly where I wanted the shower base. But it wasn't just a pile of rubble. It was solid rock, part of the original fortifications. 'We'll be here forever, breaking that away,' Piero moaned.

I nodded, regarding this as a serious setback. But Michele was delighted. He'd been waiting for this opportunity and was already standing where he thought the 70cm x 90cm shower base should go.

'We'll build up, around the rock, 40cm up from the floor, and 30cm deep, and tile it. You'll have a handy little shelf for sponges and shampoo and shower gel. You'll never regret it.'

His eyes sparkled with excitement. And I wouldn't need an expensive shower door – a curtain on a rail would be fine.

'You've won,' I smiled back. Every day since then I've silently thanked him for his foresight – a much better solution than what I had planned.

At the same time as they built up the shelf, they would raise the ceiling of the alcove over the shower and put three glass bricks along the outside wall. The boiler would be outside in the guttering on the ramparts, right outside the tiny bathroom window, so in order to be of any use, the window would also be shifted along and raised slightly. With so much more light streaming in, the room already seemed bigger, even if it wasn't. White walls and a big mirror over the handbasin would complete the illusion.

Michele was beaming with satisfaction, but Piero had more important things to discuss. 'What about the toilet? Where's it going to go?'

'Right there, where you're standing now,' we replied.

It would be at right angles to the outside wall, and as close to the wall as possible. The bathroom is a metre wide at that point, and after studying toilet dimensions in the catalogue, I'd calculated the toilet could jut out a maximum of 65cm, leaving room to get past it to the shower.

Piero retrieved the old toilet bowl from the bedroom and plonked it down in the middle of the bathroom. 'Like this then?' It formed a complete barrier between the door and the shower, and Michele was still in the shower.

'Don't be daft, Piero, *fratello mio*. Nobody's going to climb over the toilet to get to the shower!'

'It has to jut out at least 85cm,' Piero scowled at him, and at me too. No captivating smiles now.

'Think again,' were Michele's parting words as he stepped

over his brother and followed me out of the bathroom. I was glad I didn't have to handle this one myself.

Giuliano was putting down the new floor. Starting from nothing on the outside walls facing Via Garibaldi, where the old floor sat right on the old roof line and therefore couldn't be lowered, he had to raise the level of the floor to remove the slope that had been built in when the house was new. This was a typical gravity-defying technique of a hundred years ago. By sloping the floor inwards, the top floor was less likely to collapse outwards into the street. Across the six-metre depth of the flat he had to raise the level at the far wall by seven or eight centimetres, but at the same time slope it down sideways, very gradually towards the front door so that the door could open inwards. The last step at the top of the stairs was already higher than usual: it couldn't be any higher. A fine blue pencil line ran along the walls, parallel to the ceiling: the floor level would be brought up parallel to the blue line. It wouldn't feel as if I was walking uphill anymore when I crossed the living-room.

Piero wanted me in the bathroom again. 'What about the toilet cistern? That old thing up there,' he said, indicating my treasured chain-operated cast-iron cistern. 'It'll have to go.' It still had its old chain and enamelled china handle.

'No, Piero, you don't understand. I don't want to throw out *all* the old things. I want to keep that as an ornament.' I could see it, with its decorative embossed frieze, cleaned up and repainted, and hanging plants cascading off its lid.

'But it's at least fifty years old!' Piero protested.

'Exactly!' I exclaimed. 'It's at least fifty years old! That's why I want to keep it.'

Piero was speechless.

'Piero, the *signora* wants to keep it as an ornament – to put pot plants on top.' I don't know when Giuliano had joined the discussion or where he'd got this revolutionary idea about the pot plants. Piero gaped at him. Another bemused shrug of acceptance, though.

We'd need to start choosing things, Michele announced. He'd take me to Nice, to a builders' supply shop, and we'd choose a door for the bathroom and maybe a front door too.

High up in the mountains we hurtled along the motorway, past the off-ramps for exotic places – Monaco-Monte Carlo, Eze, Beaulieu, Cap Ferrat. They glistened at the water's edge, far below.

The range of doors was overwhelming, but finally a choice was made – for the bathroom at least. I decided on an armoured front door: not that it was what I wanted. I would have preferred a solid wooden door, but that was too expensive. I would find an armoured one in Ventimiglia. Piero would choose the bathroom fittings as they were included in the quote, and I already had the sink. The carpenter was making double-glazed windows and dark green slatted shutters for the guestroom, and the other windows and shutters were in good enough condition to keep. I liked their old-fashioned opening mechanism, and didn't want to change them.

For months now I'd been looking for floor tiles: the choice was staggering. To add to my range of options, Michele promised to take me to some stockists outside Ventimiglia: maybe they would be cheaper. We'd start doing the rounds the following week.

CHAPTER 6

Tiles unlimited

THEY WOULD BE 30CM SQUARE AND LAID diagonally, the same tiles throughout the entire flat. A matt finish and an irregular pattern. Warm and cool at the same time: the exact colour was hard to define – I was looking for something that reminded me of a sandy beach, but a little bit darker. Allowing for some inevitable wastage after cutting, I'd need roughly sixty square metres, I estimated.

Going around the tile stockists in Ventimiglia I saw some examples that were *nearly* right, but . . . too brown, too blue, too grey, too pink, too shiny, too regular in their pattern. I wasn't convinced. The square metre of a showroom display was one thing – how would a whole floor look? Just right or a major mistake? I wouldn't know until they were laid.

Just outside Ventimiglia on the Friday evening, on my way to choose some kitchen cupboards, I came across '*Freno – piastrelle per pavimenti e rivestimenti*'. Unimposing from the street, indoors a welcoming, friendly reception from Enzo, one of the twin brothers who own the floor- and wall-tiling showroom. I explained as best I could, seeing as I didn't really know myself, that I was looking for a new floor for a small flat. Enzo's eyes lit up.

'Signora, I have just the thing for you! Just the thing for a small floor area.' My scepticism swiftly turned to delight. Indeed, he had just the tiles for me. Sandy, salmony matt finish with roughly bevelled edges. The series was made up of several different patterned tiles so that the pattern would hardly be seen to repeat.

But how many square metres did I need? There was a catch with the exceptional cheapness of these tiles, less than half their normal price. They were the very end of the stock: only 46 square metres. Enzo scratched his head. We went over the dimensions of each room once again. The living-room is the only square one. The bathroom, kitchen and hallway are truncated wedges, while the bedrooms are rhomboids. Calculating the area of these very irregular rooms and a tapering 'L' passageway was probably the last thing Enzo needed on a Friday afternoon, but he set to very obligingly.

Careful calculations done, he arrived at a maximum area of 52 square metres. Was he sure? We went over it again, and agreed that I'd estimated too generously, but it was still too much. I considered having a different tile in either the bathroom or the kitchen. Enzo admitted to having about twenty square metres of the same tiles at home, ready to do one of his own floors. He'd check over the weekend and see how many he could spare. Then, along the wall in the kitchen where the cooker, fridge, sink and washing machine would hide them, I could use the same tile but of a slightly inferior quality, and the same in the bedrooms where the beds and wardrobes would be.

We moved on to the wall tiles. The health department requires the kitchen and bathroom to be lined in glazed tiles from the floor to a height of 1.5 metres. White was my choice for the bathroom to give the maximum illusion of space, and white with a very light tawny speckle for the kitchen. Finally, a decorative row of 6cm-high frieze tiles to insert below the top row of tiles in both rooms. The tiles were quickly chosen. The choice of friezes was daunting, and they were expensive. I'd think about it over the weekend.

On the Monday I tried to convince Michele I'd found exactly the floor I was looking for. He was as sceptical as I had been on the Friday afternoon, but I persuaded him to take me back to Freno before we started looking elsewhere. Enzo greeted him as an old school friend. I showed him the tiles I'd chosen and he nodded in agreement: words weren't necessary. A rare find. We went over the friezes together and I let Michele choose a pale blue, green and lemon scroll pattern for the bathroom: the bathroom was, after all, his special project. For the kitchen I chose terracotta with sea-green, royal blue and red diamonds. I paid a deposit and Michele and Enzo arranged delivery dates. Some of the tiles were in the warehouse; the friezes would have to be ordered. It was 15 December. Enzo guaranteed delivery for the second week in January.

'*Complimenti. Hai scelto veramente bene.*' Michele congratulated me on my choice of floor tiles. The choosing was nearly over.

The next day I ordered a cooker, washing machine, kitchen cupboards and drawers, all for delivery in early February. After what had seemed like such a hopelessly slow start, the men were racing ahead now. I was sure they would finish on schedule at the end of January.

A surprise invitation to my niece's wedding in New Zealand arrived in mid-December. 'Is it all right if I leave you to finish off on your own?' I asked Michele. 'Do you need me anymore?' A family wedding wasn't to be missed. I was struggling to imagine my little brother, two years my junior, as father of the bride.

'Leave tomorrow if you want,' he teased. Managing to find a seat on the last day of the low season, on 19 December I left Genova as, even at sea level, incredibly, it started to snow. The men in the team were pleased with the wine and panettone Christmas cakes I'd given them, and I'd given Bruna a little something too. She still had a month of construction work to put up with while I swam, sunbathed, barbecued and caught up with family and friends, and up till now she'd been very, very patient.

Michele could phone or fax if anything needed to be discussed. I trusted him, and his ability to decide on my behalf if necessary. By now he understood how I expected the work to turn out. I wanted the work finished by the end of January, so with barely a thought for the enormity of what I was doing, I gave Michele every last lire of the money that I owed him and packed my case.

I'd be back on 31 January.

On and beyond the Riviera

CHAPTER 7

The citrus fruit festival
in Menton

'COME ON! I WANT TO SHOW YOU THE NEW house!' Michele greeted me eagerly at 10 a.m. on Sunday, 1 February 1998.

After a forty-hour journey door-to-door – two long flights and a short one, and finally three hours by train from Genova – I'd reached Ventimiglia at four o'clock the previous afternoon. Getting out of the taxi I noticed that my apartment's gable end was newly painted and the shutters on that end were a new deep green. Too tired to take in anything more, I had fallen straight into bed in Marianne's basement flat, and slept through until a few hours ago. Waking up, I realised I didn't have a key for the new front door. I'd phoned Michele from Zurich airport the morning before and told him to enjoy his Sunday. 'See you on Monday,' I'd said.

He couldn't wait to show off his work though. A switch just inside the street door turned on my stair lighting: no more groping about in the dark.

Clonk, clonk, clonk, clonk, click. The four-pronged lock turned four and a quarter times and the new front door swung open. The shutters were open and light streamed in. I gasped with pleasure. The floor tiles were perfect, and in the corner of the passage there was an enormous bouquet of flowers, carnations and gladioli matching the sandy-salmony tones of the floor. *Caro Michele, grazie.*

I hadn't expected this. He was explaining that the wheat-ears among the flowers were a traditional symbol for good luck in a new house: I wasn't to throw them out. I noticed that the floor was spotless – his sister-in-law had been to do the cleaning.

We inspected the bedrooms and living-room. Was I pleased, he wanted to know. Delighted, overwhelmed, thrilled, moved. I hope he understood just how much. And what about him, was he satisfied?

'Yes,' he smiled, 'everything worked out fine. Except in the kitchen.' I gulped: surely they hadn't had an accident with my precious sink?

Actually the sink was still on end against one newly tiled wall. Partially tiled wall, in façt. Enzo from Freno had phoned in early January to say there was a delay with the frieze tiles, and last week to say they were out of production. I'd have to choose another frieze. In the meantime, shopping at Mount Maunganui, I'd chosen the kitchen curtain and cushion fabric: tropical fish and shells alternating with blocks of Greek key pattern and, as luck had it, green and blue diamonds on a terracotta oblong. Perfect. I'd already made the Roman blind for over the French door. I stifled a sigh. I was lucky that this was all that hadn't worked out.

'Michele, what about the bathroom?'

'Ah! Well! Yes! The bathroom.' He gave me a furtive, sidelong glance. I feared the worst. What else could have gone wrong?

He opened the door. The rascal, he'd been teasing me. What a transformation! Perfection! It was the most beautiful mini-bathroom I'd ever seen. The low winter sun streamed in through the glass bricks and the repositioned window. The old cistern was newly painted and just waiting for its pot plants. The toilet was perfectly positioned, and the shower with its built-up ledge along one end was far more practical than what I'd originally had in mind.

The rooms glowed. Freshly whitewashed walls and ceilings, freshly painted doors, windows and shutters. That hadn't been part of the quote, had it? I thought I'd said I'd paint the doors, windows and shutters. 'That's a gift from all of us,' Michele grinned. The floors had been swept and mopped, and the tools which were still needed to finish the kitchen were neatly stacked in a bucket in one corner. I gave Michele a big hug.

We hauled up a bed base and mattress, and I started to move back in. I'd use the basement kitchen for a few more days while mine was finished off, but spring was already on the way. Mimosa and white broom are cultivated on the hillsides here, and they were already coming into flower. I admired the colourful hillside across the valley, from the guestroom window. My spirits soared.

I wanted to know why Enzo hadn't known straight away that those frieze tiles were out of production. Now I had to find others to match my curtains. Leafing through the catalogues once again, rejecting almost all the possibilities, until . . . a terracotta tile with tiny sea-green, dark blue and yellow diamonds, alternating with tiny white triangles. I didn't let on that maybe I liked it even better than the one I'd ordered before.

Giuliano whistles as he finishes the tiling. Then he and Salvatore have to make two brick walls, faced with tiles, for the sink to rest on. They call me to come and stand in front of where the sink will be: they want the finished height to be just right for me. I'm not having cupboard doors underneath – the kitchen's too narrow. Instead, curtains will hide the shelves under the sink.

Three men come from the furniture shop to hang the kitchen cupboards. I haven't anticipated any problems, but now I find they want to hang the cupboards with the bottoms of the cupboards 1m 40cm from the floor, thus hiding six of my gorgeous frieze tiles. And they cost 5000 lire each! They have to be joking. But they aren't. I tell them to go up six centimetres, but they insist it has to be 1m 40. But why? Apparently every kitchen in Italy is installed at 1m 40. I don't believe them: Italian women aren't all the same height, and I'm not short. All the examples that I saw in the showroom were at 1m 40, they explain, getting exasperated. That doesn't interest me in the least. For the first time since work began in November, I'm getting quite cross. Michele and Giuliano are working on some scaffolding next door but I resist the temptation to call in some moral support. I tell the men to get on and install the cupboards at 1m 46 from the ground. 'We'll hang them from the ceiling if you want!' one of them says sarcastically. I won't be going back to their shop again, that's for sure.

When the job's done and the men have gone, Michele and Giuliano drop in to see the new kitchen. They both want to know what's wrong with me. I'm still seething, and they've never seen me angry before. 'We were only next door,' they say, admiring the cupboards. 'Why didn't you call us?'

Michele and I go around room by room to see if anything has been overlooked. We make a list: some beading here, a squirt of silicone sealant here, hooks in the ceiling to hang the lightshades from, an extra light on the stairs. And the instruction booklet for the thermostat-controlled central heating. Years later I'm still waiting for that, but in the meantime he has taught me how to use it.

We go over the list. It's an hour's work, two at the most. He'll be back next week to do it, with the electrician, and Salvatore, who's small and light enough to get up through the manhole to fix the hooks in the ceiling – they have to be threaded down through a hole next to the light fitting, and plastered in place from inside the roof – as soon as he's finished the job he's moved on to in the meantime.

In fact, the team's working downstairs. As soon as Bruna saw that they were working for me she decided to let them into her bathroom to fix the broken tube that's been causing the flooding in Marianne's place. But there's a catch. They can't just break the tiles and repair the tube. She wants a complete new bathroom – bath, basin, bidet, toilet, new tiles for the floor and walls. Beside herself by now, Marianne has agreed to pay for a new bathroom for her neighbour. Never-ending generosity. While Michele and I were at Freno he got me to choose three samples from the cheapest range of tiles available. 'It's a mysterious house,' Bruna cackles. I think she still believes there's a fountain in the gutter in the ramparts. She certainly isn't accepting any responsibility for the repair work.

The men trickle back to do the finishing touches. Salvatore had optimistically taken away his tools but now he good-humouredly brings them back again. If only they'd make an effort, it would be done in a morning. Some of the jobs I do myself, and they admire my workmanship. Some mornings, however, I wait for them – in vain. But I've long since learned the value of patience here, and resolve not to let the lack of lightshades or other silly things spoil my first spring on the coast.

Friends come from Milan and we go to the Fête du Citron in Menton. The annual Citrus Fruit Festival takes place in the second half of February. Themes vary: 1997 honoured 'Asterix and the Gauls'; the first time I came the theme was 'Greek and Roman Myths and Legends'. This year celebrates the adventures of Tin Tin.

The public gardens that run towards the mountains from in front of the waterfront casino are cordoned off and gigantic scenes are created using oranges and lemons – millions of oranges and lemons, each one rubber-banded onto a wire-netting framework. The amount of work involved is staggering, the results stunning: Tin Tin and his dog on a galleon in full sail in a sea of mauve cinerarias; swinging on an elephant's trunk; kilted and scaling a Highland castle wall; off on safari in a heavily-laden car; fighting a monster. Tin Tin and Snowy are life-size models; the castle, the galleon, the safari-car, the monster and so on are made entirely of oranges and lemons. The adventures unfold down the length of the gardens. Copies of the original comic strips tell us the background to the stories depicted. The static display is a blaze of orange, lemon and spring flowers: mimosa and cyclamen are at their best. Stalls offer citrus products too – marmalade, lemon meringue pie, crêpes with cointreau, orange- and lemon-scented soaps and body oils and lotions, a wide range of citrus varieties from massive grapefruit to tiny kumquats.

In the adjacent exhibition hall, craftspeople from the inland villages have set up a market of their products – ceramics, glass, leather goods, hand-dyed silk, weaving, honey, sweets, candles.

These are some of the busiest days of the tourist calendar for Menton. During the afternoon, more enormous orange and lemon statues, this time mounted as floats, parade along the waterfront. By evening we're already looking forward to next year – Lucky Luke the cowboy is the theme.

On a Friday in early March I find Michele and Salvatore doing a job for the town council in Via Garibaldi. 'See you on Monday,' they promise cheerfully. I'm not amused and am still fuming a few minutes later when Vito the architect pays me a surprise visit. In November I paid him half his fee. Now he imagines the job is finished – he's come for the rest of his money.

'So how did the work turn out? Let me see,' he says, confident that my cheque will soon be in his hand.

'How dare you come asking for money when they still haven't finished? And if you'd followed the job through to the end, you'd know that,' I rant. 'Look!'

He's astounded and speechless as I vent my exasperation. Yes, it's a job really well done in all major aspects, but why is it still dragging on towards the finishing touches? I haul him from room to room. He makes a list of all the little things still waiting to be done. Yes, it only needs an hour or two, he says. Don't I know it! Where is Michele anyway, Vito wants to know. Doing something for the council four doors down the road, I say petulantly. Vito goes off, without his cheque but promising to find some way of getting the team back.

And he does. They're back on Monday morning, slightly

apologetic but ready for action. They tell me I was right to vent my frustrations on Vito. 'If you don't do it too often, it's effective,' they say.

A concentrated effort – ladders, cement, laughter, silicone, sawdust, wire-cutters. Vito returns for a final tour of inspection, apologises to me, and I'm glad to settle my account. No hard feelings. A happy ending. But I feel sad and apprehensive when Salvatore takes away his tools again. Something totally unknown waits in the post-renovation phase of my new life.

Menton Fête du Citron

Getting there: suggested transport in **bold**
On coast road near Italian border. A8 exit Menton

Train – Paris, Nice, Ventimiglia
Bus from Nice airport

Eating and staying overnight:

Croque Chaud
Petra & JP's Snack kiosk
36 Ave Félix Fauvre
in pedestrian shopping area

Restaurants

In old port:
L'Endroit Snack Bar
Quai G Benet,
tel 0493 28 20 97

In old town:
Le Darkoum – Moroccan
23 Rue St Michel
tel 0493 35 44 88

Hotel/Restaurant Paris-Rome
79 Porte de France
06500 Menton Garavan
tel 0493 35 73 45, fax 0493 35 29 30
www.logis-de-france.com
www.hotel-paris-rome.com

Hotel de Londres with restaurant
15 Ave Carnot
tel 0493 35 74 62
fax 0493 41 77 78
e-mail HOTEL-DE-LONDRES@wanadoo.fr
www.hotel-de-londres.com

Narev's Hotel
12 bis Rue Lorédan Larchey
tel 0493 35 21 31
fax 0493 35 21 20
www.hotel_narevs.com

Hotel/Restaurant l'Auberge Provencal
11 Rue Trenca
tel 0493 35 77 29
fax 0493 28 88 88

Restaurant le Colomba
6 Rue St Michel
tel 0493 35 76 01

Restaurant La Braise,
near the Ponte San Luigi border, fine views
80 Bd de Garavan
tel 0493 51 24 16

Info and website
www.villedementon.com

Office du Tourisme tel
8 Ave Boyer
tel 0492 41 76 76, fax 0492 41 76 78
e-mail hotelmenton@wanadoo.fr
www.hotelmenton.com

Gare Routier de Menton (bus station) Avenue de Sospel
tel 0493 35 93 60

Climate and when to go:
Pleasant all year round

Fête du Citron – February

CHAPTER 8

The pine cone villages
of the Nervia valley

RENOVATIONS GIVE WAY TO FURNISHING
and decorating. Michele takes me to see a carpenter who can
make a cabinet for the hand-basin in the guestroom. It will
go in a corner where the wall curves, tapers and slopes
outwards. Aurelio makes a quick sketch, gives a rough quote
and agrees to come next week to take the measurements. He
promises to install the finished cabinet in two weeks' time.

Don't you believe it, I tell myself, anticipating, correctly as
it happens, that it will take a month. This is crucial timing as
my first guests arrive from New Zealand on 6 May, and I don't
want to make a *brutta figura*, especially as these people booked
in December. I play on this Italian weakness and Aurelio
understands – he doesn't want to make a bad impression either.

Captive in the car on the way home, Michele has something to ask me. 'Now that the house is finished, isn't it time
you started working?'

I agree, and wonder – how, when, where, for whom? 'You can start by helping my son Marco with his English homework.'

This is my own particular nightmare – going over schoolwork with kids who'd much rather be out riding their bikes after school. When I left Alba I vowed never to do *repetizione* again. But how can I say no?

I swallow hard and agree to do it. We set a time for the first lesson. Marco is eleven, in his first year of intermediate school, first year of English. I pray that he won't come to the first lesson.

And then he's there, a quiet, smiling boy, polite, motivated, bright, inquisitive, fascinated by my knick-knacks from New Zealand and China. The first lesson flits by. It's going to be a pleasure – we're both enthusiastic about next time. After six months of non-teaching I get a real buzz from doing it again. Marco has twenty-six classmates, and I feel sorry for him. I feel sorry for the teacher too. How can she keep track of all of them? Marco really wants to learn, but the brightest classmates and a core of troublemakers are getting all the teacher's attention. Two or three of the latter are still at intermediate school even though they're nearly fourteen. Marco isn't the only one who's floundering. Neither of his parents speaks English. I feel a special responsibility for him – the same special interest that his father invested in renovating my place, and he makes good progress. Shortly his cousin Chiara joins him for the lessons. Three afternoons a week, for an hour each time. It's fun and I realise that, unwittingly this time, Michele has done me another enormous favour. I'm amazed to find myself hoping this is only the beginning.

And it is. A year later I have a small group of adult beginners, two other adults and a teenager at various more advanced levels, and another twelve-year-old.

Michele and Aurelio come to install the cabinet for the bedroom, then Piero comes again to fit the basin and taps. Michele, Salvatore and I lay a row of seven frieze tiles along the wall at the back of the cabinet. Obviously, working with three in a small space, we make a mess of it – or rather Salvatore and I make a mess of it while Michele is outside cutting the seventh tile. 'You're both sacked!' he groans, and we slink off. There were eight frieze tiles left after the kitchen was finished, and considering how much they cost, neither Michele nor I wanted to admit responsibility for ordering too many. Who counted up anyway? We laugh and admire our efforts in the bedroom. It looks great once Michele has shooed Salvatore and me aside and tidied up our handiwork.

'How much do I owe you for Marco's lessons?' Michele is offering to pay me, and I don't know what to say.

'Let's do a few more lessons and then we'll see.'

The next time he asks me, I counter with, 'How much will I owe you if you come up and help me put up the mirrors and light-shades, and if you go on letting me keep my bike in your garage?'

We can do a swap – it suits us both. I couldn't manage the bike up and down four narrow flights of stairs, and renting a shed would be extravagant. Helping Marco and Chiara is a pleasure, and Michele is happy to give me a hand. My bike can stay where it is for as long as I like. Friends joke that I should arrange a similar swap with the grocer, the baker, the butcher. *Magari!* If only!

Choosing furniture takes me into the Nervia valley, to Camporosso and Dolceacqua. The main road skirts around Camporosso, with its enormous, too-classical-for-me furniture showroom. Not far beyond Camporosso, Dolceacqua's ruined Doria castle rears into view further up the valley. It presides high over the village: twin towers, roof long ago caved in, gaping holes where doors and windows were, still irresistibly photogenic.

A simple, arched, hump-backed bridge crosses the Nervia River from the newer part of the village across the river and leads into the medieval quarter. A plaque on the bridge reminds us that Claude Monet painted here. He walked from Bordighera, and did some lovely views of the castle and the bridge. Across the bridge entering the ancient village; it's like going into a giant pine cone. The narrow alleys are arched and buttressed over to give an impression, not so much of walking down a village street as of being almost inside a tunnel. People live here too – there are intriguing cave-like shops, lots of hanging pot plants, and finely embroidered linen curtains. More semi-troglodytes: children play in the big square outside the main entrance to the pine cone.

The newer part of the town is the commercial heart of Dolceacqua. Here small cellars stock the Rossese wine of the surrounding vineyards, locally pressed olive oil, Nervia valley cheeses, pesto, walnut sauce, olive and capsicum spreads, forest mushrooms in autumn – gastronomic treats. After this, the furniture showroom is a disappointment.

The quiet stone and slate villages of the Ligurian hinterland contrast strongly with the noisier, brighter, pastel-washed ones of the coastal strip. Further up the Nervia valley, as it meanders by wooded or terraced hillsides towards the foot of the Ligurian Pre-Alps, other picturesque destinations are Rocchetta Nervina, Isolabona, Apricale, Pigna, Castel Vittorio. The gradient is gentle: it's great cycling country.

Walking trails link the villages through the woods and olive groves too. The spring and autumn vegetation is spectacular. The villages are similar and yet different. Apricale is in a side valley that joins the Nervia valley at Isolabona. The two-kilometre deviation is well worthwhile – as you come round the bend in the road, Apricale comes pouring down its spur of hillside to meet you. The ancient houses reach up towards the church steeple, which has a bicycle firmly secured to its side, a gravity-defying relic from Sergio Bianco's exhibition a few years ago, aptly entitled *The power of non-gravity*.

There has been a settlement here since the Bronze Age. The main alleyways in Apricale are decorated with murals, many depicting traditional country life. At the foot of the parish church, a small sheltered piazza is the hub of village life, and the stage in summer for open-air theatre. Come up here in autumn to enjoy a long and leisurely lunch: the stewed snails, and wild boar casserole are delicious, and the traditional dessert is zabaglione – egg and marsala custard – served hot and runny with a mountain of small fried dumplings. It's too good to miss, so keep some room for it if you can.

Back in the Nervia valley, the road continues up to Pigna. A new well-being complex has opened recently beside the river at Lago Pigo, on the outskirts of Pigna. Although the thermal spring was probably known in Roman times, a local folk legend has it that the curative properties of the sulphurous waters were first discovered when a donkey fell into the river. The sores on its back healed quickly, and people began to come here to bathe in the restorative waters of the original spa.

The bridge over the river at this point is the boundary between Pigna and Castel Vittorio. Although Castel Vittorio is three kilometres from Pigna, the road winds back on itself so that the village overlooks Pigna from high above. Imagine how the two must have bristled with antagonism towards each other when Pigna was within the territory of the Kingdom of Savoy, and Castel Vittorio was under the cloak of the Republic of Genova. A winding, well-trodden mule-trail through the woods links the two villages, and passes in front of the spooky ruins of the long abandoned church of Santa Maria Assunta.

In the Middle Ages Pigna held a key position on the main thoroughfare between Liguria and Piemonte, and there would have been a constant coming and going of merchants and mule trains, pilgrims and peasantry. Nowadays it is a hub for hikers heading off into the mountains, and a pleasant place to come and relax in the thermal baths.

Furnishing my new home goes well. I choose lampshades, wall lights and mirrors, and Michele comes and puts them up for me. As he goes along I admire his handiwork and the pride he takes in it, and he usually approves my choice of furnishings. When it's the last thing that he would ever have chosen, I appreciate his honesty when he candidly tells me so.

The guestroom glows with honey-coloured wood, bamboo, pale blue and lemon fabrics, sunflower-shaped cast-iron doorstop, some prints on the walls. One is an ink sketch of the rooftops of Ventimiglia Alta, the bell tower of San Michele church and the Roya valley, the work of an English artist who holidayed next door last autumn. Another favourite is a print of one of Claude Monet's views of Bordighera – the next town down the coast from here.

We leave the hall mirror until last. It was a shabby old wardrobe door, abandoned by the vendors. I've painted the frame, and as Michele drills into the concrete wall to put in the hooks he says, 'After this there's nothing more to do, is there?'

It's the very last week before my guests arrive so I'm pleased, relieved and excited now that the work is finished. At the same time I feel glum. There has been so much uncertainty, so much to do, and now there's nothing more to choose, to decide, to worry about, and I know I'm going to miss it. I must be the only woman in the world to suffer withdrawal anguish as the builder puts away his tools. He understands, gives me a hug and leaves his ladder on the terrace, promising to come back when he can to put up some shelves.

I know it won't be until October at the earliest. In two weeks' time he'll start assembling a pre-fabricated kiosk-bar on the Calandre Beach. This is Ventimiglia's one truly sandy beach, and can be reached only by sea or on foot. He'll ferry the panels for the buildings, the cookers, cupboards, fridges, freezers, deck-chairs, beach umbrellas, plates and glasses, everything, around by boat, assemble it all, and run a thriving little business – delicious seafood meals included – seven days a week until mid-September. There isn't any sort of a jetty: the boat has to run straight up onto the beach, so we cross our fingers for dead calm seas over the next few weeks.

I teach Marco and Chiara some beach, bar and restaurant vocab, including counting hundreds and thousands of lire. It's warm enough to swim now, even though most Italians won't even consider it until the beginning of June.

After so many winter months as a builder, Michele can't wait to become a barman again.

'See you at the Calandre!' I call after him as he goes off, grinning and waving, and swinging his bucket of tools.

Nervia Valley

Getting there: suggested transport in **bold**

Dolceacqua 12km, Pigna 17km from Ventimiglia.

Buses from Ventimiglia to Dolceacqua, Isolabona, Apricale, Pigna, Castel Vittorio, Buggio

Eating and staying overnight:

The following are only suggestions: full lists are available from local tourist information offices:

Dolceacqua

Ristorante Bar Gastone
2 Piazza Garibaldi
tel 0184 20 65 77

Agriturismo Terre Bianche
località Arcagna
tel 0184 31 426 fax 0184 31 230
e-mail rondelli@terrebianche.com
www.terrebianche.com

Ristorante La Vecchia
Via Roma, 86
tel 0184 20 60 24

Pizzeria La Rampa
Via Barberis, 5
tel 0184 20 61 98

Apricale

Hotel/Ristorante

Locanda dei Carugi – rooms and adjacent restaurant
Via Roma, 14–16
tel 0184 20 90 10
www.locandadeicarugi.it

La Favorita
1 Strada San Pietro
tel 0184 20 81 86

Rifugio Escursionistico Sciacaigaglia, Hikers' Hostel,
Via Doria, 4, Apricale, contact Silvano Pisano
tel 0184 20 80 62

Bed and Breakfast Casa del Ghirosveglio
Via Martiri della Libertà, 46, Apricale
tel 0184 20 82 43
www.ghirosveglio.com

Bar-Trattoria I Tarocchi
Via Roma, 42, Apricale
tel 0184 20 86 43

Pigna

Bar Trattoria La Posta
Via S. Rocco, 60
tel 0184 24 16 66

Albergo Grand Hotel
Pigna Antiche Terme – thermal spa
località Lago Pigo
tel 0184 24 00 10, fax 0184 24 09 49
www.termedipigna.it

Ristorante Hotel Terme
Località Terme di Pigna
tel 0184 24 10 46

Castel Vittorio

Ristorante Osteria del Portico
Via Umberti I, 6
tel 0184 24 13 52

Maps for walking:
IGC number 14, 1cm = 500m

Alpi Liguri Itinerari Escursionistici Transfrontalieri 1cm = 500m

Info and website:
Dolceacqua: www.comune.dolceacqua.it

Pro Loco, Via Barberis, 1, tel 0184 20 66 66

Apricale: www.apricale.org

                   Comune – Via Cavour, 2, tel 0184 20 81 26

Pigna: Municipio, Via Isnardi, 50, tel 0184 24 10 16

Castel Vittorio: Municipio, Piazza Comune
tel 0184 24 10 48

Climate and when to go:
Check opening times at local tourist office before going.

Especially attractive in spring and autumn; numerous events during the summer –

International Harp Festival – Isolabona – July

Organic products and craft market – Dolceacqua – last Sunday of each month

Open-air theatre – Apricale – July/August

CHAPTER 9

Cervo – gateway to the Riviera of Flowers

FROLICKING IN THE WAVES, DRESSED PRETTY much as she had been created, the goddess Diana was embarrassed and annoyed when she realised that the young shepherd Atteone had been peeping at her. She flicked some water at him and he turned, or at least partially, into a stag. The rest of Ovid's tale of Roman mythology is rather grisly, and anyway it *is* only a myth: a tale adopted to account for how the village of Cervo sits upon its headland overlooking the bay of Diano Marina – formerly *Pagus Dianae*. For if you know your animals, you will know that the Latin name for the deer is *cervidae*, and so, in Italian, a stag is called *cervo*. Look down from any one of Cervo's panoramic vantage points, and it's easy to imagine how this legend appealed to storytellers of old. At your feet the resort of Saint Bartolomeo al Mare merges into the seaside town of Diano Marina. Capo Berta in the west and Capo Mele in the east protect the bay's generous curve. Cervo watches sentinel-like from a rounded nub of land, ideal for keeping a lookout. Then, if we go back to 182 BC we find the origins of the place that came to be known as Cervo.

The Ingauni were one of Liguria's three main pre-Roman indigenous tribes. Practically nothing remains now of their *castellaro* in the woods above Cervo. It was a circular construction in rough-hewn stone: a protection for men and beasts. From their *castellaro*, the Ingauni watched the Romans arriving, building a road through the woods between their settlement and the coast. Knowing the territory better than the Romans, at first the Ingauni had an advantage that let them carry out successful raiding parties. Obviously the Romans weren't going to put up with that for long, and they built a sentry post alongside their new road, the Via Julia Augusta, at the point where it dips steeply down towards the sea. Then from *their* vantage point, and with their more sophisticated techniques, honed over years of empire building, the Romans retaliated against the Ingauni.

The Ligurian tribesmen were fierce, proud and shrewd. Realising that they couldn't outwit the greater *military* might of the Romans, they decided to exploit the colonists' wealth in a more subtle way. They left their *castellaro* and crossed the gully to the Roman settlement. Here they set up stalls and eventually a whole range of small service businesses, offering food, fodder and labour. Whoever was available to work for the Romans put out a sign reading '*Servo*' – I serve. These first Ingauni businesses and buildings were at the side of the Via Julia Augusta as it began its steep descent towards the coast in the lane that is Cervo's present-day Via Romana. The Romans called the cluster of enterprising Ingauni *Servo*, and the name stuck. Well into the sixteenth century the by now important and wealthy little town was still named Servo. It wasn't until the 1600s when Latin was displaced by the common language that was to become Italian, that the name mutated to Cervo, and the first stag appeared as the town's emblem.

Coastal Liguria is a palette of pastel-washed villages and towns, earthy greens, browns and greys, and every hue of blue that sea and sky can offer. The region's western provinces are Provincia di Imperia and Provincia di Savona; Cervo, just inside Imperia Province, is perched near the border between them. Facing the setting sun, today it is perhaps the prettiest and liveliest of all the coastal destinations. Totally traffic-free, it beckons to artists, photographers and lovers of the picturesque.

At the bottom of the hill, where the main road and the railway line run just a few metres from the coast, a steep ramp of cobbled steps is aptly named Salita al Castello – the way up to the castle. Salita al Castello becomes Via al Bastione, and from here you have a choice of nearly a dozen narrow lanes, all leading up to the castle. It doesn't matter which lane you choose – each one is as pretty as the other. And so, up and up. Why hurry? Savour the colours of the houses – lemon, apricot, cream, salmon, cherry; the elegant dark green doors of the noblemen's *palazzi*; the pot gardens set off against wrought-iron railings and gates. Enjoy the handicrafts on sale in cave-like shops with low, vaulted ceilings. When you begin to feel a bit puffed, turn around and look back down the alley. Back-lit succulents glow translucent-green around the edges. Multicoloured washing billows out overhead. Far below, for the lanes rise steeply, you'll catch a glimpse of the sea. Up and up then, until your lane opens into Piazza Santa Caterina.

TOP: *My secret roof-top garden*   BOTTOM LEFT: *Ventimiglia Alta*
BOTTOM RIGHT: *Porta Canarda, Ventimiglia*

TOP LEFT: *Perinaldo – old shutters, new shutters*   TOP RIGHT: *Cervo*
BOTTOM LEFT: *Perinaldo*   BOTTOM RIGHT: *Dolceacqua – Delia admires*
'L'estendales' banner

TOP: *Tende, Maritime Alps*   BOTTOM LEFT: *Trophy of the Alps, La Turbie*
BOTTOM RIGHT: *Tende, Maritime Alps*

Top left: *Cervo, looking towards Capo Berta and Diano Marina*
Top right: *Cervo* Bottom: *Capo Cervo*

TOP LEFT: *La Mortola with Ventimiglia in the background*
TOP RIGHT: *Entrance to Hanbury Botanic Gardens*
BOTTOM: *Il sentiero delle Calandre, winter 2003*

TOP: *Barrême, on the Route Napoleon, and on the Chemins de Fer de Provençe scenic railway*
BOTTOM: *Il porto, Marina San Giuseppe di Ventimiglia, as seen from my terrace*

Top left: *The Citrus Fruit Festival in Menton* Top right: *Ventimiglia –*
The Battle of the Flowers
Bottom left: *The engravings of Mont Bégo – ploughman with oxen*
Bottom right: *The grave of William Webb Ellis, Menton*

TOP: *Gaspard's Lair, Massif de l'Esterel*
BOTTOM: *Massif de l'Esterel*

On the northern side of the square, Clavesana Castle occupies the site where the Romans built their sentry post. The castle grows directly out of the rocky headland. Dating from the twelfth century, it is a sturdy, unpretentious stronghold. Over the centuries it has been castle, fortified church and hospital, and today houses the Tourist Information Office and the Western Liguria Ethnographical Museum. Catch an insight here into what life was like on the Riviera in the nineteenth and early twentieth centuries. Endearingly lifelike figures, shaped in papier-mâché by local historian, writer and museum curator Franco Ferrero, are intent on the everyday pursuits of generations past. Wearing the workaday clothes of the period, the women are engaged in wool-carding and spinning, lace-making and knitting, butter-churning and washing in an enormous metal bucket. Carved butter pats, hair-crimping irons, wash-stands, pots, plates and babies' cradles all vie for space. Two centuries-old brocade bodices hint at a more luxurious past. A precious centrepiece is the bound volume of the 1878 issues of *La Mode Illustrée*. In its nineteenth year of publication, this fine French illustrated magazine let Cervo's fashion-conscious women know what was the latest from bonnets to corsets, as well as hints on sewing and crocheting, and a serialised romance too.

In the next room, the men are busy about such tasks as turning a small olive press, corking wine, grinding, cobbling, sharpening a scythe, mending a fishing net. Alongside these figures are reed baskets for gathering chestnuts and mushrooms, and pans for roasting the chestnuts too, cheese strainers, a centrifuge for separating honey from the comb, tools and implements, straw-stuffed saddles, cork buoys and sailmakers' needles. It wasn't all work: here is a sailor making a model of his ship, and another making an intricate 3D picture frame with tiny pieces of interlocking wood, each piece not much bigger than a match. Other exhibits include old coins, from the days when every bank in Italy minted its own money and the five-lire coin, with a lovely bunch of grapes on one face, was a reasonable amount of money; photos of boats being launched from the yard at the bottom of the hill; an 1884 issue of *L'Epoca* showing the shooting of a policeman in Palermo, and a map from 1570.

Saint John the Baptist church is nicknamed *dei corallini*, the coral fishermen's church. The town's merchants, ship owners and nobility gave generously for its construction, while the coral fishermen offered their winters and the use of their boats to help in a practical way, transporting building materials and marbles from the quarries in Tuscany. These products were unloaded on the beach and the fishermen carried them up the hill on their shoulders. Under the local architect Gio Batta Marvaldi, the church took nearly fifty years to complete: it was finished in 1736. Frothy and curling like a foaming sea-green wave, the slightly concave façade is washed in pale green and coral pink. Statue niches, windows, cornices and the door, which is reached from the square by a long and broad flight of steps, are all bordered, framed and embellished in delicate stucco motifs. Stucco – a concoction of dehydrated lime, powdered marble and glue – makes the perfect time-and-weather-resistant material for the exuberance of Baroque flourishes. It is used just as lavishly inside, and sets off the warm mauve-red marbles, the greens and pinks, and the centuries-darkened paintings. The graceful, curvaceous, galleon-like altar almost seems afloat on its pedestal. Above the door, look up as Saint George – a favourite of Ligurian sailors – slays a magnificent black dragon. Outside, pause at the top of the steps. In late summer, chamber-music concerts are held in the square at your feet. The audience are seated on the steps of the church, with the sea and the twinkling lights along the beach as a backdrop for the stage.

Cervo's well-to-do built or modernised their *palazzi* during the seventeenth and eighteenth centuries, and you can admire a number of these homes in your stroll around the village. They have fine, aristocratic doorways and deep green doors with imposing bronze or metal knockers and knobs. If the door is ajar, you'll catch a glimpse of wide low-rise stairs in spacious, airy stairwells. To maximise the entry of sunshine and light, the *palazzi* were built around the edge of the village. A favourite is in Via Multedo, behind Saint Catherine's oratory. Called Palazzo De Simoni del Pulcin, it has a yellow chicken emblem painted in the centre of the door. The doorway itself is in black slate. A few doors down from here, you'll see another slate doorway. Look carefully at the boat etched into the slate, it shows a two-masted *tartana* with lateen sails – a fishing boat of long ago.

Down past gorgeous wrought-iron gates you can take a peek at olive trees, lemon and oleander, cacti and succulents, climbing roses and grapevines, lavender and cascading rosemary, all thriving in an assortment of pots and enormous terracotta urns that once stored olives and their oil.

Around and behind Cervo, the olive groves and pine woods thrive right up to the edges of the medieval town. A network of walking paths takes you to panoramic lookout points and past the characteristic *caselle:* structures which the farmers made by stacking up the stones in the fields and shaping a small, squat storage area for tools and equipment.

And you may like to hike up to Colle Castellaretto: the remains of the Ingauni stone stockade are barely discernible, but sit a while and relax. Enjoy the view, the scent of wild broom and pine, look carefully and you'll find delicate wild orchids (a protected plant in all of Italy). And perhaps there, among the stones of long ago, you can still catch a whiff of Cervo's fiery and enterprising founders.

Cervo

Getting there: suggested transport in **bold**

50km from Ventimiglia on coast road. A10 exit
S. Bartolomeo

Trains to Cervo, or more often to Diano Marina (3km)

Frequent buses from San Remo via Diano Marina

Eating and staying overnight:
Hotel/restaurant San Giorgio, Via Volta, 19,
tel 0183 40 01 75

Hotel/restaurant Bellavista, Piazza Castello, 2,
tel/fax 0183 40 80 94

Maps for walking:
Edizioni Multigraphic 106,1cm = 250m,
or IGC 15
1cm = 500m

Info and website:
www.cervo.com

Information: Piazza Santa Caterina
tel/fax 0183 40 81 97
www.apt.rivieradeifiori.it

Climate and when to go:
Pleasant all year round.

Museo Etnografico, Piazza Santa Caterina, open every day
9–1 p.m., 4–7.30 p.m.

Open-air classical and chamber music concerts July and
August.

CHAPTER 10

Green vegetable pie

THE FIRST NEW ZEALAND VISITORS TO THE
little house in the ramparts of Ventimiglia Alta are both
seasoned travellers, with just a small backpack each, and a
suit-carrier because Ian has to go to a business meeting in
Veneto. I've been looking out for them from time to time, and
now they're at the top of the stairs, huffing a bit but so glad
to be here after that long flight from Auckland to London,
and then on to Nice. Nice to Ventimiglia is a breeze as long
as there isn't a train strike. It's only an hour by train, with
frequent departures, and the line clings to the scenic shoreline
nearly all the way.

When we met in Auckland in December I'd showed then
my 'before' photos, and now they gasp and exclaim with
delight at the transformation, admire the floor tiles, are
captivated by the little terrace in the ramparts, the sea view
on one side, the bird's-eye view of the *Via* on the other. Later
we sit down to supper: raw ham with cantaloup melon, small

but tasty Ligurian olives, some of my favourite cheeses – creamy stracchino, smoked scamorza, soft Triora with its nutty, ugly but fully edible rind, and mixed salad. And *torta verde*, a Ligurian speciality. I used to buy it ready-made by the slice until one of my friends wanted to know why I didn't make it myself.

'It's so easy,' she assured me. 'And much cheaper.'

'But I haven't made pastry for years, wouldn't even want to,' I protested.

What a dunce I am. It turns out that you can buy 230g rolls of fresh, unsweetened short pastry, rolled out on baking paper and ready to use. I just give it a quick, final roll and line my pie tin, leaving plenty of pastry hanging over the edge. Then it's ready for the filling. Nothing could be easier than that!

Of fillings there are as many variations as there are friends, *nonnas*, *mammas* and *suoceras*: as I've never had an Italian granny, mother or mother-in-law, my friend Annamaria's version has rapidly become my own. It's my favourite type of recipe: a handful of this and that. Generally I sauté a finely sliced onion or two – a white and a red one if possible – then add other, predominantly green vegetables, according to season. A sliced capsicum, several sliced zucchini, a few handfuls of spinach, several sliced leeks, slivers of finely chopped raw artichoke hearts. All of these are fine and others too if you like – the quantity depends on the size of your pie dish. While the vegetables are cooking, heat the oven to 200°C and, in a big bowl, mix two beaten eggs with roughly half a cup of ricotta cheese and a really good handful of grated Parmesan. When the vegetables are just cooked, and all the liquid has evaporated, mix them with the cheese and egg mixture and season to taste. If it looks as if you have too much liquid, toss in a handful of cooked rice. Smooth into the pastry case, in an even layer about 1.5cm deep, and cover with a lid of finely rolled pastry. Roll up the overhanging pastry to form a rim: it will be friable and crunchy when the pie is cooked. Drizzle olive oil over the top and use the tips of the kitchen scissors to clip slits in the crust, then bake for forty to fifty minutes. It's delicious warm, even more so cold the next day. Thanks, Annamaria!

Ian and Lynnette and I have worked out their itinerary for the next two weeks, and I've booked their accommodation, and have provided some orientation info, maps and train timetables. All they have to do is avoid train strikes (it's that time of year when a lightning strike can hold you up for twenty-four hours), get themselves from place to place and enjoy each destination.

After two days in Ventimiglia, a circular route takes them to Lake Como, to Thiene where Ian has to meet a man whose firm makes sausage machines, then to Padova. From there I join them for the trip down the Brenta Canal on *Il Burchiello*. The boat takes us past the Ville Venete, the country retreats of the Venetian nobility of old, and cruises through locks and past pontoon bridges. The highlight is coming out into the Venetian Lagoon in late afternoon – Venice shimmers in the distance and materialises as we cruise nearer and nearer. Magical. We dock at St Mark's Square. Although I've already studied the route to our hotel, I'm just as surprised as Ian and Lynnette are when we get there within a few minutes of stepping out of the square: it's so easy to get lost. From Venice I head home, and Ian and Lynnette go on to Orvieto via Vinci – the birthplace of Leonardo with its small, fascinating museum dedicated to his inventions and the delightful walk up through the olive groves to the house where he was born. Their final stop before returning to Ventimiglia is to Vernazza in the Cinque Terre.

The Cinque Terre – 'five lands' – are a favourite Ligurian destination for most of my visitors, provided they're reasonably fit and enthusiastic walkers. Lynnette and Ian are lucky to be there mid-week, as almost all year round the trail is crowded at the weekend. Lucky to have found a room in the annex of Hotel Sorriso down near the sea, as Vernazza is by far the prettiest of the five villages. Lucky too to be travelling by train, as road access is breathtaking but torturous – gasps of delight, or fright, from the passenger, but the driver's eyes are glued to the road. There is no direct road access between the five villages: a series of five side roads wind down from a link road high up in the mountains. The villages are each only two or three kilometres apart, but it's at least half an hour between any two of them by car. Far better the *locale* train between La Spezia and Sestri Levante or Genova, which stops at all the stations.

From west to east the five villages are Monterosso al Mare, Vernazza, Corniglia, Manarola and Riomaggiore. Eleven kilometres in all, in a direct line. The clearly sign-posted hiking route between the villages takes the walker through terraced olive groves and vineyards, vegetable gardens and maritime scrub. The sea breaks directly onto the rocks far below the trail: the only real swimming area is at Fegina Beach at Monterosso, or off the breakwater at Vernazza.

The total walking time, Monterosso to Riomaggiore, is roughly five to six hours, but the route itself, and the villages, are so photogenic that a full day will soon slip by. At Prevo, between Corniglia and Vernazza, a solitary café clings to the rock face, jutting out precariously, and offering a spectacular view to the sea far below. If the sea is calm, the trip back to base by boat is a relaxing treat. If you get tired, a train will rattle into the tiny station and whisk you on or back. Don't count on seeing very much by train, though: outdoor space is so precious that most of the line and several of the stations are in tunnels.

Corniglia is the only one of the *terre* that isn't a fishing village. It's perched up high on a headland, the oldest and, in solemn stone and slate grey, the least colourful of the five. From here the route to Manarola is possibly the least interesting part of the trail, but the descent into Manarola makes it worthwhile.

If you're in Manarola during Christmas and New Year you can admire the *presepe*, the Christmas scene erected on the terraced hillside above the town – a life-size Holy Family with wise men, shepherds and sheep, and piped Christmas music. All the figures are outlined in coloured lights and illuminated until late at night. Beyond Manarola the last part of the trail is the romantically named Via del'Amore. This part of the path is flat and paved: an open-air art gallery dedicated to love and lovers, although the original path was in fact access to an ammunition storage bunker. Tiny Riomaggiore, squeezed into, spilling out of, its crevice in the rocks, completes the excursion.

Happily feeling like old Ventimiglia hands, Ian and Lynnette are back again for two more days before going on to the south of France. I throw their sweaty gear from the Cinque Terre into the washing machine and Ian and I go out to talk to Signor Barbero the butcher. Ian is a wholesale butcher, curing his own hams and corned beef and making his own sausages. He's interested in finding out how it's done here. Barbero is cheerful and obliging, readily explaining about salting and hanging and curing, and I translate for them. Ian and I buy a metre or so of Italian sausage. We wind it up like a pinwheel, skewer it together and pan-grill it. It's delicious, discreetly spiced with fennel seeds, not at all fatty. We enjoy it with rice, salad and a glass or two of the local red wine, Rossese di Dolceacqua.

CHAPTER 11

Perinaldo – reaching for the stars

THE OLD-TIMER IN FRONT OF ME, IN THE first seat on the bus, is telling the driver how to grow prize pumpkins: an above-ground technique that involves letting the seeds sprout on so many cubic metres of fresh cow dung. And it doesn't need watering: it stores up to eighty per cent of its volume in water for up to three months, he says. The bus driver nods, storing the hints away. It's a method better suited to another region of Italy, where cattle graze on rolling pastures. Where, in the steep terraced valleys of Liguria's hinterland, will a man find even one cubic metre of fresh dung? This is the last run of the day, and the men both live at the end of the line, at the head of a valley that fêtes the pumpkin and champions the green-thumbed wizard who grows the biggest one or the longest and straightest marrow. Pluck off most of the flowers. Just leave four or five, no more than six or seven, to grow to maturity. That explains why courgette flowers, stuffed with a savoury filling and lightly fried, are such a delicacy. The local name for them is *meesana*. The hints keep coming as we leave the valley floor and start the final climb, zig-zagging up and around, and up some more. It's nearly eight o'clock on a May evening. The Verbone valley is narrow and V-shaped: for the first eight kilometres after leaving the coastal town of Vallecrosia Mare, the road – barely wide enough for a bus and a bicycle – stays close to the stream that, after heavy rain, lives up to its name of Torrente di Vallecrosia.

It's already dusk in the villages of San Biagio and Soldano, but as the road climbs, Perinaldo still glows in the sunset. As the gardening focus moves on to tips for cantaloup and watermelon cultivation, I glance back down the valley. What was at first a tiny triangle of sea across the mouth of the valley is growing rapidly with every bend in the road. Just as we arrive in Perinaldo, the sea, by now twelve kilometres away and 572 metres below, spills out of the confines of the valley and stretches across the horizon.

Glad to be home, and no doubt itching to get out into his garden, the bus driver drops us off in the twilight. Outside the village bar, a heated discussion is in full swing about goodness knows what – it's in Perinaldo's distinctive dialect: when the discussion is as animated as this, they call it *gaggian*, a local name for the squabbling call of seagulls or *gabbiano*.

It'll be dark soon, but first there's just time for a delicious plate of *coniglio al ligure* – Ligurian rabbit stewed in white wine with tasty black olives, rosemary, thyme and sage, and a handful of minced pine nuts to thicken the sauce. There's no need to be dainty with a knife and fork: it's served with a lemon-garnished finger-bowl and chunks of bread to mop up the gravy. The perfect meal, complete with potatoes oven-baked with rosemary, green beans, and a sea view.

Night-time. The sky is swept crystal clear and cloud free; the moon in its last quarter, and stars galore. After two disappointing, storm-cloud-thwarted previous visits, at last conditions are ideal for an evening visit to Perinaldo. First stop is the GD Cassini Astronomic Observatory, named after one of Perinaldo's most famous sons, the astronomer Giovanni Domenico Cassini, born in Perinaldo in 1625.

Cassini spent his entire life exploring space and the stars. He discovered another four of Saturn's satellites, and determined that Saturn's ring was in fact a darker outer ring and a wider, lighter inner one, with a fine space between them. Although his instruments weren't accurate enough for him to identify exactly what was in this dividing space, he concluded that it probably contained a myriad of tiny particles, resembling for Saturn the Earth's Milky Way. In the nineteenth century James Maxwell's observations confirmed Cassini's theory, so that the space between Saturn's rings is still known as Cassini's Division.

Established in the early 1990s, the observatory occupies part of the former seventeenth-century convent of Saint Sebastian. It opens on fine Saturday evenings two or three times a month. By early May Saturn has dropped from view below the western horizon, to reappear in the autumn, so the ideal time to visit is during a session in April, when it is warm enough to comfortably spend the evening outside. Sessions are run by local astronomers and star-lovers, and are fun and informative. The mobile telescope in the courtyard magnifies up to 200 times, and is best suited for observing the western sky. What a thrill to see the moon's pitted surface and the streaky sphere that is Jupiter. The evening's treat of treats is Saturn, glowing jewel-like in its ring. Then it's up the spiral staircase to the fixed telescope in the revolving dome, for a view of the northern and eastern sky, with magnification of up to 400 times. Nebulae, galaxies and star clusters are suddenly, startlingly, more than just anonymous pinpricks of light. When the sky is clear, the evening can go on for as long as the audience can stay awake. As the Earth turns towards dawn, more and more stars move across the sky.

However long you stay, don't leave without taking a stroll through the village. It is strung out along the very top of the ridge, with the houses getting progressively older as you move west. By muted street light the pastel-coloured houses, the cobbled streets and older, bare stonework glow warmly, even in the dead of night.

Cassini was born in Castello Maraldi in Via Maraldi, the main street running along the top of the ridge. The sweet-faced angel over a side door contrasts with the more austere aspect of the castle with its crenellated tower, which you glimpse through an overgrown garden as you approach the village from the coast.

Further along the ridge the *via* opens out into a spacious belvedere. Below the southern side of the square, and in line with the parish church behind you, floodlights pick out the unadorned façade of the church of Our Lady of the Visitation. Sited on a flat-topped spur overlooking the valley, the church is oriented, according to Cassini's suggestion, precisely along the Ligurian meridian so that it casts no shadow at the summer solstice. The parish church, dedicated to San Nicolò, dates from the late 1400s, as recorded in the bas-relief sculpture of the stone lintel. The lane to the left of the church opens into a small north-facing square. The Alps form a backdrop to the villages of Apricale in the valley below and Baiardo further off, higher to the east.

With the first hint of dawn it's time to slip away. Perhaps
after this visit the night sky will never be the same again.

Perinaldo

Getting there: suggested transport in **bold**
16km from Ventimiglia
Buses from Ventimiglia

Eating and staying overnight:
Hotel Ristorante La Riana
Via Genova, 12,
tel/fax 0184 67 24 33
e-mail info@hotelLaRiana.com
www.perinaldo.com

Maps for walking:
IGC number 14,1cm = 500m
Alpi Liguri Itinerari Escursionistici Transfrontalieri 1cm = 500m

Info and website:
www.commune.perinaldo.im.it
Comune do Perinaldo, 1, Piazza S Antonio
tel 0184 67 20 01

Observatorio Astronomico G. D. Cassini, information
Tuesday and Friday 9.30–11.30 a.m.
tel/fax 0184 35 66 11

Museo G. D. Cassini, Comune di Perinaldo, Mon-Sat,
except public holidays, 9 a.m.–1 p.m.

Climate and when to go:
Check opening times at local tourist office before going.

The Observatory is open, weather and cloudless sky
permitting, at night, usually at weekends. Sightings vary
according to the time of year. Saturn is visible from autumn
through to the end of April.

CHAPTER 12

Triora – in memory of witches past

IMAGINE AN ISOLATED MOUNTAIN VILLAGE. Rough-hewn stone houses, clinging to each other, spill down a steep spur above neatly terraced patches of cultivated land.

Imagine this village – its name is Triora – in early autumn, 1587. For the third successive year, the grain crops have failed. The villagers are desperate. Autumn leaves shuffle down, murmuring in the still air. A chill fog shrouds the neighbouring villages. Slivers of bitter cold penetrate all but the cosiest of homes. Villagers dart about, hoarding every tiny morsel of flour or goat's cheese, every handful of dried chestnuts, every precious stick of winter firewood. Misery and anxiety nurture fear and suspicion: surely this ghastly famine cannot be a natural occurrence. Searching for a scapegoat, furtive whispers become bitter charges of spells and sorcery. A witch-hunt begins. A search for someone to blame.

Triora – in memory of witches past

The Argentina River flows into the Mediterranean Sea at Arma di Taggia, just twenty-five kilometres east of Ventimiglia. At its mouth the valley is quite wide and the road climbs gently at first. As the valley begins to narrow, small, ancient settlements mark the route. Montalto Ligure rises above Badalucca, tiny Glori nestles in the curve of a hillside, Aggaggio Inferiore is little more than a widening in the road. After twenty-five kilometres the valley opens out at Molini di Triora. Past the last houses on the edge of the village, the mountains close in again.

The hamlets of Andagna and Corte guard one side of the valley and on the other, sentinel over all at 780 metres above sea level, looms Triora. The road winds narrowly on and around and cuts back along the side of the mountain for another 5.5 kilometres. As the road curves around for the final approach to Triora we gasp as we look straight down onto the rooftops of Molini di Triora lying far below: it's practically an aerial view from 316 metres above.

With the onset of winter 1587, Triora was gripped by famine and poverty; fear and suspicion. Determined to have the witches rooted out, the village parliament began an investigation. Both the bishop, eighty kilometres away in the prosperous coastal town of Albenga, and the Inquisitor in Genoa sent representatives to make their own enquiries. In an atmosphere of mounting tension, the inhabitants were asked to make their accusations. Desperate to find an end, *any* end, to the famine, they came forward willingly and accused their neighbours of practising witchcraft. Initially thirteen women were arrested, but in turn they implicated others, so that by January 1588, thirty or so women had been charged. As the trial gathered strength, accusations included dancing with the devil, drinking human blood, and stealing and killing

125

children. An etching of that period shows witches playing 'ball' with a baby in swaddling clothes, and it was claimed that they tossed the baby back and forth across the valley from Triora to Corte. Worst of all, the women were charged with casting spells over the countryside to curdle the milk, to rot the grain, to freeze the wine in the barrels, to pelt the crops with hail.

Brutal torture was legal at that time, and it worked quickly. The women admitted to the charges from terror rather than from guilt.

Triora is a perched village where on a still morning you can hear a dog barking a kilometre away down the valley. Eventually the screams of the women being tortured in a nearby dungeon must have stabbed into even the hardest of Triora's hearts. Those who had scurried to accuse their neighbours of witchcraft began to have doubts about the trial. They began to fear too for their own impunity, as the tentacles of the investigation snooped into every cranny of society, from the poorest to the richest. Popular protest welled up in the village, demanding an end to the torture and horror. On 27 June 1588, the thirteen who were originally accused were sent to Genoa to appear before the chief magistrate. What a forlorn sight they must have been, huddled into the cart, as it set off on that long, grim journey.

In Genoa the children were released from prison. The adults were condemned to death, but as the investigators began to wrangle among themselves five of the women died while awaiting execution. Eventually those who had survived imprisonment for so many months had their sentences revoked and they were sent home to Triora.

Various aspects of this disturbing and tragic event have become the core of Triora's Museum of Local Lore and

Witchcraft – *Il Museo Regionale Etnografica e Della Stregoneria.* Among the fascinating exhibits in the museum are extracts from the transcript of the trial. This is a rare example of an Italian witch-trial where the names of the accused and the transcripts have been preserved.

Other exhibits in the witchcraft section of the museum, formally the village prison, include models of traditional witch activities, a torture chamber, a vast selection of books relating to witchcraft, black magic and casting spells from all over the world, and a report from a witchcraft conference held in Triora in October 1988. Upstairs there are exhibits of everyday rural life – tools and implements used in the fields, in working the grain, producing cheese, winemaking, drying and grinding chestnuts which were a staple winter food, and so on. An intriguing instrument is a butter drier – a sort of roller that pressed out excess moisture. Spare a thought for a woman going off to work in the fields. She isn't smiling for the camera, although photography must have been quite a novelty when this shot was taken: two small children are clutching her skirt and the baby is in its wooden cradle balanced on her head. It wasn't all hard work though – in one showcase we can admire the early twentieth-century piano accordions that Domenico Alberti played at festivals and rural gatherings.

Finally, there is another room in commemoration of Luigia Margherita Brassati, a saintly Sardinian noblewoman who settled in Triora and was a great and loved benefactress for the village until her death in 1927.

Visit Triora today and you will find the witches rehabilitated. Just outside the museum you will see a statue of 'The witch of the 21st century'. She's young and beautiful, and smiling a welcome: a deliberate attempt, in recognition of the injustice of the trials of 1588, to eradicate the more sinister concept of a witch. On the edge of the village the handful of ruined houses known as 'La Cabotina' is marked by a simple plaque noting that on this spot it was believed that the accused met on the Sabbath and danced with the devil.

Let your imagination finish the story, but don't neglect to explore the nooks and lanes and vaulted alleys of the rest of the village. Fine local slate has been used to set off the doorways of many of the houses. The lintels are carved in religious, allegorical or aristocratic symbols. Slate is still mined in the Argentina Valley, and some of it is of such high quality that it is exported worldwide for making billiard tables.

Very little remains of Triora's castle but a fine view can be enjoyed from its ruined tower, and from in front of the ruins of San Dalmazzo church. These ruins are a reminder of the damage wrought here by the earthquake of 1887.

Short walks out into the country will take you to the fifteenth-century San Bernardino chapel (closed for restoration at the time of writing) or to the picturesque ruins of Santa Caterina chapel, built by a local noble family in 1390. Follow a mule path to the spring where the witches are said to have gathered, and on to the stunning Loreto bridge that spans a river gorge. Listen to the tinkle of goat bells – perhaps you will even meet a goatherd with his snow-white nannies and their frisky kids.

It is also claimed that the witches gathered at the communal laundry tubs on the edge of the village. These tubs are still in use – an ideal place to scrub some especially dirty overalls or a cumbersome carpet.

Longer walks lead through chestnut forests to isolated,

sparsely populated hamlets (one of these is referred to in Triora as the village of thirteen street lamps and one inhabitant) and up over the crest of the Alps and into France. Buzzards soar and cry overhead, and the undergrowth rustles with lizards and snakes. Abandoned farm buildings built long ago with dry-stone walling crumble back into the undergrowth. Beyond the ruins of Santa Caterina, the dirt track continues on to Ca' Bruciata – an enormous chestnut tree struck by lightning many years ago. (The name *Ca'* is an abbreviation of *castagna*, the Italian word for *chestnut*.) You can walk for hours and almost become spooked by the sensation of total isolation, pulsating with presence. Turn around, but there's no one there, and yet . . .

Before you leave Triora, you might like to buy some goat's milk cheese or some products bearing a label with a witch at work in front of her cauldron – *I Prodotti Tipici della Strega di Triora*: locally produced jams and honeys; bottled mushrooms, or walnut sauce.

Triora

Getting there: suggested transport in **bold**
Triora is 36km from the coast at Arma di Taggia.
There are **buses** from San Remo a couple of times a day.

Eating and staying overnight:
Hotel Restaurant Colomba d'Oro, Corso Italia 66,
tel albergo 0184 94 051, restaurant 0184 94 060
fax 0184 94 089
e-mail colombadoro@libero.it
www.colombadoro.it

Maps for walking:
IGC Alpi Marittime e Liguri, no 8
1cm = 500m

Info:
Comune tel 0184 94049, fax 0184 94164

Museo Etnografico e della Stregoneria – Ethnographic and
Witchcraft Museum – and Pro Loco, Corso Italia, 1,
tel 0184 94477 – at least during the summer months, the
museum is open every day 2.30–6 p.m., and on Saturday
and Sunday morning, 10.30–12 p.m.

Climate and when to go:
Check opening times at local tourist office before going.

Pleasant mild climate during the summer, cold in winter.

Mushroom Fair – Festa del Fungo – in September, Village
Fair with roast chestnuts – Fiera e Castagnata – in
November, other events throughout the year.

CHAPTER 13

Spring in the
hanging gardens

I GIARDINI PENSILI DELLE CASE NOBILE DI Ventimiglia. The posters announcing the Spring Festival promise a rare treat, a guided tour of some of Ventimiglia Alta's hidden treasures: two of the privately owned 'hanging gardens' will be open to the public. At the same time, there will be visits to the medieval medicinal herb garden high up in an elevated courtyard in the convent next to the cathedral. The convent of *Le Suore dell'Orto*, the Sisters of the Kitchen Garden, has been recently restored – brought back from the brink of decay to become a sanctuary where children of working parents can be sheltered before and after school, fed and helped with their homework, and the little ones can take a nap. With many of the parents here going off early to work in factories, hotels and the homes of the wealthy, and on building sites in and around Monaco, the three nuns and their helpers are a second family for the children. The convent building is ancient and protected as part of the national heritage. The original stone floors, worn into uneven humps and hollows, are still visible under clear perspex plates, and the herb garden has been replanted. Ligurian rosemary takes pride of place with the traditional medicinal and culinary herbs: sage, calendula, mint, thyme, oregano . . . a scented delight.

The nobility of Ventimiglia Alta built their wide-staircased, high-ceilinged homes along the south-western side of the town, facing out to sea and catching the sun all day long. The main entrances are in Via Garibaldi, modelled on the aristocratic façades of Via Garibaldi in Genova. From the second floor of each house, a little footbridge over the alley that runs behind Via Garibaldi connects the main part of the houses with the roofs of their former stables, carriage houses and storage buildings. In all, ten of these quaint, balustraded bridges span the alley. On the roofs of these utility buildings each noble family had its own private vegetable garden: a large cultivated area, right in the heart of the town, ingeniously well drained, sunny all year round, protected from the wind by a wall on the seaward side. In the late nineteenth century, the popularity of Thomas Hanbury's botanic garden at nearby La Mortola saw a decline in the kitchen gardens, and they were remodelled into more fashionable miniature 'botanic' gardens. The exotic vegetation flourished here, just as it did at La Mortola, and vines of wisteria, bougainvillaea, grape and plumbago intertwined on trellises and pergolas. Proud palm trees became the focal point of each garden. The noble houses and their gardens are all privately owned. Tantalising glimpses of the upper branches of the gardens are all that is visible from Via Colla, so being able to visit two of them is indeed a treat. One of these two gardens has been converted from a miniature 'Hanbury Garden' into a more modern garden, with open, well-groomed lawn space and flowering plants contained in tidy borders. Trees have been limited to citrus varieties, and the former utility rooms at the end of the garden areas have been fashioned into summer flats and a work studio. The garden must be alive on summer evenings with outdoor dining and partying. The owner welcomed us into the main part of the house too, so that we could admire his recently restored ceiling frescoes.

The second garden on show is still a profusion of vegetation, as it was planted a hundred-odd years ago – a wild, gnarled contrast to its more modern neighbour two doors away. It would be shaded and splendidly cool all day long here in summer, dank and shadowy maybe in winter. I thought about the palm tree, with its roots no doubt by now an integral part of the roof of the storage room on which it is growing, and shuddered to think of upkeep and maintenance costs.

One of the two men in the tour group admitted to an academic interest in the gardens as his university thesis is on the nobility of Ventimiglia; the other told me that he was home from his diving school job in Thailand and had recently bought a flat in Ventimiglia Alta. We swapped notes about renovation costs and addresses. 'But you have a hanging garden of your own!' he exclaimed. 'Right over Porta Nizza, too.'

My garden is little more than a square metre of built-in planter box, with lots of pots along the Via Garibaldi side of the parapet. 'Does it qualify as a hanging garden?' I wonder, amused by the idea, and invite him up to have a look. I'm encouraging herbs and salad greens – there's no scope here for a palm tree. By now some of the fruit stones which I tossed, compost-minded, so nonchalantly into the pots last summer have sprouted. A miniature peach, plum, apricot, loquat, cherry – even an avocado and some lemon seedlings come up from pips, all vying for space in a pot of their own. They'll never bear fruit, my horticulturist friend Riccardo tells me. A lecture on grafting follows, one that I remember from my childhood when I grew an apple tree from a pip. Dad was also a horticulturist and just as my little apple tree was the exception to the rule then, in due course, I'll eat my own stunted but delicious peaches and plums: not bad after three years in a 40cm tub.

There's a great surge of activity in Ventimiglia in spring, as preparations for the summer get top priority. In the bars and restaurants along the waterfront, awnings are wound out and washed, outdoor furniture gets fresh cushions and tablecloths, planter boxes and pots are filled with bright, sunny colours. The beaches are cleaned – the debris washed up in the spring storms is bulldozed up, bonfired or taken away. In some places lorryloads of crushed river sand are brought in and levelled out over the pebbles, probably to get washed away in the first rough sea, but in the meantime it makes a good impact. Gaily coloured deck-chairs and beach umbrellas are arranged in readiness for the first intrepid swimmers. An open-air cinema is set up with a different film starting each evening at dusk. Spruced-up signs advertise sailing and skin-diving lessons, beach volleyball competitions, rowing and sailing regattas, open-air concerts and dances for every taste, for every age group.

In Ventimiglia Alta, doors, shutters and windows are flung open wide in little flats and bed-sitting rooms that have been closed up since last September. The air circulates, taking away the mustiness. Mattresses and carpets are hauled over balustrades and window-sills, beaten and aired. Excited chatter from neighbours as they discuss who's coming to stay this summer, and what accommodation they still have available for relatives, friends and, better still, short-term tenants and paying guests, from all over Italy and from France, Germany, Switzerland . . . Soon the carpark will be overflowing with visitors' cars from every European country; shops, cafés and restaurants become a multilingual babble. The towns and cities of northern Europe close down, become ghost towns stifled by the heat and humidity, drained of everyone who can possibly get away. The coastal towns and inland villages blossom and bustle and bulge with holiday activity. Some of the inland villages, gradually abandoned due to population drift towards the coast and the bigger towns, have been revitalised in recent years by Swiss, German, Dutch or Belgian input. What began with one couple buying an isolated holiday home quickly multiplied to become a northern/middle-European enclave. The long-neglected medieval shells have been renovated, redecorated, lovingly rescued from the final indignity of dereliction.

Town councils and the National Heritage Trust keep a watchful eye out for any exterior modernisation that would detract from the original architectural character of the village. Suspicious at first of what foreigners, and holidaying ones at that, would bring, the villagers have come to welcome the surge in building work and increased general well-being which the newcomers have brought to the villages. Property values have begun to creep up so that even a semi-abandoned village house, its power supply disconnected years ago, is no longer a bargain buy. As the suspicion of foreigners fades, smiles, gestures, a smattering of Italian and another language prevails, and the youngsters thrive on multinational experiences. At Calandre Beach young Marco is hopping up and down, excited behind his father's bar counter, telling me that yesterday an English boy asked him for a sticking plaster and he understood! We're both thrilled. I hope that something similar happens every day.

'Meloni! Meloni! Dieci mila lira la cassa! Meloni!' We can all hear him coming up Via Garibaldi, the man with the fruit and vegetable lorry, selling cantaloup melons, 10,000 lire for a case of five or six. It's good value now, and as they become more plentiful they'll be 8000 or even 5000 lire a case. He sells tomatoes, onions, potatoes, capsicums, artichokes: whatever's plentiful at the moment. Sometimes a couple of lorries come around, vying for space in the parking area outside Porta Nizza. Keeping to the cool shade in Via Garibaldi, a fisherman comes around too with his morning's catch. *'Acciughi, sardine belle fresche.'* Juicy fresh sardines and anchovies.

Colourful stalls in the covered fruit and vegetable market in Ventimiglia Bassa overflow with tempting produce. It was opened in 1922 as a fresh flower market, and although there are still a handful of stalls selling flowers and plants, most of the floor area is now dedicated to fruit and vegetable stalls. On one side are the bigger displays of the stallholders who buy at the produce auction, while on the other side the smaller stalls of the local market gardeners. Seasonal crops follow each other, week by week: strawberries, cherries, apricots, peaches, plums, grapes, apples, pears and persimmons; asparagus, beans, massive sun-ripened ox-heart tomatoes, aubergine, zucchini, broccoli, crunchy fennel, red and yellow apple-sweet capsicums, leeks, forest mushrooms and pumpkin. Buckets of small but tasty Ligurian olives, bottles of home-pressed olive oil, jars of fresh pesto sauce, bunches of fresh-picked herbs, plaits of garlic, garlands of chilli peppers and free-range eggs complete the choice from the market gardeners.

If you want to cure some olives yourself, you can buy them here too, for about three Euro per kilo. Take them home and put them in a bucket of water. Change the water every day for about ten days. Then boil up a brine solution with a good 100g of salt for every litre of water – enough water to completely cover the olives. When the water is cold, put the olives in a large jar with some rosemary, a couple of bay leaves, as many cloves of garlic as you like and a lemon, cut in half, for every kilo of olives, and pour the brine over them. Close the jar and leave in a cool place for at least six weeks. Check it from time to time and if you see any signs of mould forming, just drain off the liquid, rinse the olives in cold water and make some fresh brine, being more generous with the salt.

I prefer to shop on the market gardeners' side of the market: my favourite stallholders appreciate my custom – their gift of a lemon or a bunch of basil or laurel is always welcome. Along one edge of the market are the remnants of the once-thriving flower market. The stalls that remain are incredibly colourful: most of the flowers are skilful silk imitations. The other wall of the market is lined with kiosks selling cheeses from all over Italy, hams and sausages and salamis, fresh pasta in every shape from tagliatelli to ravioli and tortellini. Shopping bags overflow with fresh flavours and aromas.

The produce market is open every morning, Monday to Saturday. A market of a very different sort takes place on Fridays. By pale dawn light, stallholders line up their kombi vans, bumper to bumper – a hundred vans at least, just along the riverbank and part of the waterfront, and more right around the public gardens. Setting up their tables, heaving their enormous canopies into position in a rhythm perfected over the years, they are soon laying out their wares in the biggest street market on the Riviera and the Côte d'Azur. Busloads of tourists come from as far away as Nice, and coach tours from England and Germany include it in their itinerary. Clothing for men, women and children; leather bags, shoes, sunglasses and trinkets; football team and Formula One souvenir shirts, caps, scarves and flags; bedding – the mohair blankets are a popular buy; lingerie, tablecloths, saucepans, coffee pots, household goods . . . The choice goes on and on.

By 8.30 a.m. the throngs of shoppers are happily looking for bargains or reminders of a visit to Ventimiglia. Both abound, as do crushed toes and tales of woe – it's a pickpocket's paradise. By five or six o'clock the almost mechanical packing-up process is under way. The stallholders quickly stow their goods in their vans and make way for an army of street sweepers and cleaners. Very soon, almost by magic, it's as if the market had never been. Tomorrow, and throughout the week ahead the stallholders will circle round the other, smaller street markets, every day the same routine in a different town.

Ventimiglia/Hanbury

Getting there: suggested transport in **bold**

Ventimiglia is on the coast, 10km inside the Franco-Italian border, and 150km from Genova. There is a busy international railway station, with direct **trains** to Nice, Paris, Turin, Genova, Milan, Rome, Venice, Strasbourg, Basel, and Irun and Port Bou on the Spanish border.

Riviera Trasporti buses run to most inland villages, and coastal destinations.

Villa Hanbury botanic gardens are in the hamlet of La Mortola, between Ventimiglia and the French border, and there are buses to the gardens and on, to the border, ten times a day.

The roads become very congested during the summer, especially at weekends, and all year round on Fridays, which is market day.

Eating and staying overnight:
The following are only suggestions: full lists are available from local tourist information offices.

Restaurants

Bar Pizzeria Porta Nizza, Piazza Funtanin, Ventimiglia Alta, tel 0184 23 84 37

Pasta e Basta, 12, Passeggiata Marconi, Ventimiglia, tel 0184 23 08 78

La Caravella, 1, Passeggiata Marconi, tel 0184 35 18 40

La Greppia, fish restaurant, 107 Corso Nizza, Latte (between Ventimiglia and Villa Hanbury Gardens) tel 0184 22 60 63

Hotel Restaurant: XX Settembre, 16A Via Roma, tel 0184 35 12 22

Albergo Sole Mare, Passeggiata Marconi, 22, tel 0184 35 18 54, fax 0184 23 09 88, www.hotelsolemare.it

Hotel Restaurant La Riserva di Castel d'Appio, Via Peidago, Località Castel d'Appio tel 0184 22 95 33, fax 0184 22 97 12, www.lariserva.it

Apartments to let and B&B in Ventimiglia Alta, tel Yvonne Molinari, 0184 35 27 74, e-mail carolynmckenzie@libero.it

There is a pleasant snack bar within the grounds of Villa Hanbury Gardens.

Maps for walking:

IGC no.14 San Remo – Imperia – Monte Carlo 1cm = 500m

For general touring, Touring Club Italiano Liguria, 1cm = 2km

Info and website:

www.apt.rivieradeifiori.it

Information, Via Cavour, 61, Ventimiglia,
tel/fax 0184 35 11 83

Villa Hanbury Gardens tel 0184 22 95 07, open daily April–
September 9 a.m.–6 p.m., October–March 10 a.m.–5 p.m.,
closed Wednesday

The garden's summer evening programme includes open-air
concerts and stargazing: ask for programme.

Battaglia di Fiori – Battle of Flowers www.battagliadifiori.com

Biblioteca Civico Aprosio, 10 Via Garibaldi, Ventimiglia Alta,
tel 0184 35 12 09. Check opening times before visiting, but
generally the Library is closed on Sundays, open in the
mornings during school summer holidays, and on Monday
and Saturday morning in winter and in the afternoons until
7.30 Tuesday to Friday.

Climate and when to go: check opening times at local tourist
office before going.

Pleasant all year round. Mild winters, mimosa in full bloom
late winter/early spring (February/March). July and August
can get very hot and crowded.

Battle of the Flowers in June

Medieval Pageant in August

Market day all day Friday – the biggest street market on the
Riviera

Fruit and vege market and fish market, mornings until
lunchtime

CHAPTER 14

The Battle of the Flowers and the Hanbury Botanic Gardens

WINE, OLIVES AND FIGS WERE THE AGRI-cultural basis of the economy of Ventimiglia and the surrounding countryside from the thirteenth century onwards. Records regarding their cultivation, harvest and earnings date back to the mid-1200s. Later on, citrus fruit, particularly lemons and oranges, became the fourth most important crop. Climatic conditions in this area meant that the quality of the harvest was generally assured, and the produce was recognised and valued throughout the known world.

Towards the end of the nineteenth century, various factors caused a change in the agricultural base of the Ventimiglia area. Plant diseases, a scarcity of water and falling prices caused concern among the growers of traditional crops. At the same time, contemporary fashion was creating an ever-increasing demand for cut flowers. Although many long-term residents were dismayed to see the vineyards, olive and fig groves, and citrus orchards being rooted out, the more adventurous growers decided to face the risk, and turn their land over to floriculture.

Whereas nearby San Remo was known popularly as 'The City of Dreams', Bordighera as 'The City of Palms' and Menton glowed as 'The Pearl of the Riviera', Ventimiglia was readily defined as 'The City of Flowers'. It was the most important centre of floriculture in Italy, and the spectacular afternoon flower market was soon a tourist attraction as well. Every day at 1.25 p.m. a special train pulled out of Ventimiglia station, laden exclusively with flowers, bound for Genoa. Other wagons containing ornamental plants and foliage from Tuscany were added, and the train continued northwards with its colourful, perfumed cargo, distributing it in fifteen European countries, as far away as Scandinavia.

The first bi-annual floral exhibition was held in 1924. These exhibitions would always close with a colourful street parade of floral floats, held as a competition among the major growers. In time this parade became the annual Battle of the Flowers, which is still held today.

The so-called 'battle' or competition is held annually in June or July. Three months before the parade, the various groups of growers and their supporters construct an enormous, temporary shed. Enthusiastic teams of up to fifty workers devote every free moment to constructing the gigantic polystyrene figures for the float. Eventually these figures are entirely covered in flowers and other vegetable matter – leaves, dried seed heads, moss. The floats must be ninety per cent vegetation, so the volume of flowers that will be imbedded in the polystyrene in the final hours before the parade is breathtaking – around 100,000 carnations are used for each float. Initially the floats were decorated with bunches of flowers, but later the mosaic technique was introduced. Only the heads of the flowers are used, with each head being pinned to the polystyrene base. Once the polystyrene base is ready, scaffolding is built up all around the structure, and the floral mosaic-makers go about their work, perched on the scaffolding, lying on it if need be, to get at the really tricky parts. This final stage of preparation has to be done at the last minute, especially since the flowers would soon wilt in the summer heat. Work goes on long into the night before the parade. At this stage there is no longer any real need for secrecy. The sheds are opened up, and in a balmy late-night party atmosphere the floats' supporters stroll along to watch the final hours' work, to chat and maybe sing and enjoy a glass of wine and or an ice-cream. Somehow, as those final frenetic hours tick by, the buckets bursting with rainbow-coloured carnations are transformed into people, animals, birds, cars, planes, globes, spaceships, dinosaurs . . . all picked out in perfect detail in flowers.

Since flower cultivation has diminished in importance over recent years, and in any case carnations require quite a lot of attention in their cultivation, nowadays the groups that prepare the nine or ten floats have to buy the carnations: if they are lucky the town council will, in the interests of tourism, help out with a grant.

Each year the parade follows a different theme: the countries of Europe, famous personalities, the songs of the 1960s and so on. Carnations form the basis of each float's figures, and if necessary white blooms can be dyed to obtain blues and greens. From early morning on the Sunday of the parade, the streets in a rectangular circuit around the public gardens and the town hall are cordoned off, and a series of tiered seats erected. This is the circular route of the parade.

As well as viewers in the tiered seats, standing spectators throng the footpaths, and there is a lively festive atmosphere with music, balloons, and candyfloss. The parade starts in mid-afternoon, with the tractor-drawn floats making a slow, introductory circuit. They tower high above the crowd: the few people on each float seem to be Lilliputians among the gigantic floral Gullivers. Each float is separated from the next by other entertainers – bands and marching girls, ceremonial-flag throwers and whip-masters, jugglers and clowns.

After the first circuit of the gardens the finale begins. This time the floats are laden with masses of loose flowers and small bouquets, and the attendants on the floats blithely toss these flowers out to the crowd while more attendants follow on foot, tossing still more flowers to the spectators and deep into the back rows on the footpaths or high into the stands. It's a joyous occasion as, float by passing float, old and young alike gather posies of carnations and roses in particular, but other flowers too. The flowers that fall short of the crowd lie briefly on the road, but the spectators nearest the road dart forward, in spite of the protests of the police, and rescue these blooms before they are crushed by the next float. Twice around the circuit the shower of gorgeous colours continues, and when the floats finally come to a halt the streets are carpeted with rejected greenery and battered flowers. Later in the day the winner of the competition is announced amid singing and celebrations in the central square, which is lined with the parked floats. The next day they are still on display, and awed passers-by can admire the details of their construction from close up – gigantic figures and their surroundings, with every feature – lips, teeth, eyes, eyelashes, fingernails, buttons, buckles, watch faces – all made with flowers and vegetable matter.

Following the rocky coastline from Ventimiglia towards Menton, a promontory spills down a myrtle-green slope into the sea, forming the western arm of the Bay of Latte. This headland has taken its name from the myrtle, *mirto* in Italian, *murtula* in Ligurian dialect, evolving in time to Mortola, and so Capo Mortola. In the 1860s the cape was planted in vineyards, olive and citrus groves, peaches and artichokes, and sheltered an elegant seventeenth-century mansion. An Englishman, Sir Thomas Hanbury, bought this 112-acre property in 1867, and transformed it into one of the most important botanical gardens and acclimatisation centres in Europe. Just as the mild climate had long favoured the cultivation of food crops, it now enabled the creation of a paradise of rare and exotic plants: an enchanted acclimatisation garden where plants from all over the world flourished side by side in the open air. The land was terraced and planted, and to add to the pleasure of a visit to the gardens, statues, ornamental temples, fountains and fish ponds were added. Pathways zigzagged down the slopes from the entrance to the gardens, high up on the hillside in the village of La Mortola Inferiore, down to the seashore. Tantalising glimpses of the sea occurred naturally through the trees, and wider vistas were created by the shrewd counter-play of paths and unplanted areas. Trellises and pergolas completed the landscaping, and in time the ornamental tombs of the Hanbury family were also incorporated in the gardens.

A visit to the gardens is a pleasure at any time of year. Each season brings its own particular flowers and fruits, aromas and colours. The visit starts at the ornamental gates on the old Ventimiglia-Menton road, and a clearly marked red zigzag route saunters down to sea level, passing species from Australia, Africa and subtropical America – agaves, aloes, cork oaks, papyri (this is the most northern locality where they are cultivated outdoors), a citrus grove and an exotic orchard, a garden of heady perfumes. The species are clearly labelled and interest is added by the inclusion of several Japanese bronze sculptures. Towards the end of the downward path, a small bridge takes you over a trench that runs across the width of the garden. Deep in the trench is one of the better-preserved original stretches of the Roman road Via Aurelia, the highway which was built 2000 years ago and was a link in the chain of wide, paved roads from Rome to Arles.

This section of the road owes its preservation to the fact that it has remained for centuries within the protective walls of the gardens. A plaque names the famous travellers who have passed this way: Pope Innocent IV on May 7 1251, St Catherine of Siena in June 1376, Nicolò Macchiavelli in May 1511, the Emperor Charles V in November 1536, Napoleon Bonaparte on April 3 1796.

Beyond this historic piece of the gardens, the path passes through an olive grove to reach the sea wall. A pergola, blessedly shaded in summer and sunny in winter, is outdoor seating for the café-snack bar – the ideal spot to sit quietly before heading uphill again. The beach isn't accessible from here, but the sea can be seen, lapping serenely on the rocks or pounding furiously on the shore according to the weather, just a few metres outside the gate.

Turn your back to the sea and the gardens rise steeply towards the pretty pastel-washed villages of upper and lower La Mortola. Villa Hanbury peeps through the vegetation, and the mountains rear up behind. 'Do we have to walk all the way back up there?' friends moan as we leave the café, refreshed with drinks and delicious *panini caldi* – toasted buns with ham, tomato and runny-cheese fillings. Far over to our right as we head up the blue path, we catch a glimpse through the trees of Calandre Beach and Ventimiglia. In spite of the initial dismay, the return path meanders easily up the gradient, and the species that we encounter catch at our imagination: *Cedrus deodara* from the Himalayas, Australian eucalyptus growing at their most northerly latitude, a pergola of climbers, an avenue of palms, ginkgo . . . We wander gradually upwards, until at last it's time to turn and face the sea again, one last time from the gates of the gardens.

CHAPTER 15

A walk around
Ventimiglia Alta

BRING YOUR CAMERA AND COME WITH ME.
Let's start under the arch of Porta Nizza, at the top of Via
Garibaldi. The ironclad doors are always open, though once
they would have been heaved closed at night and stoutly
bolted in troubled times. We're in Piazza Funtanin – the
stagecoach doesn't leave from here any more, although there
are plenty of old photos showing the loaded coach, and the
wheelwright's business which was built onto the outside of
the wall where there is a private home now. The natural
spring that fed a fountain giving the square its name was
blocked up about forty years ago. In the times before everyone
had indoor plumbing – that is, before the 1950s – the fountain
was a precious source of clean water for drinking and
washing. After it was stoppered in the 1960s, the water built
up underground until a massive landslide carried away the
hillside, including the road that was then the only one to

the border. Until it could be repaired, Ventimiglia was cut off from France.

Looking up at Porta Nizza from the outside, we can see the rough outline of the original stone arch. The more decorative opening of today is a legacy of Napoleonic times. Notice how it was chipped, high up on the left-hand side, by an Allied bomb during World War II.

Next to the pizzeria, a signpost indicates the start of a five-hour tramp up and over the mountains to Castellar, and we'll go up here, but just a little way, skirting the medieval walls, until we come to another entrance through the fortifications. This sentry post and arched gateway has changed very little in structure over the centuries. The walls were built by the Genovese Republic from 1529 onwards, and Porta Nizza would have been built then in the same style as this gateway.

We turn under the archway and down the ramp to a point where we can see out over the lower Roya Valley, dominated now by light industry, the railway line and main road to Piemonte, and crossed by the motorway. The little house here on our right is one of very few with a garden within the walls – a real haven, especially during the summer.

On down the lane, then first on the left into Via Appio, which even by medieval standards is extremely steep. Down and down, until we reach Piazza San Michele. This square was originally outside the town walls – the ones built in the twelfth century – and was surrounded by olive groves that were tended by the Benedictine monks. In the tenth century a simple chapel stood on the site of San Michele church, and over the next hundred years or so it was enlarged. Because of its strategic position on the approach road to Ventimiglia Alta, the bell tower was designed to double as a lookout post. The church was part of a hospital complex where road-weary travellers were cared for. Under the church a fascinating little crypt is supported by columns that were transported here from the Roman township and reused in building the church. One column is a Roman milestone, dating from the time of Caracalla, AD 211–17, and confirming the distance from Rome to Albintimilium as 590 Roman miles. A second milestone, from the earlier reign of Augusto stands just inside the front door of the church, and is used as a holy water font. Services are held in the church on special occasions, and although it isn't always open, it's a treat to visit.

We'll continue along Via Piemonte – notice how some of the houses were once quite smart, with frescoed walls and elaborate windows and doorways. Past a baker's and a grocery shop the road narrows, and we turn off to the left at Piazza Morosini – notice the squat little building on the corner. It was built by the brothers Guido and Ottone Guerra, two Counts of Ventimiglia who were also Knights Templars. The building served as a refuge for travellers. Even after the order of Templars was suppressed in 1312, pilgrims continued to stay here. Eventually it became a simple hospital, and continued as such until the eighteenth century.

Across the square we duck down Vico Coperto – true to its name, this is a covered alley, passing directly under some of the houses that face onto the square. It will take us right around the back of the houses that overlook the valley. All of these houses were built long before the advent of flushing loos, so it isn't uncommon to see that the toilet has been built onto the outside of the house, jutting out from one end of the balcony. Vico Coperto continues into Vico Rocchetta, and then into Vico Buio. The houses here are some of the very oldest in Ventimiglia Alta, and date back to the 1400s. Just at the start of Vico Buio a few metres down the lane on the left you'll come to Salita Lago. This lane, Lake Rise, on the very edge of the township, passes under one of the oldest gates in the fortifications, and was the way down to the small lake that had formed at the foot of the hill from a loop in the river. The town's laundry women did the washing in the lake; if you continue down Salita Lago, you'll come to Vico Lago and Vico Lavandaie – Lake Alley and Washerwomen's Alley – and eventually into Vico Mulino, named for the water mill which was powered by the river.

Back though to Vico Buio – Dark Alley; it bends around to the right, and is so dark that it's almost like going into a cave. Luckily the street lighting is usually on day and night. If we had continued straight on in Via Piemonte instead of turning into Piazza Morosini, we would have reached Vico Buio by way of Vico Scuri. This alley, where the name also suggests darkness, referred in the past to the darker, danker, working-class part of the town, crammed in under the larger, lighter, airier middle- and upper-class houses on the floors above.

Vico Buio takes us up into Vico Olivi, running parallel to Via Giudici and Via Garibaldi. Around to the right and up the last few steps in Via Fallerina and we're outside the cathedral. Now we are right at the core of Ventimiglia Alta's origins. The steep stone wall to the side of the cathedral is all that remains of the castle of the Counts of Ventimiglia – an imposing edifice that would have dominated the ridge, with an unhampered lookout in all directions. As we see them today, the cathedral and octagonal baptistery are mainly early-to-late Romanesque, with a baptismal font engraved with the year 1100 and the porch over the main entrance to the cathedral dating from 1250, along with the triple-arched window above the porch. In the 1500s the baptistery was modified to create another chapel in the cathedral, but the older part can be partially seen through the perspex floor of the chapel, or reached on special occasions from behind the cathedral. The present-day bell tower was built on the remains of a former defence tower; it retains its baroque aspect in the upper part, while being clearly much older near the base.

Vico Battistero takes us down the left-hand side of the cathedral – I don't want you to miss what must surely be the narrowest and most intriguing house in Ventimiglia Alta: it reminds me of a lighthouse. Here it is, bright purpley-pink (the colour known in Italian as *fucsia*, pronounced fooks-ee-ah) on the corner of Salita San Giovanni Battista. It even has a rooftop terrace. Sometimes the shutters are open, but I've never seen any other sign of life. How would you furnish those tiny horseshoe-shaped rooms?

If we follow the road out to the *belvedere* we can enjoy the same view that the Counts of Ventimiglia had. Just hidden from view, to the immediate left, the steep-sided wall of Porta Marina originally rose sheer out of the river. Directly in front of us, at Marina San Giuseppe, a number of enormous rocks were scattered along the beach. The best known of them, Scoglio Alto, the High Rock, was almost seventeen metres high, and since earliest times had been used as the base for a lighthouse for the boats that anchored in the river mouth. In November 1917, it was carried away during a storm, although old photos showing it are quite readily available still in the bric-a-brac markets.

Returning to Piazza Cattedrale, between the cathedral and the castle wall, we head for home, up Via Garibaldi. The main street is lined with fine aristocratic houses, especially on the left-hand side. If a doorway is open you can peep inside – notice the wide staircase with shallow rises and marble treads, and elegant iron balustrades. This aspect of Ventimiglia dates from the 1500s and in many respects is modelled on the finer streets of the same period in the city of Genoa, which controlled Ventimiglia at that time. Near the beginning, on the right, we pass Ventimiglia's library. It was founded by the Ventimiglia-born Agostinian monk Ludovico Aprosio in 1642, and was one of Italy's first public libraries. Aprosio was such an avid book collector, with wide-ranging interests, that he amassed a total of 10,000 volumes before his death in 1681. In spite of their age – some of the books were already old when Aprosio bought them – there's nothing musty about this library, and the books can be consulted in special conditions or obtained on CD: students of the Baroque come to Ventimiglia from all over the world to do research in the library.

On the corner of Vico Pignone, notice the bas-relief of Saint George fighting his dragon. Saint George was a popular saint in medieval Genoa, and English sailors visiting the port there are believed to have introduced his cult into England.

The second covered alley on the left is Salita Colla Bassa. Especially on sunny afternoons, when Via Garibaldi is already in the shade, the bright warm sky beckons at the end of the alley. As we cross Via Colla Bassa, we can see the little footbridges that link the noble houses with their own private hanging gardens. Such luxurious growth – palms, vines, plumbago, wisteria and bougainvillaea; so tantalisingly near, and so totally inaccessible. Even the little arch over the end of the salita is part of two gardens, very decisively divided with a spiked iron grill!

Our walk ends here as we face westwards to take in the view from Passegiata Colla. Tete di Chien, the flat-topped, snub-nosed mountain above Monaco, dominates the horizon, and beyond it on a clear day we can pick out Cap Ferrat, Cap d'Antibes and the two humped summits of Massif de l'Esterel, roughly sixty-five kilometres away. In super-clear conditions, the misty outline of Cap Camarat is visible too, just beyond St Tropez and a good eighty kilometres away in a direct line across the sea from our vantage point.

The skyscrapers of Monte Carlo loom up over Cap Martin, and the Trophy of the Alps at La Turbie is visible on the mountainside, above and slightly to the right of them. Very early in the morning or on a crisp winter's day, the view extends to Corsica, standing out on the southern horizon.

CHAPTER 16

Sospel – on the salt route

A PSYCHEDELIC TRIO OF PARAGLIDERS drifts up over Mont Agaison, fuschia pink, spring green and brilliant blue – revolving lazily in a cloudless sky. Higher still a lone hawk hovers above them, watchful over its territory.

It's mid-morning in Sospel, in late spring. Daffodils are out, fruit trees and forsythia are in full bloom. Shaded road banks are speckled with pale lemon wild primroses and wild violets. Sospel lies in the Bevera River valley. In a direct line from Menton it's only thirteen kilometres from the sea, but in spite of the valley being wide and sunny, there's no sense of the sparkling Mediterranean here. This is a rural valley surrounded by the Alpes Maritimes: steep, ravine-riddled mountains that soar up to 600, 800, 1000 metres and more above sea level. Getting here is an adventure. The road from Menton winds up and up for fifteen kilometres before crossing the Col de Castillon and then drops down, one tight hairpin bend after another, for a further seven kilometres. Buses from

Menton make the trip several times a day, and the scenery is spectacular. The forty-three kilometres up from Nice follow a similar pattern. These roads are not for the faint-hearted or queasy-stomached, so if you're driving yourself, an easier approach from Ventimiglia is up the Roya Valley to San-Michele and then up to Olivetta, where the road crosses the border and then wends its way down into Sospel. Alternately, on the Nice-Turin railway line, you can reach Sospel by train from Nice in about an hour, or roughly an hour from Ventimiglia, with a change of train in Breil-sur-Roya.

And even if most people arrive by car or motorbike these days, Sospel is still a popular destination for trippers from Piemonte, Liguria and the French Riviera. And a few hardy souls do still arrive on foot: walking trails are well sign-posted and documented. Heading out of town in any direction you can easily pick up pleasant paths through the woods that trace the muleteers' routes from village to village. And in these back-to-nature days, you may even meet someone clopping along with a mule or two.

Whatever the approach, the effort is well rewarded. In fact the name Sospel derives from the village's original name of Hospitellum, and hospitality is still a genuine part of a tradition here that dates back over 900 years. As early as the twelfth and thirteenth centuries, Sospel was already a bustling market town. In the 1200s the first bridge was built over the Bevera, right in the centre of the village, making it easier for northbound mule trains carrying salt, coffee, olives, citrus fruits, fish and silk to cross the river on their way north to Cuneo and Turin. Later on, this bridge became the first toll-gate in the Alpes Maritimes.

As we see the two-arched bridge today, with the French flag flying jauntily from the roof of the toll-house, it's sobering to reflect on how Sospel was repeatedly bombarded during the last months of World War II. The toll-gate was partially destroyed in October 1944, but in the 1950s the stones were retrieved from the river and the bridge was rebuilt exactly as before. Known simply as Le Pont Vieux, it is the symbol of Sospel today, and a picturesque starting point for our tour of the village.

Come to the end of the bridge by the main road, and turn right. In just a few metres we come to a small square that spans the road: Place de la Cabraïa. 'Cabraïa' is an old word for goat in the local dialect. Early in the morning in not-so-long-gone-by times, the square would have rung to the tinkle of goats' bells as they and their goatherds gathered here before heading out into the pastures. Goats' milk cheese is still sold here on the Thursday and Sunday morning market stalls.

Fountains abound in Sospel: one of the more unusual ones is in Place de la Cabraïa. On one side the fountain rim is at about waist height: you would rest your water carriers here to fill them in the days before everyone had running water in their homes. On the other side of the fountain there's a much lower trough: this is where cattle stopped to drink.

A short lane leads from the fountain to Place Saint-Michel. It's an irregular, wedge-shaped space, light and airy and paved in rounded stones gathered from the riverbed and carefully sorted into greys and whites to form a geometric pattern. Two small chapels sit either side of some steps that take you up to the ruins of the fourteenth-century castle and ramparts. They are the chapels of the Chapelle Gris and the Chapelle Rouge. In the Middle Ages groups of charitably minded laypeople formed confraternities that helped the poor, offered hospitality to pilgrims and travellers, and prayed for special intentions. Each group was simply named according to the colour of the tunic that its members wore. Sospel had a total of five confraternities: Pénitents Noirs, Rouges, Blancs, Bleus and Gris. Curiously, the penitents' chapels weren't painted in the same colours as their names: in Place Saint-Michel the Grey Penitents' chapel, on the left of the steps, is painted in a warm salmon-pink, and the Red Penitents' chapel, on the right of the steps, is a bluey-grey. Services are still held from time to time in the Chapelle Gris, but the Chapelle Rouge has been converted into a cinema/theatre, an intelligent use for a former church.

Across from the two chapels, there are some lovely arcaded buildings along the other long side of the wedge, while the blunt end is dominated by the Baroque Cathedral of Saint Michael, its thirteenth-century bell tower and the russet-red and mustard façaded, lavender-blue shuttered public library.

La Cathédrale Saint-Michel was built, and then embellished, over a period of many years starting in 1641. It's the largest church in the Alpes Maritimes: almost fifty-seven metres long, and over twenty-six metres wide, with a height of twenty-two metres. Visit it on a Sunday morning while that faint incense whiff of its former splendour still lingers around its pillars and in the two chapels on either side of the main altar. Look up as you enter: I was captivated by the fresco on the ceiling. In true baroque style, Satan is scrambling desperately to escape from Saint Michael – big brown eyes bulging in terror and long, dark, wavy locks streaming down his shoulders. Saint Michael is about to run his sword through Satan, but passing time has warped the plaster surface under the painting so that his sword has some strange kinks in it. The two figures behind the saint seem to be whispering about his chances of nabbing Satan before he gets out of the picture altogether.

In the little chapel on the left-hand side of the main altar you can admire a painting of the Virgin Mary. It is a masterpiece of mid-sixteenth-century religious art, and shows the Virgin in a gorgeous gold brocade dress. The artist was from Nice – he has placed the Virgin on a hilltop, with the sea in the distance behind her. In this chapel there's also a fine oak tabernacle, inlaid with ivory and mother-of-pearl.

The Chapel of the Relics is to the right of the main altar. It contains an astonishing collection of bone fragments from the martyrs of the Roman catacombs. Gilt casks and glass cylinders are arranged in wooden cabinets lined with red velvet, while phials containing the tiniest fragments are arranged in geometric patterns on cream satin. Each one is labelled in the finest of fine minuscule writing.

As we leave the cathedral, the paintings on either side of the door are of Our Lady of Lourdes and Our Lady of a Safe Trip – the seventeenth-century Notre Dame de Bon Voyage: what more could we want?

The narrow Rue St Pierre leads out of Place Saint-Michel. It was one of the main thoroughfares of old Sospel, and some of the nobility had houses here. Unfortunately, very little remains of their fine doorways or lintels carved with noble coats of arms. Opposite Number twenty-three there is still a hint of former importance in the building that was the Hôtel de la Gabelle: it was a bonded salt warehouse. Old Sospel caters for the present too. Further along the street there's a small guesthouse, a trendy clothes shop called Billy Boop, and a cosy restaurant serving local specialities, such as rabbit and duck stews.

We return to Le Pont Vieux by turning down Rue du Pont Vieux. The old bridge is at the end of the street, but before crossing over, let's pause for a moment and look across the river to the houses along the riverbank. We're looking at the backs of the homes of the well-to-do of old Sospel. They enjoy a lovely sunny position overlooking the river, and there's a long wrought-iron balustraded balcony on every floor. During the summer the balconies are a joyous confusion of washing, pot plants and coloured sun umbrellas. In the nineteenth century it was fashionable to paint the south-facing wall of your house in a decorative *trompe-l'oeil* pattern. Some of the decoration has been restored on some of the houses: one in particular is painted in a yellow and tan pattern that is reminiscent of old-fashioned wallpaper.

Life overlooking the river can't always have been very pleasant. Apart from the obvious problems of damp and the danger of floods, the river was also an open sewer. The culverts that open into the river between the houses carried excessive rainwater and sewage down from the street behind. Some are wide enough for you to walk down to the grassy area along the river bank, where there are a couple of popular fishing spots.

Passing under the toll-house on Le Pont Vieux brings us to Place Saint Nicolas. This has always been another of the town's important meeting places, and still bustles today. The town's governors met in the rust-red building that faces into this sunny little square. Nowadays it's a pleasant place for a leisurely lunch, either in the sun or in the cool of the arcades. On one side of the square a baker sells delicious quiches, onion and olive-topped *pissaladière* bread, irresistible fattening pastries and intriguing *pane irlandais* – hot cross buns disguised as 'Irish bread'. Fountains gush and splatter all over Sospel: you're never far from the sound of running water, and if it makes you want to go, follow the sign outside the baker. A short lane leads through to Place Garibaldi. The women's loo is especially unusual. It's very discreetly placed in a small room under the arcades of the *lavoire*, the public washing area. You can dabble your fingers in the water of the laundry troughs and be thankful that you don't have to lug your washing here to soap and scrub and wring and rinse, all in cold water. On the plus side, it was a lively meeting place for the village women, and any amount of gossip and hints must have been exchanged here. The troughs are still used – you can bring your floor mats here to wash them and then lay them in the river, anchored down with stones, to rinse. For the new millennium the town had the walls of the *lavoire* decorated with frescoes. One shows a young couple frolicking by a river while their clothes dry, draped around on bushes and branches.

We finish our stroll around Sospel by passing back through Place Saint Nicolas, and turning down Rue de la République. This road follows the salt route out of town – in the past it was the main road north. It was lined with shops, which were sheltered under arcades similar to the ones in Place Saint Nicolas and Place Saint-Michel. Unfortunately the arcades have been walled up, so that very few traces linger of the street's former importance and charm – except for the dog carved into a stone pillar at Number nine. He's running for his life, trying perhaps to catch a whiff of bygone days. Not far from the running dog pillar is an extremely narrow lane called Rue des Tisserands. The tisserands were the weavers, and the alley reminds us that hemp and mulberry trees for silk-worm cultivation were grown in this valley. The alley is so narrow that, from side to side, you can't stretch out both arms, and the eaves of the houses almost touch overhead. At one point, if they weren't placed one above the other, their spoutings *would* touch. At the end of the alley we're in Place

Sainte Croix, whose north side is taken up by the bright blue and mustard-yellow wall of the chapel of the White Penitents, Sospel's oldest and longest-serving confraternity. It was founded in the late fourteenth century, and is still active. Today the *Pénitents Blancs* still wear their white tunics, but since they no longer need to maintain their anonymity they have thrown back their all-equalising hoods.

Sospel

Getting there: suggested transport in **bold**

22km from Menton, narrow, winding road.

43km from Nice, winding

24km from Ventimiglia via Olivetta San Michele.

Buses from Menton

Trains from Nice; from Ventimiglia via Breil-s-Roya

Eating and staying overnight:

La Cabraïa, 1,
Place de la Cabraïa tel 0493 04 00 54

Hotel des Etrangers
7 Boulevard de Verdun, tel 0493 04 00 09
fax 0493 04 12 31
www.sospel.net
www.logis-de-france.com

Maps for walking:
IGN TOP25 3741 ET 1cm = 250m

Detailed maps and walk descriptions available from Tourist Information Office.

Info and website:
Office de Tourisme et d'Animations de Sospel, Le Pont-Vieux
tel 0493 04 15 80, fax 0493 04 19 96

Climate and when to go:
Cold winters, mild summers.

Baroque concerts June/July www.lesbaroquiales.org

Scarecrow contest – early August

Maginot Fort Saint Roch open 2–6 p.m. Sat and Sun April, May, June and October, every day except Monday July, Aug and Sept. www.alcyonis.fr/st-roch

Market day – Thursday

Guided tours of town during summer months. White Penitents' Chapel open Thursday mornings in summer.

CHAPTER 17

The Valley of Wonders
and the Valley of Fontanalba

THE BEARDED MAN HOLDS HIS ARMS UP
straight above his head, fingers outstretched. A narrow
moustache droops down and touches his beard and seven
teeth stand out clearly in his wide-open mouth. His eyes are
high up under his eyebrows, so that he looks, if not exactly
fierce, then certainly fully concentrated on the slopes of the
mountain directly opposite him across the valley. His is a face
alive with expression and movement: an ageless face that,
across four millennia, still has the power to grab our attention. As we don't know exactly who engraved this picture,
barely two hand spans wide and 31cm high, or precisely why,
we laypeople can make our choice from the interpretations of
the various scholars who have studied and analysed the
drawing over the last hundred or so years. By common
consensus the incision in the streaked rusty-tan rock face is
variously called *the Magician, the Sorcerer, le Sorcier* (in French)

and *il Mago* (in Italian). He is at least 4000 years old. For some specialists in Bronze Age art and culture he is the god of the sacred mountain himself, the bringer of rain and nourishment for the earth; for others he is the exorcist of danger, warding off the threat of crop-destroying hailstorms and thunder and lightning; for others he represents a negative force and invokes danger in the form of those same violent thunderstorms. Whichever interpretation you choose, and I certainly prefer a benign one, you will easily recognise the Magician: he is the symbol of the mystery and grandeur that is the Vallée des Merveilles.

When an electrical storm breaks in the Vallée des Merveilles – which happens often, even in the height of summer – it strikes with a ferocity that is both terrifying and fantastic. Lightning is drawn earthwards by the iron deposits in the rocks, and the thunder is magnified over and over as it crashes and reverberates and, echoing again and again, rumbles around the cliffs and rock-strewn amphitheatre of this awesome open-air museum.

Terrifying. Awesome. Fantastic. It sounds like hype, but it isn't. The Vallée des Merveilles deserves all these adjectives and more. Beyond the larch forests on the eastern edge of the Parc National du Mercantour lie glacial valleys and lakelets surrounded by a towering surreal moonscape of crags and boulders and waterfalls and icy streams. If this were all, it would still have been enough to earn the valleys their names: the Vallée d'Enfer – the Valley of Hell – and opening out of it, the Vallée des Merveilles – the Valley of Wonders. But this is only the beginning.

Nowadays, when we go tramping in the Parc National du Mercantour, rain is the last thing we want. But if it comes, as it so often does at this altitude, even in summer, bringing a dive in temperature and perhaps snow, we're equipped for it, with a jumper and waterproof gear, and proper waterproof hiking boots with non-slip soles, wet or fine. And in the evening we'll enjoy a hot cooked meal and snuggle up in our sleeping bags in a mountain refuge, or between the sheets of our own bed.

As we drift off to sleep, thankful that it didn't rain today, or that twenty-first-century fibre and textile technology kept us warm and dry if it did, it's so difficult to imagine a small group of men – pilgrims driven on by faith and need – as 4000 years ago they trudged through the last of the winter snows towards Mont Bégo, the sacred mountain of the god of life-giving water. Their pilgrimage would last a week, maybe ten days or a fortnight, in each direction.

Try to imagine those determined little bands of pilgrims, heading doggedly for one or other of the valleys that surround Mont Bégo, where they would leave signs of their devotion to the god of the mountain using the tips of their daggers to peck at any flattish surface in the rock face.

The Ice Age had done its work in the valleys long before them, rubbing the bedrock irresistibly smooth and bare, and leaving the erratic masses of greeny-grey schist flat and clean, and propped, one great chunk wedged against another, all around the valleys. Because the schist in this area has a high iron content the surfaces oxidised – you could almost say *rusted* – and turned tan and rusty orange, even dark dry-blood red. The Bronze Age pilgrims drove the tips of their metal daggers and quartz flints down through this oxidised crust, and point by point, they pecked out their symbols and drawings. Plunge the dagger down, break the crust, grind the point deeper into the rock, re-gather your strength, strike down again, over and over again. It must have taken hours, because many of the engravings are picked out in hundreds of overlapping indentations. In an area of about 4000 hectares, and in seven distinct zones around Mont Bégo, roughly 40,000 drawings have been identified and catalogued.

The Parc National du Mercantour – Mercantour National Park, created in August 1979 – covers a vast mountainous area of south-east France, and protects Mont Bégo and the Valleys of the Merveilles and of Fontanalba within its far eastern limits. Whether for the spectacular natural landscape, a true manual of glacial action, for the precious and unique rock engravings, or for the fauna and flora that abound here (with 2660 identified plant species it is the area of greatest botanical interest in all of France) the protection of this wonderful site is paramount. Access is controlled and limited, but with a minimum of preparation and planning, a visit to the zone can become a very memorable experience.

The adventure begins in the small town of Tende, high in the Roya Valley, just outside the boundaries of the Mercantour National Park. Here the ultra-modern Musée des Merveilles sets the scene: a pre-excursion visit is highly recommended because each showcase helps us to understand the background to the open-air exhibits – the glacial rock formations and the rock engravings – in the park.

And now for the hard part. This is an excursion to make in two parts: let's start with the Vallée des Merveilles. Faced with the choice of (a) walking uphill for three or four hours from outside the boundary of the National Park to the mountain hostel at the foot of the Vallée des Merveilles and then walking in the valley itself to see the glacial action and the rock drawings close up, or (b) going up to the hostel by four-wheel-drive and then walking with a guide in the valley,

I chose the latter, and would recommend this for all but the very keenest of walkers.

There are seven qualified guides with permission to take walkers into the valley by 4-wheel drive vehicle: several of these employ other guides, so that there is a total of twelve vehicles providing access to the two main valleys and to nearby Valmasque as well. Only these guides and hostel and forestry staff have vehicle access to the National Park – no private vehicles are allowed. I chose Luc Fioretti, the only one who advertises that he speaks both Italian and English. I couldn't have made a better choice: here is a highly professional guide whose job is obviously also his passion – the perfect combination.

With my tramping boots long since broken in and, according to Luc's instructions, a picnic lunch, jumper and waterproof jacket in my rucksack along with camera and binoculars (for animal spotting) I'm raring to go when we meet in Tende at 8.30 a.m. After a thunderstorm the day before, the air is crystal clear and not likely to get too hot. Luc drives a modern open-top 4WD and there's plenty of room for his other passengers, a young French couple and their daughters Barbara and Julie. We head down the Roya valley a few kilometres to St-Dalmas-de-Tende and then turn north-west on a good country road. At St Dalmas we pass in front of the massive railway station built by Mussolini when the zone was still Italian territory. It is an enormous, solid building, largely boarded up and neglected now that the mines further up the valley have closed and the village is no longer the gateway to Italy. As we continue up the Vallon de la Minière, the road begins to climb, and after ten kilometres we reach the first of the day's lakes. Lac des Mesches is the site of one of the valley's hydro-electric plants, built by the

Italians early last century. For visitors arriving by private car, the ten-kilometre walk up to the *Refuge des Merveilles* – Merveilles Hikers' Hostel – starts in the carpark here beside the lake. Luc changes into low gear and we begin the bumpy ride through the forest. The track is extremely rocky and we jig and bounce about, holding on tight. In less than a kilo-metre we come to the disused mines that gave this first valley its name. The mines were already known in the Bronze Age. The fierce little statue of a thick-necked, helmeted warrior that is on display in the Museum in Tende was found in a mineshaft here, and has been dated to around 1000 BC. Zinc, lead, iron and silver have all been mined here, and there was quite a substantial community living near the mine last century.

We're soon deep in a forest of larch with the occasional, much darker cembro pine. In the undergrowth Luc points out wild strawberries, blueberries and raspberries; bright pink *semprevivum dei monte* with its miniature artichoke-like clusters of leaves; blue and yellow aconite . . . We pass a grove of rhododendrons: in June the forest glows with their pink and red flowers. Stout-hearted hikers heading up and down the valley wave to us when we meet or pass them. There are marked shortcuts for them through the forest – it must be a relief to get off this stony track and onto an earth path. We have been climbing steadily and have reached 1700 metres above sea level when we pass through the gates into the National Park. We'll soon be above the treeline, and as the larches thin out we see where wild boars have rooted up the ground around some trees.

Then suddenly we're out of the forest and gasp with amazement. In just a few metres we've emerged from a dappled green grove into a stark, desolate, wide open valley.

There isn't a cloud in the sky and peaks and ridges loom all around us. The landscape is unearthly: rocks and boulders and more rocks and cliffs spilling and plunging down from the peaks. Hardly anything grows, the ground is peaty and boggy, and torrents gurgle along. Small wonder that in earlier times this vast barren space was named Vallée d'Enfer, the Valley of Hell.

The grey stone hostel overlooks Lac Long and the various authorised paths through the Vallée des Merveilles and up over the mountain passes to other valleys branch out from here. If we weren't with the guides we wouldn't be allowed to leave the designated paths.

The first incision that we see is of a dagger. It's on a flat rock quite near the hostel, and we could easily have walked past it and not noticed anything. Luc shows us how easy it is, if the engraving is in the shade, not to see anything, and he points out how the lichens that have partially covered it have also protected it. Later on he shows us where someone has rubbed away the lichens and at the same time has buffed and dulled the outline of the incision itself. Soon we come to some horned-bull symbols, more daggers and some halberds. Sometimes we see oblongs divided into small sections: scholars believe these represent the engraver's home fields, and that the engravers drew a representation of their own fields and pastures, so that when they called the gods and prayed for rain, the gods would know where to send the rain.

As we climb we catch sight of other small glacial lakes, each with a name evocative of a legend or superstition or reflecting the deep blue and green and even blackish colour of the water, depending on the mineral deposits in it: Lac Saorgine, the lake of a drowned shepherd from the village of Saorge; Lac de l'Huile, Oil Lake; Lac de la Muta, Deaf Lake;

and high up near the Cime du Diable (Devil's Peak), the two tiny Lacs du Diable.

Just before lunch we see the engraving known as *Christ.* The incision seems to have been done quite carelessly, with the dagger marks across the top of the head stabbing here and there in the rock, so that the lean, bearded face seems to be wearing a crown of thorns.

We eat our picnics by a stream and look far down the valley: beyond the hostel and over the forest to more mountains on the horizon. Luc has brought flasks: one with coffee and a smaller one with a sip of home-made honey brandy for all of us. It's delicious. We scan the mountainsides with our binoculars and see cheeky marmots and high up near the skyline I spot the first chamois for the day.

As we move off again after lunch Luc points out more and more mountain flowers: there are flowers here for making aperitifs and digestives, for medicines and for making poisons to kill wolves (wolfbane). He tells us that forty of the plant species found in the park are endemic to it: later on we *might* see a rare example of *saxifraga florulenta* – it flowers once every thirty-five years!

The outing gets progressively more challenging now as we leave the designated path and our guide leads us up steep rocky slopes and we clamber up onto *les ciappes*, the rock wave that is the mountain's bare bedrock. There are engravings all around us and we tread carefully, keeping to a strip of rock that has been marked out for walking on. What look like rusted nail heads in the rock surface are actually globules of raw iron.

Near the top of the rock wave we see where local shepherds made their own engravings, dating from the early Middle Ages on. Some of these are quite elaborate and Luc explains that for them coming to this bedevilled place also needed a tremendous amount of courage, but they came to leave their engravings in order to ward off the evil that they believed dwelled here. It's a beautiful place and a superb day. Even when clouds puff up from behind Mont des Merveilles in the west, there's no feeling of anything malign lurking here. Only family groups of chamois standing still and proud a few hundred metres away. We watch and they watch, and then they drift sedately away.

At last we reach the top of *les ciappes* and here is the *Magician*, waving his hands high above his head. What a treat to see him 'in-the-rock' at long last. It's getting on for five o'clock now, and the day is cooling off. We're all relieved when Luc tells us that there's no more climbing to do. In fact we have crossed a ridge behind *les ciappes* and now a gentle grassy slope leads back down to the hostel. But Luc has one more treat for us – it's the engraving known as *the man with the zigzag arms* – he's holding them down by his side, while his torso merges with a symbol of cultivated fields. He is interpreted as representing the god of thunder and lightning, bringing rain to the earth. Next to him another figure seems to represent a female lower torso with the bull-god upper part – the fusion of the divine couple.

Then down the grassy slopes we go, behind *les ciappes*, tired but happy. As we come near to the hostel a shepherd is bringing in his flock of Roman-nosed *Brigasca* sheep, white and black, and a handful of goats too. I'd like to stay the night here in the hostel, but my train leaves Tende for the coast in just under two hours and I need to get home: what a fabulous day out this has been. Thank you, Luc!

I catch the 8.30 train back to Ventimiglia: when I get back, tired but very contented, it's exactly fifteen hours since I set out. In the fast-fading light as I cross the bridge over the

Roya River I can just pick out the summit of Mont Bégo: only thirty-four kilometres away as the crow flies. But from four millennia away, a spell has been cast and filtered down through spectacular scenery, distinctive mountain flora, the whistle of marmots and the tinkle of sheep bells. Before I fall asleep I'm already plotting another outing: this time to the Vallon de Fontanalba, on the north-western side of Mont Bégo.

During the summer months a bus leaves Tende and St Dalmas for Casterino every morning, and returns in late afternoon. I decide to use this service and book in for an overnight stay in the Refuge de Fontanalba – the Hikers' Hostel. Casterino isn't exactly a village – there aren't any shops here, so if you're planning a picnic or camping, bring your provisions with you. It lies at just over 1500 metres above sea level in a wide, grassy valley, and caters for visitors with a hotel, a hostel and several restaurants. There's an information centre, a guide who can take you up the valleys by 4WD, and guided horse trekking.

The 4WD track up the valley of Fontanalba to the hostel leaves Casterino quite steeply, but soon levels out to a gentler slope, and is pleasant walking through a larch forest. The track is fairly rocky, so sturdy hiking boots are essential. In mid-August the forest is shady and cool: in a few months' time the larches will turn vibrant golden before losing their needles. After a steady two hours' walk I reach the hostel and a warm welcome from Yvette, the keeper. This hostel is smaller than the Merveilles one, and belongs to the Nice Ski Club, whereas the Merveilles one is the property of CAF – the French Alpine Club. In either case, non-members are welcome, but it always pays to book ahead.

Although it is at 2018 metres, the hostel is still within the forest: this valley is in fact far greener than the Vallée des Merveilles on the other side of the mountain range. After lunch I continue up the valley on the designated 'discovery itinerary' that lets visitors see some of the rock engravings and enjoy the valley's natural beauty without the walking being too strenuous. I meet people of all ages, including families with small children. The itinerary is a circular route, and in order to be going down on the steepest part, I follow it around in an anticlockwise direction. Even when the trees thin right out, there are still some dotted here and there, and grassy slopes where enormous white cattle graze: there isn't the same feeling of desolation and of dramatic glacial action that there is in the Vallée des Merveilles. The valley's main features are its lakes and a natural rock feature named *La Voie Sacrée*, The Sacred Way. At the high point of the walk, it is an inclined rock surface, seventy metres long, forming one side of a rocky crevice in the mountainside. By clambering up the natural stairway made by the rubble in the base of the crevice, we can see the numerous Bronze Age incisions that cover the flat rock surface: bulls and ploughing scenes; weapons and tools; and geometric figures representing fields. Unfortunately some of these engravings have lost their original clarity through the effects of weather and abrasion from other rocks tumbling down the crevice. At the top we are on an outcrop where an orientation table identifies all the surrounding peaks: Mt Bégo to the south-west; much nearer Cime de Chanvrairée's jagged peaks loom over the hostel; behind us to the north, the slopes of Mont Saint Marie are dotted with white cattle; over to the north-west the bare Ciappe de Fontanalba. Far away to the north-east we can just make out the Col de Tende, the pass between France and

Italy. Almost due east, Casterino hides in the trees at the foot of the valley. With binoculars you can pick out the details, including more intrepid hikers crossing the passes – the Baisse de Valmasque and the Baisse de Fontanalba, both at just over 2500 metres. From here they will make their way down into the Vallée des Merveilles and the Vallée de la Valmasque to the north. These tracks are old military routes: abandoned barracks still perch among the rocks near the summits.

Below the orientation table lie the Lacs Jumeaux – the Twin Lakes. Their water is dark and still, and the surface covered with strands of silvery weed. The ground all around is oozing with damp – it's a peat bog. The cattle grazing here are enormous and wear bells the size of a small bucket on massive collars. These bells don't tinkle as sheep and goat bells do: they clank and ding and dong as the leaders move about, each one ringing differently. Near the end of the walk, we reach Lac Vert – and it really is a green lake. Trees grow down to the edges and reflect in the still water, and lots of hikers have chosen this attractive spot to picnic and rest. As in several other places along the walk, there's a ranger perched Pan-like on the rock nearby, keeping an eye on everything, making sure we resist the temptation to pick flowers or venture off the path. And making sure we don't drop litter – the entire park is incredibly litter free.

Back at the hostel, all the other hikers have come in: about thirty in all. There's no electricity, so we make up our beds in the communal bunkroom before dinner. There's a really cheerful atmosphere: people poring over maps and swapping route notes, and laughing their way through the cold showers. It's simple but fun, and although the twilight lingers and lingers, we have dinner inside by candlelight. I'm the only New

Zealander: nearly everyone is French, with a couple of Italians. Vegetable soup, chunks of brown bread, beef stew and polenta, local cheese and custard is followed by a wander outside in the rapidly dropping temperature.

We're up with the dawn, just after 6 a.m. Everywhere is tinged a vivid lime green, and the hostel catches the first of the sun's rays as it comes over the Cime du Plan Tendasque. After breakfast it's goodbyes and *'Bonne marche'* – enjoy your walk!

I'm off marmot-spotting, taking a long route back down the valley to Casterino. Marmots are inquisitive animals, but they won't let you get too close. To watch them reasonably close-up it's best to set out fairly early, before the mountain-side is crowded with lots of other people moving about and frightening the marmots back down their burrows. They're furry, pear-shaped animals, a tawny brown colour that blends in with the rocks and tree stumps that litter the grassy slopes where they love to graze. They have a canny habit of being able to stay perfectly still, in an upright position, resting on their haunches, nose in the air and their front paws held up in begging position. They're the size of a biggish cat or small dog, with a long tail and wide rear, and, belonging to the rodent family, they have long, sharp gnawing teeth.

As an alternative to the shorter route down to Casterino through the forest, I've chosen a longer way down the valley from the hostel. It follows an old, paved military road, and curves quite gently around the opposite side of the valley to where I came up yesterday. This is the valley's sunny side, and the trees are thinner, so there are lots of marmots, including mothers and young ones, basking on rocks or loping about eating flowers and grass. They call to each other in hoots and whistles; when they're anxious, the whistle becomes a frantic, shrieking signal like a burglar alarm. Then they'll scamper off or shoot into their burrow if it's near enough. This is your best chance for a close-up view. Squat down a few metres from the burrow. You won't have to wait very long. Out comes a little grey nose, nostrils wriggling, then the head, dark eyes alert for any movement at all. All clear? Yes! Shoulders first, short front paws resting on the edge of the burrow. No one around? Okay, heave out the rest of the body, keep close to the ground. Sniff here, nibble there. Scamper about. You've been lucky to see all this, because now here comes a family of humans, the father striding along, the child running about, the mother calling out to the child: suddenly all the marmots are far-off furry, anonymous blurs.

A short deviation takes us up over a hillock to Lac des Grenouilles, Frog Lake. A dairy-farming family has their summer base beside the lake, and they're moving among the cows, squatting on one-legged stools, hand-milking into blue buckets, as the herd stands quietly in a paddock. Freshly made butter and cheese are for sale at the farm – perfect souvenirs if you've brought your cooler bag along.

Tende – St Dalmas – Vallée des Merveilles

Place names: vallée – valley; vallon – a small valley; cime – peak; refuge – hikers' hostel

Getting there: suggested transport in **bold**
Tende – 44km from Ventimiglia, 80km from Nice, via Sospel

Trains from Ventimiglia (1hr) and Nice (90mins) Certain departures from Nice of 'Le train des Merveilles' have live, onboard introductions to the Valley and the rock engravings.

St-Dalmas-de-Tende is 4km south of Tende. This is where the D91 road branches off to Les Mesches and Casterino. At Les Mesches, 10km from St-Dalmas, there is a parking area, and from here only foot access, or authorised 4WD access to the Vallée des Merveilles. Private 4WD vehicles do not have access to the Vallée des Merveilles.

The Park is in effect an open-air museum: do your bit to protect it in every way.

Eating and staying overnight:

Tende: Restaurant Auberge Tendasque, 65, Avenue du 16 Septembre 1947,
tel 0493 04 62 26

Hotel Restaurant Miramonti, 5–7 Rue Vassalo,
tel 0493 04 61 82, fax 0493 04 78 71

St-Dalmas-de-Tende: Hotel Restaurant Le Terminus, 1, Rue des Martyrs,
tel 0493 04 96 96, fax 0493 04 96 97
www.loges-de-france.com

Hotel Restaurant Le Prieure Rue Jean-Médecin,
tel 0493 04 75 70, fax 0493 04 71 58
e-mail contact@leprieure.org www.leprieure.org

La Minière: Neige&Merveilles – this accommodation and activity centre in the former mine buildings can be reached on foot (800m) from Les Mesches car park. The centre will collect your luggage from St Dalmas railway station.
tel 0493 04 62 40, fax 0493 04 88 58,
e-mail Neige.merveilles@wanadoo.fr
www.neige@merveilles.com

Vallée des Merveilles: Refuge Merveilles – hikers' hostel, can be reached after 3–4 hours' hike from Les Mesches,

or by authorised 4WD. Open June to mid-October, weather permitting.
tel 0493 04 64 64
Book ahead for meals and accommodation
Out of season contact Alex Ferrier,
tel 0493 04 69 22, 40 Rue Lascaris, 06430 Tende.

Maps for walking:
IGN TOP 25 3841 OT. Unless accompanied by an authorised guide, hikers are not permitted off the designated paths.

4WD access with guide:
Luc Fioretti
tel/fax 0493 04 69 11, e-mail lucfioretti@9online.fr
http://merveilles.4x4.online.fr

Info and website:
www.tendemerveilles.com

www.parc-mercantour.fr

www.royabevera.com

www.traintouristiques-ter.com/traindesmerveilles

Office de Tourisme de la Haute Roya, Ave 16 Septembre 1947, 06430 Tende
tel 0493 04 73 71, fax 0493 04 35 09

Climate and when to go:
Altitude varies from 800m above sea level around Tende to over 2000m in the Vallée des Merveilles. Even in summer it can be cool in the morning and at night, and the weather can change very quickly. Thunderstorms are violent, but afterwards the air is especially clear and the view far-reaching. Warm and waterproof layers are essential for hiking in this region. Well worn-in hiking boots are a must. Take plenty of drinking water with you, sunscreen, camera and binoculars. Metal-tipped walking poles are not allowed in areas around the rock engravings.

For **safety reasons**, remember that mobile phones are out of range in the valleys: you are advised to carry a whistle in case you need to call for help.

Access to the Vallée des Merveilles is only from June to mid-end October.

Rhododendrons flower in June, spectacular autumn foliage in October. All plants are protected – do not pick them.

Casterino – Vallon de Fontanalba

Getting there: suggested transport in **bold**
As above to Les Mesches, and then on by road or footpath through woods to Casterino – 4km from Les Mesches.

At Casterino you can walk to the Fontanalba hostel in 2hrs, or in just over 3hrs from second carpark about 3km north of Casterino. The circular route, starting at the hostel and taking in the Voie Sacrée, Lacs Jumeaux and Lac Vert de Fontanalba takes about 2 hours. This route is easy to follow unguided – just follow the yellow signs – but to see the most rock engravings it is better to go with an authorised guide, leaving the hostel at 8 a.m., and the Lacs Jumeaux chalet at 11 a.m. and 2 p.m., at weekends in June and September, and every day in July and August.

If going without a guide, follow the circuit anti-clockwise for less-steep climbs up between the lakes.

The Fontanalba hostel is about 5 hours' hike over the Baisse de Valmasque pass, 2549m, from the Merveilles hostel, and about 5 hours from the Valmasque hostel via Lac du Basto, Lac Noir and Lac Vert.

Eating and staying overnight:
Casterino: Hotel Restaurant Les Melezes,
tel 0493 04 95 95, fax 0493 04 95 96
www.logis-de-france.com www.lesmeleze.free.fr

Refuge Fontanalbe, tel 0493 04 89 19, June to end Sept.

Out of season contact Yvette Ferrier,
40, Rue Lascaris, 06430 Tende, tel 0493 04 69 22

Refuge Valmasque, June to end Sept. There is **NO telephone** at the hostel.
Out of season contact Michel Duranti,
tel 0492 31 91 20

Maps for walking:
IGN TOP 25 3841 OT

Info and website:
As above

Climate and when to go:
Check opening times at local tourist office before going.

As above – in addition, there is horse-riding in Casterino – from 30 minutes to a full day – and cross-country skiing in the Casterino valley in winter.

CHAPTER 18

Places in the sun

THROUGH EACH OF THE FOUR SEASONS, THE Riviera sparkles and offers a warm welcome to visitors. But, where exactly are its boundaries? Last century it was defined in general terms as the coastline from Genova to Marseilles. In 1887 the poet Stephen Liégeard holidayed on the Riviera. What really struck him were the hues and shades of blue that predominate all along the coastal strip. Sea-blue, sky-blue, mauvey lavender-blue. Liégeard wrote enthusiastically about the Riviera in a book that he cleverly entitled *La Côte d'Azur*. He used the name as an appropriate contrast to the already renowned Côte d'Or, the 'Golden Hillside' wine-growing area that stretches south of Dijon in his native Burgundy. The name had flair and style, and was eagerly adopted. Although Liégeard had intended the term Côte d'Azur to encompass a much wider area, it soon came to refer exclusively to the French Riviera, stretching from Menton to Cannes, St Raphaël or to St Tropez, which is generally accepted now as the western limit. Nowadays the Italian Riviera begins in Marinella di Sarzana, on the Tuscan border near La Spezia. It stretches to Ventimiglia, and is divided into the eastern Riviera *di Levante*, referring to the rising sun, from Marinella di Sarzana to Genova; and the western Riviera *di Ponente*, referring to the setting sun, from Genova to Ventimiglia.

Liégeard coined a catchy name for an area that was already well established as a pleasant and healthy place to spend the winter, especially if you were an invalid. However, less than sixty years earlier, hotels and holidaymakers had been far fewer than they were when he visited the area, and most of the flourishing resorts of the twentieth century were then modest fishing villages.

As the area became popular with British travellers, Protestant churches were built along the Riviera to cater for the wintering population. The church of Saint John the Evangelist, for example, was consecrated in Menton in 1868. At the height of its popularity as a winter resort, Menton had other Protestant churches too, but St John's is the only one that remains consecrated and active into the twenty-first century. Like so many other non-Catholic churches along the coast, the Scottish church in Menton has become a cultural centre – a venue for exhibitions and presentations.

Just one short block back from the waterfront, St John's is an unmistakable remnant of a bygone era. Built in sombre grey stone, it sits, in marked contrast to the pastel-washed buildings that surround it, on the corner on Avenue Carnot and Avenue de Verdun, directly opposite the Menton Casino. Flower beds against the side of the church struggle defiantly against the exhaust fumes in Avenue Carnot, and daffodils flower jauntily towards the end of February. A resident chaplain looks after a small but enthusiastic congregation of

English-speaking expat residents from Menton and the surrounding towns and villages. Visitors are always welcome. Services are held every Sunday and on other key occasions throughout the year, such as Remembrance Day, Easter and Christmas. There's a garden party for the Queen's birthday too.

Three or four times a year the church gardens are also the scene of the fundraising *braderie* or jumble sale. Tables are set up under the trees, laden with clothes and shoes, furnishings and household items, books and bric-a-brac. Refreshments are served, and the delicious home baking is a treat. The first time I was asked to help on the second-hand shoes I went along more out of curiosity then commitment to the cause. How many hundreds of pairs of shoes did we have that morning? More than would fit on our trestle tables: they overflowed onto chairs and upturned cartons. Dainty or chunky; tottering stilettos or clompity tramping boots; elegant black or startling green, or red, or yellow; first shoes for toddlers or cosy slippers; tennis shoes and skates or plastic beach shoes; even a pair of flippers – and the furry *après-ski* were constantly being mistaken for a pair of sleeping dogs. Belts and bags and berets completed our display. By 9.55 a.m. we had everything neatly arranged, with the shoes lined up pair by pair. An eager crowd of buyers had gathered at the gates and at 10 a.m. they surged in. Within minutes our display was in chaotic disarray. Bargains were snapped up: 10FF for the most worn pairs, 20FF for the ones that were nearer to new. Even though it was a church fair, some buyers still wanted a discount. My French is seriously limited, but I quickly came to recognise the two most urgent customer questions. 'What size is it?' was answered by inviting the customer to try it on, while 'Where's the other one?' led to frantic searching in the tumble of shoes until the partner was found – usually at the far end of the table. We scampered up and down, and round and round our trestle table, re-matching our goods, and untangling belts. Foreign tourists bought some of our wares – at 20FF a pair, snazzy French shoes, even if slightly worn, are a bargain souvenir in any currency.

Within an hour the crowd had thinned, and a quick count of the contents of our money pouches revealed that we'd sold hundreds of pairs of shoes. In fact, we could finally see the surface of our table.

Welcome refreshments came round on a tray and we ordered our toasted sandwiches for lunch. What fun this was turning out to be. That first time, some friends from Alba were down for the weekend and they came to see how I was getting on. 'Do people really buy second-hand shoes?' they asked, scandalised: jumble sales aren't part of Italian culture.

Special stall-holder rates applied on the bookstall, so I stocked up there. The press came round too and I found myself being photographed, and eventually printed in *Nice Matin* with a black court shoe in one hand and something white in the other, and a scowl that says 'Now, where's the other one of these?'

And then it was time to prepare our stall for the last burst of activity: the hardened bargain hunters who knew that we would rather reduce the price than have to store any leftover shoes again. By mid-afternoon we were packing up. To my surprise, I found myself promising to do it again.

For some visitors to the Riviera, Menton became their final resting place. From the Bay of Garavan, the view of old Menton is crowned by the stark white tombstones of the international cemetery, and in turn, the focal point of the cemetery is a little Russian chapel among the cypresses. The cemetery was established on the ruins of Menton's castle, and is reached from the waterfront by following the lanes up through the old town, up and up until at last you are right under the wall of the cemetery. Towards the end of Rue du Vieux Chateau, opposite number sixty-eight, look up to the left. Originally there was an arched gateway here, and the first Protestant grave was placed on top of it. Continue up to the cemetery, and follow the path around to the left. The view is spectacular – over the rooftops of old Menton, around the Bay of Garavan to the Balzi Rossi, and up the hill to Villa Woronoff.

A plaque is set in the wall where the archway would have jutted out in 1851. At the base of the tombstone, the weather-worn inscription honours Gustavus Adolphus Fahrener, lieutenant of the Infantry of Copenhagen. He was born in Denmark in 1828, and when he died on 26 December 1851, permission for the burial of a Protestant was obtained after a certain amount of difficulty. Thus he was buried on the very edge of the cemetery – in it, but only just.

Later on, a section of the cemetery was set aside for Protestants in a small area surrounded by a little wall opposite Fahrener's grave, and most of the graves in this enclosure date from the early 1860s. The path continues to the Russian chapel, which is embellished with a frieze of colourful ceramic tiles and dark-blue ceramic roof tiles topped with an onion dome. The main path turns around to the right and just beyond the chapel the view opens out to the west, over the modern town of Menton towards Cap Martin and Monte Carlo. Look over the wall here to the graves on the lower terrace. One of them, slightly to the right, stands out because a number of commemorative plaques have been placed on the grave. It is the grave of the Reverend William Webb-Ellis, who died in Menton on 24 February 1872. On the first centenary of his death a commemorative stone was laid here, bearing an inscription to remind us that in 1823 'in fine disregard for the rules of football as played in his time, he first took the ball in his arms and ran with it, thus originating the distinctive feature of the Rugby game'.

Although Bordighera, further along the coast, was never as fashionable as Nice, Menton or San Remo, its success as a wintering resort was assured by its sunny mild climate and the stunning beauty of the palm plantations. An elegant winter colony was established on the flat land along the coast, with spacious hotels, villas and gardens. The wintering visitors were catered for by an English church, library, bank and bakery, and their clubs and tennis courts were established too. From 1883 and for the next fifty years, the locally published *Journal of Bordighera* kept them up to date with details about concerts and plays showing at the Victoria Hall, and news of who was expected on the next train; who had just arrived, and which parties were being planned. When Queen Victoria was forced to cancel her planned trip to Bordighera in 1900, because of the Boer War, it was a bitter disappointment to all of her subjects who were so earnestly preparing to welcome her. With changing economic times and two world wars, wintering on the Riviera eventually declined in popularity. Today, if you peer through the gates of Hotel Angst in Via Romana, you will see a ghost hotel, derelict and decaying, the garden gone to weeds. No trace remains now of those more elegant, aristocratic times when the English had their own separate dining room and the hotel was graced with a fine ballroom and a private bridge club.

Nonetheless, because of its mild winter climate Bordighera is still a popular winter destination for many Italians from the landlocked regions north of the Alps. The link with England is kept up too by the Anglo-Ligurian Club. In the late 1990s the club's incoming president and lively vice-president made a concentrated effort to attract new members. Weekly meetings have become more focused, and an ever-increasing membership always enjoys a short bilingual talk on such varied topics as 'the blue train', 'New Zealand', 'the Euro currency', 'toe and fingernail diseases', 'keep fit', 'Dylan Thomas' . . . Visitors are always welcome. If they have a special interest and volunteer to share it with members, then all the better.

The climate also favours the cultivation of palm trees and the town goes under the name of 'The City of Palms'. Tradition has it that Saint Ampélio brought the first palms to Bordighera from the Middle East in the fourth century. A small chapel, dedicated to the hermit who became Bordighera's patron saint, nestles into the rocks on Capo San'Ampélio. From here a path leads up through the gardens to Bordighera Vecchia. This, the oldest part of Bordighera, is unusual among medieval settlements because it was built to suit the specific requirements of the thirty-two families who decided to make their home here in the 1470s. These founding families, farmers and fishermen, lived a short distance away in Borgetto San Nicolò, in a closed and steep-sided valley. In a time of relative peace and prosperity, but still mindful of the pirates and marauding bands who had attacked their homes in the past, they drew up a deed for the foundation of the new town on 2 September 1470. They had chosen a slightly elevated site on the San Ampélio headland which could be fortified and defended. At the same time, it was pleasantly ventilated and luminous and commanded a wide view down the coast and out to sea. Each family chose a site for their new home, and the relatively wide streets were laid out in an orderly fashion. Having been built to such precise and clearly thought-out specifications, the old town is in contrast with surrounding medieval settlements. It is less of a maze of confusing, narrow alleys, connecting steps and dog-legs and vaulted passageways, and higgledy-piggledy housing than Ventimiglia Alta, Dolceacqua or Pigna, to name just three, and more sedate and tidy: a custom-built settlement, rather than one that just grew and grew.

The Giardino Esotico Pallanca is a showcase garden for Pallanca Landscaping, specialists in Mediterranean and cactus gardens. The gardens, which are open to the public, are on the coast road, just a few kilometres east of the centre of Bordighera. Like so many of the gardens in this area, they are laid out on terraces, built with stone walls on a steep hillside. The main path follows the time-worn cobbles of an ancient trail used by mule trains. Newer paths branch off at each of the successive terraces, where there are beds of cacti and succulents of every description. Some of the cacti are well over a hundred years old and have grown to massive proportions. Ferocious spines contrast with seemingly furry surfaces and delicate cerise, lemon, orange and white flowers. Typical Mediterranean specimens grow alongside exotic varieties from Africa and South America. Forbidding thorns protrude from the bark of some of the more unusual trees, almost defying you to approach them, while some of the cacti are such exquisite shapes that they seem to be sculpted in smooth green stone: the temptation to touch them is immense. The cacti are in flower from March to April, reaching a

shimmering peak of vibrant colours in June and July, and then
tailing off as the autumn approaches.

Cannes to Bordighera – A Place in the Sun

Getting there: suggested transport in **bold**
The main centres mentioned above are all on the coast.
Traffic congestion can make driving and parking frustrating
and time-wasting – **use public transport if possible**.

Staying overnight:
The following are only suggestions: full lists are available from
local tourist information offices.

Cannes
Centre International Marie Eugénie Milleret (CIMEM) –
accommodation in a convent with peaceful garden
just minutes from the centre of Cannes.
37 Ave du Commandant Bret,
tel 0497 06 66 70, fax 0497 06 66 76
e-mail assomption.cannes@wanadoo.fr
web – perso.wanadoo.fr/cimem/

B&B Eve and Henri Daran, L'Eglantier, 15 Rue Campestra.
06400, Cannes,
tel 0493 68 22 43, fax 0493 38 28 53

Mougins – between Cannes and Grasse
Le Manoir de l'Etang, 66 allée du manoir, 06250 Mougins,
tel 0493 900107, fax 0492 92 20 70

Montauroux
B&B between Cannes and Grasse – Pierre and Monique
Robardet, Fontaine d'Aragon, Quartier Narbonne, 83440
Montauroux,
tel/fax 0494 47 71 39, e-mail p.robardet@wanadoo.fr

Nice – see chapter 20

Villefranche-sur-Mer
Welcome Hotel, Quai Courbet,
tel 0493 76 27 62, fax 0493 76 27 66
www.welcomehotel.com

Monaco
B&B Villa Nyanga, Michelle Rousseau, 26 Rue Malbousquet
tel/fax 0377 93 50 32 81,
e-mail michelle.rousseau@mageos.com

Hotel Cosmopolite, 4 Rue de la Turbie, La Condamine,
tel 0377 93 30 16 95

Abela Hotel, 23 Ave des Papalins, Fontvieille,
tel 0377 92 05 90 00

The world-famous luxury Hotel de Paris, is in Place
du Casino,
tel 0377 93 50 80 80, www.monte-carol.mc

Nearby, Hotel Hermitage, Place Beaumarchais,
tel 0377 93 50 67 31, www.monte-carol.mc

Roquebrune-Cap Martin
Hotel les Deux Frères, Place des Deux Frères,
Roquebrune Village,
tel 0493 28 99 00, fax 0493 28 99 10,
e-mail 2freres@webstore.fr

Hotel Westminster, 14 Ave Laurent, Cap Martin,
tel 0493 35 0068, www.westminster06.com

Menton – see Chapter 7

Ventimiglia – see Chapter 13

Bordighera
Hotel Villa Elisa, Via Romana, 70,
tel 0184 26 13 13, fax 0184 26 19 42,
e-mail villaelisa@masterweb.it www.villaelisa.com

Albergo Parigi, Lungomare Argentina,18,
tel 0184 26 14 05, fax 0184 26 04 21,
e-mail info@hotelparigi.com www.hotelparigi.com

Pensione Villa Garnier, Suore San Giuseppe, Via Garnier, 11,
tel 0184 26 18 33

Maps for walking:
Details of local town walks with maps from tourist offices.
Highly recommended is the walk around Cap Martin from
Menton/Carnoles to Roquebrune beach and then on to
Monte Carlo.

There are also pleasant walks on Cap Ferrat and Cap d'Antibes.

Info and website:

Cannes Office de Tourisme,
Palais des Festivals,
La Croisette,
tel 0493 39 24 53, e-mail tourisme@semec.com
www.cannes.fr

Nice – Office du Tourisme 5,
Promenade des Anglais,
tel 0492 14 48 00, fax 0493 92 82 98,
www.nicetourism.com

Monaco-Monte Carlo www.monte-carlo.mc
Office du Tourisme, 2a Bd des Moulins,
tel 0377 92 16 61 16

Menton – Office du Tourisme,
Palais de l'Europe, 8 Ave Boyer,
tel 0492 41 76 76, www.villedementon.com

Bordighera – Information,
APT Via Vittorio Emanuele II, 172,
tel 0184 26 23 22/26 44 55, www.bordighera.it

Instituto Internationale di Studi Liguri, and Bicknell Museum and Library, Via Romana, 39,
tel 0184 26 36 01, www.iisl.it

Climate and when to go:
These destinations have mostly mild, dry winters. They become very hot and crowded in July and August and during special events, such as the Cannes Film Festival in May, Nice Carnival in February, and Jazz Festival in July, Monaco Grand Prix in May. These are the times to avoid if you don't like crowds and the times to come if you want to spot some celebrities.

CHAPTER 19

Taking the train

Part 1 – The Roya Valley Scenic Route

DURING WINTER, NO MATTER HOW DULL OR cold or foggy the days are on the northern side of the Alps, for the people of Italy's north-western regions – Aosta Valley, Piemonte, Lombardia – there is always that enticing promise of sunshine and warmth on the other side of the mountains. Likewise, during the summer when the oppressive humidity of the Po plain and the northern industrial cities causes one stifling day to follow another for weeks at a time, northerners sigh for the caress of a sea breeze. For anyone headed to Italy's western Riviera, or perhaps even to the eastern Côte d'Azur, easy access from Turin is provided by a small two-carriage train that makes the journey up one side of the Alps and down the other several times a day from Cuneo to Breil-sur-Roya. Here this two-nation line divides, with carriages continuing to either Ventimiglia or Nice.

Cuneo is a wedge-shaped town (in Italian *cuneo* means wedge) on a plateau above the confluence of the Gesso and Stura di Demonte rivers. It is an attractive town, and as befits the northern gateway to the coast it has a fine, ornate railway station with high-ceilinged rooms and elaborate wrought-iron railings and balustrades. The mountains come right down to its doorstep. At 534 metres above sea level, it's a pleasant enough place to be in summer: in winter the fountain just outside the station freezes over for months on end.

As soon as the little coast-bound train heads out of Cuneo, it begins its climb, spiralling, tunnelling and zigzagging up into the mountains. As the fertile fruit and grain-producing Piedmontese plains are left behind, inside the carriages spirits soar too. Up and up, out of the winter fog, into crisp blue-skied sunshine. Up and up, out of the summer mugginess, into cooler, drier mountain air. Up and around, past Borgo San Dalmazzo, Roccavione, Robilante and Vernante.

Attillio Mussino, the original illustrator of *Pinocchio* retired to Vernante in the early 1900s. After his death two local artists, Carlet and Meo, decided to honour him by decorating the outside walls of their homes with large, bright murals of Mussino's works depicting Pinocchio's adventures. The idea caught on and now, strolling around Vernante village, there is a reminder on every corner, on every open wall space, of one of Pinocchio's escapades. These are scenes that we all remember from childhood, but with a difference: Carlet and Meo faithfully reproduced the style of Mussino's drawings, but superimposed them on a backdrop that is obviously old Vernante: the church bell tower, for example, can be seen from the window behind Master Geppetto as he puts his finishing touches to Pinocchio; the tower of the ruined thirteenth-century castle stands out on the hilltop beyond the field where Pinocchio encounters the fox and the cat.

On and up then, through the first of the line's coiled tunnels, to Limone Piemonte, the popular skiing resort at 1000 metres. The name of this small town derives not from lemons – in any case somewhat improbable considering the altitude and the climate – but from the ancient Greeks, who colonised Marseilles, Antibes and Nice in about 600 BC. They called the place *lei mon*, meaning a grassy place, fields or pastures: they came here with their sheep and goats for summer grazing, and returned to the coast laden with fresh cheese and butter in the autumn.

The railway line reached Limone in 1891. Excavation had already begun on the tunnel through the mountains, but it wasn't completed until 1898. In 1900 the line was extended through to Vievola on the far side of the mountains. Nowadays, once out of Limone station, the line plunges into this 8100-metre tunnel, emerging into France and sunshine, or at least fine weather more often than not, on the seaward side of the mountains. The mountains are more rugged on this side, climbing steeply from the floor of the valley where the Roya flows swiftly towards the sea. Rocky terraces, sometimes cultivated, sometimes abandoned and crumbling, isolated farmhouses and shepherds' shelters dot the mountainsides. The train gathers speed past Vievola, Tende, La Brigue, Saint Dalmas de Tende, Fontan and Breil sur Roya. These small towns and villages have been in the far south-eastern corner of France for only a little over fifty years – their names reflect their origins in the Italian kingdom of Savoia. As the train leaves Breil behind, the line divides. One line, with cosy red, yellow or grassy-green SNCF carriages, dives down through the mountains to Nice on a line that was constructed in the late 1890s. Meanwhile the blue and grey Italian carriages cross the border back into Italy. Past Olivetta-San Michele and Airole, the valley widens and the lines straighten out, leaving the mountains behind. Any minute now, between Bevera and Ventimiglia, there's a glimpse of the sea. Ventimiglia occupies the only wide part of the valley, the Roya's flood plain. Since leaving Cuneo, we have travelled ninety-six of the most scenic and spectacular railway kilometres in Italy, and this in spite of there being forty-four kilometres that are inside the eighty-one tunnels. I never tire of making the trip, even though those ninety-six kilometres can take almost two hours if the train stops at every station.

In autumn the valley's vegetation turns deep russet red, orange and luxurious, luminous golden yellow. The fiery colours glow against the valley's pale grey rock face. Here on the coast, much of the vegetation is evergreen, so we don't have the same startling colour changes as further inland. Late October and early November are ideal times to head up the valley to enjoy this spectacular seasonal change.

Out of Ventimiglia and once past the village of Bevera, the mountains rise steeply on either side. The river narrows dramatically and becomes a lively, boulder-strewn torrent, foaming and swirling, dark green and blue. The last station in Italy is Olivetta-San Michele. San Michele is just a little roadside cluster of houses with a bar and grocery shop: the main village of Olivetta is three kilometres away up a side road, high on a saddle in the mountains, and only a few hundred metres from the French border.

The train chugs past the village of Fanghetto – there isn't a station here anymore, although there still was in 1979 when the line was re-opened after being closed since it was destroyed by bombing in 1945. All along the line that day villagers partied and waved and cheered as the first train made its way along the newly repaired rail track. Even though the station has gone, Fanghetto can be reached by bus from Ventimiglia. It is a popular holidaying place for northern Europeans too. The Roya tumbles under an ancient single-humped bridge and widens enough to make a deep, sheltered swimming hole.

For more energetic types, a hiking trail links all the villages along the route from Ventimiglia to Tenda. A pleasant day out in the mountains could start by using the train to get to the departure point, and for returning to base after walking from Airole to Fanghetto, or even all the way to Breil and perhaps beyond. The paths are well marked and wend their way through olive groves and stands of myrtle. The river and the railway line are never far away.

The next tunnel after Fanghetto crosses the border into France. At Breil-sur-Roya the river has been dammed, forming a pretty lake on the edge of the village. Swans glide across the lake, and in summer concerts are held under a marquee on the shore. The railway line from Nice joins the line from Ventimiglia here, so we wait for an extra carriage to be hitched on. Beyond Breil, the valley is ever narrower. Olive groves give way to forest. The terrain is rocky and imposing, and largely uninhabited. Occasionally the vegetation is interrupted by a barren scree slope.

The village of Saorge comes into view across the valley, and at the foot of the village we catch a glimpse of kayakers skidding down the Roya. As we continue up the valley, we look across the river to another railway line running parallel to the line we're on, but higher up the mountain slope. The two lines run parallel for about a kilometre, climbing steadily as the village of Fontan drops away behind us. Then our line tunnels into the mountain. There isn't any real impression of circling around, but when we come out onto the mountain-side again it's a surprise to find that we're above Fontan again, but higher up and on the opposite side of the valley – on the section of the line that we were looking up at before. Where we were a few minutes ago is below us, across the valley, and Fontan drops even further behind us.

Spiralling on, up into the mountains, we reach St Dalmas-de-Tende. Outside the station, a secondary road leads off to the north-west, into the Parc National du Mercantour. Rough trails for four-wheel-drive vehicles and designated hiking tracks connect the mountain lakes and the Vallée des Merveilles (Valley of Wonders) at the foot of Mont Bégo.

Leaving the train at Tende we explore the village, through narrow lanes and cobbled alleyways, and climb up to the terraced cemetery surrounding the ruins of an ancient castle. We're surprised to see a young shepherd driving his flock of long-legged sheep through the maze of village streets.

On the outskirts of the village a modern museum is dedicated to the Bronze Age culture in the Vallée des Merveilles, with displays explaining the significance and symbolism of the rock drawings in their context of 4000 years ago. With the opening of this museum in 1996, Tende – or Tenda as it was called when it was in Italian territory – has made a conscious effort to move forward in time, and it's a village in constant evolution. Some new shops have opened recently, one of them catering for trekkers and mountaineers, another stocking a mouth-watering array of local cheeses; façades have been repainted, and the *trompe-l'oeil* retouched, so that the bright, decorative colours shimmer illusively. Nowhere more so than the Cathedral of Our Lady of the

Assumption which, although tucked into a narrow cobbled lane, stands tall over the nearby houses, a splash of deep red decorated with yellow and blue in contrast to the grey stone and slate, and creamy stucco and terracotta that surrounds it.

Early on a mid-October afternoon, after a delicious lunch of baked trout with toasted almonds in Tende, it's time to head back down the valley: we have decided to leave the train at Fontan and visit Saorge. From the old station, all closed up now, but a thriving holiday camp for youngsters during the summer months, it's a twenty-minute walk up the road to Saorge. Far more challenging is the hike up over the mountain that is signposted directly across the road from the station. On an impulse we decide to go that way. The first forty-five minutes zigzag relentlessly up and up. Stopping to catch our breath we admire the wild flowers, bright pink and blue and pure white. We wonder too at signs of digging in the undergrowth and realise it must be the work of a boar. Eventually the track reaches a grassy clearing and our path turns down to the right, while the path leading straight ahead continues up further into the forest. It's downhill to Saorge now, and soon we're looking down on its rooftops, many of which are still in the original deep purple slate that is characteristic of this village. When we're nearly into the village we meet a group of young people heading up the trail. They warn us that they've just seen a snake: we tell them to watch out for a boar.

The village is built on a series of terraces, in a wide curve around a natural amphitheatre on the steep, steep mountain-side. The streets around the curve are relatively flat, but too narrow for traffic, while the various terraces of the village are connected with steep steps and cobbled ramps. Exploration is rewarding: about 300 people still live here, and the village is cared for. Attractive eye-catching window boxes and balconies are splashes of colour. On a hot day, the benches in a shady clearing near the open-air laundry tubs are a refreshing haven. The arc of ancient houses faces south, looking down the valley towards Breil-sur-Roya catching the sun all day long. A simple Romanesque church at one end of the village is countered by a baroque steeple at the other end of the crescent, its dome decorated in yellow and green glazed tiles. The name Saorge is a contraction of Saint George – look out for him fighting his dragon in various frescoes and bas-reliefs around the village. Listen too for the sound of a game of boules or petanque in progress – you'll have a bird's-eye view as the pitch is on the terrace below the car park, at the north-western end of the village, where the road down to the station starts. Leaning over the railing, watching the games unfold, time loses its importance – don't miss your train.

Trains – Roya Valley

Getting there: suggested transport in **bold**
Northbound **trains** depart from Nice and Ventimiglia for Cuneo, via Breil-sur-Roya, Tende and Limone.

Eating and staying overnight:
The following are only suggestions: full lists are available from local tourist information offices. For hotels and restaurants see the Nice, Ventimiglia, Sospel, Merveilles and Notre Dame des Fontaines chapters.

In addition:

Breil-sur-Roya:
Restaurant Le Bianchéri, Place Bianchéri
tel 0493 04 40 11

Hotel Le Castel du Roy, 146 Chemin del'Aigara,
on outskirts of village,
tel 0493 04 43 66, fax 0493 04 91 83,
www.logis-de-france.com

Saorge Gite d'Etape, Le Bergiron,
tel 0493 04 55 49

Fontan Hotel-restaurant Le Terminus,
tel 0493 04 34 00, e-mail terminus.fontan@freesbee.fr

Maps for walking:
IGN TOP 25 3841 OT

Info and website:
French Railway information www.ter-sncf.com/paca

www.trainstouristiques-ter.com/traindesmerveilles

Italian railways information www.fs-on-line.com

www.royabevera.com

Office du Tourisme, Breil-sur-Roya
tel/fax 0493 04 99 76
e-mail tourismebreilsurroya@wanadoo.fr
www.breil-sur-roya.fr

Saorge Mairie,
tel 0493 04 51 23

Vernante (Italy) Pinocchio murals – Pro Loco
tel/fax 0171 92 05 50

Climate and when to go:
Check opening times at local tourist office before going.

Pleasant all year round, pretty in autumn, mild in summer.

Using this line in winter it's feasible to spend a day skiing in
Limone Piemonte, and return to the coast in the evening.

Cuneo market day is Tuesday – one of the biggest street
markets in Piemonte.

Part 2 – Les Chemins de Fer de Provence

SEEMINGLY IN THE MIDDLE OF NOWHERE, the train comes to a halt. The tiny hamlet of St-Benoit sits atop a chalky hillock a couple of kilometres away across the fields. It is almost lunchtime on a mid-summer's Sunday morning, and we're only five kilometres from our destination. Temporarily though, the little train has quite literally run out of steam. Laughing and chatting we hop down onto the gravel beside the rails, while the stokers top up with water to regain optimum boiler pressure. We've come fifteen kilometres in little over an hour, steadily gaining altitude, but the remaining stretch of the journey is the steepest of all. However, this is only a short halt. A lively toot-toot summons us all back on board and we scramble back into our ruby-red carriages. Chuff-chuff-chuffing, the train climbs through a long anti-avalanche tunnel. Sunlight beams through the arched windows on the downward face of the mountainside, and looking back down the tunnel we can see just how steep it is here. The engine is pulling with all its might. The line levels out briefly and the train gathers speed for the final slope. One last effort and we draw triumphantly into the Annot station.

A typical outing on the Train des Pignes, drawn by a 1909 steam locomotive, covers these twenty kilometres from

Puget-Theniers to Annot on most Sundays each month from May to mid-October. Whether as a passenger or as an onlooker it's a fun way to relive a bygone age and to enjoy the spectacular scenery of the valley of the Var as it slices through the Alpes Maritimes on its way to the sea from its source in the Alpes-de-Haute-Provence.

In all, there are 151 kilometres of narrow-gauge railway linking Nice to Digne-les-Bains, adding up to a three-and-a-quarter-hour journey on the regular railcar service. With the first departure from Nice at 6.42 a.m., reaching Digne at 9.53, and the last departure from Digne at 17.25, arriving in Nice at 20.35, it is theoretically possible to make the return trip in a day. But narrow-gauge trains jiggle and rattle along, and I find it less tiring to make the trip in at least two stages, with an overnight stop. It's a perfect way to explore some of the ancient, history-laden villages along the way.

In Nice's Rue Alfred Binet, the railway station bustles as workers, students and commuters mingle with locals bound for or returning from a shopping trip to Nice, and a few tourists heading up into the mountains. On this particular June Sunday, though, the platform is positively jingling with excitement as a French line-dancing group set off for one of their themed outings: and what better theme for country-and-western enthusiasts than a scenic steam-train ride.

The chartered feeder railcar departs Nice at 8 a.m. As soon as it leaves it begins to climb, pulling up through the western suburbs, up behind the glittering onion domes of the Russian Cathedral, and then burrowing through the hills to descend into the Var Valley. Shortly the sprawling commercial and industrial sites on the outskirts of the city have dropped behind, and Mediterranean-ness gives way to a distinctly mountain ambience. The valley closes in quickly. More often than not the Var seems an insignificant stream, making its way innocently towards the sea in a stony riverbed that appears to be far wider than it could ever need. After torrential rain it can rapidly become a destructive force, raging along, overflowing its banks and carrying away anything in its path, including the railway line, in the worst floods. As the Vesubie River flows into the Var, the valley narrows into the Defile du Chaudan. The light takes on hues of blue and green and grey as sheer cliffs soar straight up out of the river. The scenic road and the railway line hug the cliffs side by side and the Var tumbles along frothy and green. Where the Tinée flows into it, a secondary road branches off to the north, through the Gorges de Tinée and de Valabres, and up to the Isola 2000 skiing resort.

The line has turned westwards by now and the valley opens out again. We pass ancient Touët-sur-Var, rooted tenaciously to the mountainside, and its tiny station in the valley. Yet another river, the Cians, flows into the Var and a precarious narrow road leads into the lower and upper Gorges du Cians. From its source on Mont Mounier, the Cians plunges 1600 metres along its twenty-five-kilometre length: small wonder that it has gouged out a breathtaking spectacle of narrow fissures, roaring waterfalls and vertical rock faces.

Olive groves and orchards dotted with beehives and small market gardens border the line as we arrive in Puget-Theniers. The steam train is waiting at the platform, billowing black smoke as we mill around it admiringly. As well as the intending passengers, a small crowd of curious passers-by has also formed. The four carriages are all fully booked – a month ago I was lucky enough to get the very last available seat.

We reached Puget-Theniers at 9.45 – fifteen minutes

before the steam train's departure. We dart about, taking photos and admiring the polished teak interiors of the 1892 vintage wagons, while the stoker makes his last-minute preparations. His face is black and glistening with sweat – he has been stoking since just after dawn, in order to have steam up at 10 a.m. In all, in the twenty kilometres to Annot, the train will consume 6000 litres of water, 1000 kg of coal and ten litres of oil.

Siffler – to blow a whistle: a cheery French word that seems just right for an outing on a steam train. At the first warning toot we climb aboard. The two front carriages are occupied by a sedate group who have arrived at the station by coach, while the lively country-and-western group have the two back carriages. At the very back of the train, the station master points out the four seats reserved for the only individual passengers: I'm sharing with a pair of French grandparents and their little granddaughter. The grandmother tells me that she spent all her working life with the railways – it's in her blood and she's still enjoying it. We're delighted with our seats because we can go out onto the rear platform and feel the wind in our faces as we rattle along.

For the first seven kilometres the road and the railway line run close together alongside the river. There are several level crossings and we pass with much reciprocal waving to drivers, cyclists and level-crossing operators. Some drivers have seen us coming and have stopped to photograph or video us.

If it weren't for its backdrop, Entrevaux would be just another charming medieval village: tall and narrow pastel-washed houses with earthy roof tiles and lavender shutters. It's a small, walled village on the banks of the Var, at a point where it curves around in such a way that the village is surrounded by the river on three sides. Rounded watchtowers stand either side of the drawbridge that guards Porte Royale, the main entrance to the village. Porte de France Gate in the western wall and Porte d'Italie (formerly Porte de Savoie) in the east are the only other openings in the bastioned wall: appropriate names since for nearly 500 years, until 1860, Entrevaux was a French border post on the frontier with the Kingdom of Savoy. Behind the village, on its northern side, there was no need to build a wall, as the rocky mountainside rears up almost vertically, at the same time tapering to a craggy point which was crowned with a turreted fort in the 1690s.

The steam train doesn't stop long enough in Entrevaux for a visit to the town, but the line-dancers make the most of the stop anyway. They have a small portable drum and recorded music, and a crowd gathers round them as they dance on the station platform. They're thoroughly enjoying themselves, and their vitality adds a festive air to the outing.

Continuing on our excursion we wave to kayakers having a great time on the river. Not far beyond Entrevaux, a cry comes through from one of the front carriages, repeated down the length of the train. 'Tunnel! Tunnel!' and just in time we get the blinds down to filter out the smoke as we're plunged into darkness.

Then the Var veers off to the north while we continue westwards along the banks of its tributary, the Coulomp, past fields where sheep and goats graze and even one full of quails – no doubt destined to turn up on a menu as Caille a la Provençal. Three more kilometres and apparently in the middle of nowhere, at the foot of St Benoit, we come to a halt.

The steam train arrives in Annot just before midday and remains there for three hours, so there's time to explore some of the village. The line dancers have booked in at a restaurant for Sunday lunch, but I decide to take the path out of the village to the church of Our Lady of Vers la Ville. The country lane that leads to the chapel is an outdoor Stations of the Cross. The scenes from the crucifixion are painted in vivid colours on glazed tiles, and each one is protected inside a stone shrine. They are the work of Claude Renoir, son of Pierre Renoir, the painter.

Annot is a village of fountains – water gushes in every little square. Situated midway on the railway line between Nice and Digne, it's an ideal place to spend a short break. The village is overlooked by a forested bluff known as Le Baou du Parou. A cross at the summit marks the point where Saint Peter is said to have left the imprint of his walking stick when he came to the area as a missionary. Le Baou du Parou is quite a challenging walk from Annot, but the view from the cross makes it worthwhile.

While the line dancers are performing for an appreciative crowd in Annot's main square, the steam engine is being prepared for the return to Puget Thenier. It is shunted onto a turntable and turned around by manpower. The crew's spirits haven't flagged at all, even though they've been at work since long before the excursion started and grabbed only a quick snack during the lunch break before getting on with tending to the train. When the group gets back to the station, steam is up again and the train sets off for the relatively quick downhill return to Puget Thenier.

A couple of times a year the steam-train excursion continues all the way to Digne, but for now, let's board the regular blue-and-white railcar on its way north-west towards Digne from Annot. The villages of Le Fugeret and Méailles are only a few minutes' ride from Annot, the one quite low in the valley and the other perched high above it. They have retained their quiet rural character, and the people are friendly and helpful to wandering foreigners. As in Annot, walking trails fan out from both villages: a determined hiker could follow an ancient mule trail from Annot to the mountain hamlet of Argenton, and then descend to Le Fugeret and return to Annot by train, or hike from Méailles to Le Fugeret and on to Annot. There are options for every level of energy and ability. Unpretentious village restaurants are tempting rewards for a challenging mountain hike.

Not far from Méailles the railway tunnels through the mountains and emerges in the Verdon Valley. There isn't so much a village at Thorame Gare as a lone station which serves the village of Thorame Haute, seven kilometres away to the north, and its hamlet of Thorame Basse, another five kilometres west of Thorame Haute. In spite of the station's apparent isolation, it's a popular stop for hikers headed to the upper Verdon Valley, and the alpine villages of Colmars-les-Alps and Allos. During the winter a shuttle bus takes train passengers up to the ski fields, so that it's possible to leave Nice in the morning, spend the day skiing and return to the coast in the evening. And during the winter, if only for the magical snow and frost-encrusted landscape, the trip is well worthwhile.

From Thorame Gare the line begins to head downhill towards Digne. Saint-André-des-Alpes is popular as a centre for hang-gliding and delta-planing. World championships take place here, as well as initiation lessons for beginners. Next comes Le Lac de Castillon, at the foot of Saint André. Cool off here, swim, row or sail, or take an excursion south to the Gorges of Verdon.

The Train des Pignes has nearly run its full course. Digne

is only thirty minutes away. Since leaving the outskirts of Nice there has hardly been a single village where, had you decided to get off and explore, you wouldn't have found something interesting to see or do.

Trains – Les Chemins de Fer de Provence

Getting there: suggested transport in **bold**
Trains depart Nice from the CP station at 4 bis Rue A Binet (a short walk back behind Nice SNCF station) and in Digne from the joint CP-SNCF station.

There are 4–5 departures daily in each direction.

Steam trains depart Puget-Theniers at 10 a.m. and Annot at 3.50 p.m. Throughout the summer there are departures most Sundays, and some special departures to other destinations: see www.chez.com/gecp

Eating and staying overnight:

Puget-Theniers
Hotel Alize
tel 0493 05 05 13, fax 0493 05 06 20
www.logis-de-france.com

Entrevaux
Hotel-Restaurant Vauban
tel 0493 05 42 40

B&B Chambre d'hôtes Annie Saissi
tel 0493 05 42 92

Annot
Hotel Restaurant – Beauséjour, Place du Revély,
tel 0492 83 21 08, fax 0492 83 39 67
e-mail ALBERTALAIN@aol.com

Saint-Andre-les-Alpes
Hotel Restaurant l'Auberge du Parc, Place Charles-Bron,
tel 0492 89 02 39

Maps for walking:
IGN TOP 25 3541 OT

Info and website:
Chemins de Fer de Provence: 4 Rue A Binet, Nice,
tel 0493 82 10 17

Ave P Sémard, Digne
tel 0492 31 01 58, www.trainprovence.com

Puget-Theniers Maison de Pays, information
tel 0493 05 05 05

Entrevaux Bureau du Tourisme
tel 0493 05 46 73, fax 0493 05 40 71
e-mail tourisme@entrevaux.info
www.entrevaux.info

Annot Office du Tourisme, Boulevard Saint-Pierre,
tel 0492 83 23 03, fax 0492 83 30 63
e-mail otsi.annot@wanadoo.fr www.annot.fr

St-Andre-les-Alpes: infos tourisme
tel 0492 89 02 39

Climate and when to go:
Mild summers, lovely in autumn and spring, can snow
around Annot in winter.

Steam train only runs between May and October. Regular
services all year round.

CHAPTER 20

A long way from St Petersburg

NOWHERE ON THE RIVIERA DO THE GLITTERING fragments in the kaleidoscope of cultures and nationalities, of famous names and distinctive architecture tumble into more fascinating patterns than in Nice. Even the city's name tells a story: it derives from Nikaia, or Nike, the Greek goddess of victory, reminding us that the city was founded by the Greeks in about 600 BC. The Romans moved into the area to help the Greeks defend Nikaia from the local Ligurian tribes: on the hilltop at Cimiez, the Matisse Museum is surrounded by a park containing the remains of the substantial Roman settlement. Almost 2000 years after the Romans, the English and Russians came to Nice in search of winter sunshine, found it greatly to their liking, and left their cultural imprint too.

The eastern boundary of Nice is dominated by the promontory of Mount Boron, and the charming town of Villefranche-sur-mer nestles in a small, extremely sheltered bay between the eastern flank of the mount and Cap Ferrat. Founded as a free port, it provided shelter for a fleet of Russian ships in 1770.

It's harder to imagine any greater contrast than a port on the Baltic Sea and the mild climate, pastel-coloured buildings and verdant backdrop of Villefranche. So it didn't take long, on the seamen's grapevine, for enticing descriptions of this lovely haven to get back to ice-bound Saint Petersburg and to Paris, where, taking advantage of the greater opportunities for education, cultural activities and freedom of expression, there had been a Russian quarter since the late 1600s.

With the Russian fleet still using the port of Villefranche in the nineteenth century and the royal family now spending their winters in Nice, the Russian community there flourished. A Russian newspaper was printed in Nice, Russian shops and restaurants opened, and gradually more and more Russian families decided to stay permanently on the Riviera.

Alexander II's mother, Tsarina Alexandra Feodorovna, saw that Nice urgently needed a Russian Orthodox church of its own, so she sponsored the construction of a small church dedicated to Saint Alexandra and Saint Nicholas in Rue Longchamp. It was inaugurated on 12 January 1860: today it is the oldest Russian Orthodox church outside Russia. Because a law at the time forbade the construction of non-Catholic churches on the ground floor, it is built over the Russian library, and is reached by a wide double staircase. As a result, it is light and airy – the ideal setting for time-darkened icons trimmed in gold that gleam by the light of slim beeswax candles. Paintings of Saints Alexandra and Nicholas grace the intricately carved oak iconostasis. Saint Alexandra is wearing a gorgeous blue robe trimmed with gold; Saint Nicholas's vestment is deep red and gold.

Over to one side, behind a screen, a layman begins to chant: a vibrant, melodic voice that will accompany the entire service. Chanting in an ancient Slavonic language – the equivalent of Latin – now gathering momentum, almost singing, then ebbing away, slower, sometimes incredibly mournful, chanting, intoning, setting the pace for the handful of worshippers, echoed from time to time by the priest's chanted reply from behind the closed doors of the iconostasis.

Never mind if you don't understand: close your eyes and let the rhythm of those ancient prayers take you back to a far-off land whose religion still follows the Julian calendar. A faith where the worshippers bow humbly to kiss an icon, and where the air is soon laden with the haze of incense. From time to time the double doors of the iconostasis swing open, and the priest moves into the main body of the church. He rarely faces the congregation: instead he and they both face the altar. Watch discreetly: this is a place of profound devotion. When the iconostasis doors are open the most devoted worshippers, irrespective of their age, kneel on the carpeted floor and bow low, their foreheads touching the floor. Others remain standing: there are very few chairs in any Russian Orthodox church. There's a homely atmosphere in this little church: it's as if each of the worshippers truly regards it as part of her home.

By the late 1800s the Orthodox congregation had outgrown the church in Rue Longchamp, so construction of a cathedral began in 1903. In January 1910, on the fiftieth anniversary of the first church's inauguration, the first cross was positioned on the cathedral.

From Boulévard Tsarevitch, it stands out at the end of a short lane. Warm ochre bricks, and finely cut pale grey stonework; marble, majolica and mosaics; turquoise, green and gold leaf – and all set in a large wooded park. (It doesn't often snow in Nice, but when it did, in January 1985, the cathedral was frosted, and glistening white. Overnight it seemed, as if by magic, to have been transported back to a Russian winter setting.)

As we step into the cathedral it's difficult not to gasp with astonishment. In our Catholic or Protestant churches, we usually enter from one end, so that the main body of the church is in front of us, while the altar is at the far end. In the Russian Orthodox churches we enter in the centre of one of the long sides. The main body of the nave is to our left and right. It doesn't have to be as big as our churches because there aren't any pews, so the iconostasis, which is in the centre of the long wall opposite the entrance, is surprisingly near us as we go in. There is a sense of immediacy and intimacy that is often lacking in western churches.

Icons are everywhere: some in simple wooden frames, others in elaborately carved ones: covered in beaten gold and silver, copper and bronze, precious stones and pearls and enamel work. Then there are small folding triptych icons of your favourite saint to slip into your travelling trunk for that long journey from Saint Petersburg or Moscow. And fascinating calendar icons: barely two handspans high and wide, they are divided into thumbnail-sized squares representing the weeks of the year and the feasts of Our Lady. Each week is painted with minuscule pictures of the saints, twelve or so per week, each saint scarcely bigger than a grain of rice and over their heads each one's name in tiny writing.

The cathedral of Saint Nicholas was dedicated in November 1912, and is one of the most beautiful Russian Orthodox churches outside Russia. Tourists and faithful alike visit every day. An icon of Saint Nicholas the Miracle Worker is one of the most devoutly venerated: it belonged to Crown Prince Nicholas. After he died his mother gave it to the church in Rue Longchamp, and later it was hung over the door of the chapel built in memory of Prince Nicholas, where, exposed to the elements, it soon became darkened and practically unrecognisable. When the cathedral was finished, this icon, now very badly damaged by long exposure to the sun and rain, was placed beside the altar behind the iconostasis. Suddenly, in 1915, in a process that art experts were unable to explain, and which the faithful readily defined as miraculous, the icon began to lighten, until it returned to its original beautiful condition.

Nice's Caucade suburb is on a hillside overlooking the airport. This was once the marble workers' quarter of the city: engravers and sculptors were as much a part of the scenery as flower sellers are today; flower sellers, because the hillside is the site of Nice's cemeteries. Up a lane opposite the entrance to the main cemetery you'll see first the British and Commonwealth cemeteries, and then the Russian cemetery at the top of the lane. In spring the wild irises and freesias bloom among the graves, and visitors bring primulas, cyclamens and tulips. Some of the graves have been long forgotten; others were tended yesterday. A small tomb with three blue-enamelled domes and three bronze ones catches the eye: a lady-in-waiting to two Tsarinas rests here, and just beyond lies the Princess Catherine Dolgorouky, the second wife of Tsar Alexander II. She died in 1922, but there are still fresh flowers on her modest marble tomb: fresh freesias and white broom in a simple vase, while some roses and carnations have been laid to dry beside the altar. Other graves remind us of people whose surnames have become part of western

A long way from St Petersburg

European culture too: Smirnoff and Stroganoff, for example.

A plane takes off at the bottom of the hill. On one side of the airport, the Promenade des Anglais ends abruptly; on the other side the Var flows purposefully into the sea. Turn the kaleidoscope. Let another pattern emerge. Explore and enjoy.

Russians in Nice

Getting there: suggested transport in **bold**
Nice is easily reached by **train** and **bus**. The city has an excellent urban bus service, and the international airport is only 30 minutes from the city centre.

Staying overnight:
The following are only suggestions: full lists are available from local tourist information offices.

Hotel Windsor, 11 Rue Dalpozzo,
tel 0493 88 59 35, fax 0493 88 94 57,
e-mail windsor@webstore.fr www.webstore.fr/windsor

Hotel L'Oasis, 23 Rue Gounod,
tel 0493 88 12 29, fax 0493 16 14 40,
e-mail mail@hotel-oasis-nice.com.fr www.hotel-oasis.com.fr

Hotel Negresco, 37 Promenade des Anglais,
tel 0493 16 64 00, fax 0493 88 35 68,
e-mail direction@hotel-negrsco.com
www.hotel-negresco.com

B&B Le Castel Enchanté, Mme J Olivier, 61 Route de St Pierre de Féric, 06000 Nice,
tel 0493 97 02 08, fax 0493 97 13 70,
e-mail castel.enchante@wanadoo.fr

Maps for walking:
From tourist information office.

Info and website:
Ave Thiers, next to railway station
tel 0493 87 07 07, fax 0493 16 85 16

5 Promenade des Anglais,
tel 0493 87 60 60, www.nicetourism.com

Russian Cathedral – Cathédrale Russe St Nicholas,
Ave Nicholas II,
tel 0493 96 88 02 – open for visiting every day except
Sunday morning and during services.
With slight seasonal variations, 9–12 a.m. and 2.30–5/6 p.m.
Service times are published each month.

Russian Restaurant, grocery and craft shop Matrouchka,
10 Bvd. Tzarewitch,
tel 0493 44 98 90

Climate and when to go:

Pleasant all year round

CHAPTER 21

The Route Napoleon –
the return of an emperor

THERE WAS A LITTLE INN HIGH IN THE MOUNtains on the edge of north-eastern Provence, about thirteen kilometres from Digne. Imagine a band of weary travellers stopping there for refreshments during a chilly morning in early March. They'd been on the move for a week, first by sea, and then across inhospitable country, most of them on foot, a few on horseback. Trudging through snowstorms and over rocky mule trails; moving as furtively as a thousand or so men can move, avoiding the main thoroughfares for fear of being apprehended; grabbing a few uncomfortable hours' sleep in the dead of night, and on the move again at or before daybreak.

And now, here was the cunning innkeeper charging an outrageous twenty francs for a couple of eggs.

'Are eggs *really* so rare here?' their leader enquired.

'No, sire, eggs aren't rare,' was the ingratiating reply, 'but emperors are.'

It was early morning on Saturday, 4 March 1815. Napoleon Bonaparte was on his way back to Paris to reclaim his Empire. The innkeeper at La Clappe has gone down in local history as the perpetrator of 'l'épisode des oeufs'.

On 1 March 1815, a little fleet anchored in Golfe de Juan. Sheltered between Cap d'Antibes and Cannes' Cap de la Croix, today we know the landing place as the popular seaside town of Golfe-Juan. In 1815 it was just a quiet sandy beach – the ideal place for Napoleon and his men to come ashore from Elba about 5 p.m. The exact landing place has since become a marina for leisure craft, but a plaque showing an eagle in mosaic on a sea-blue background marks the spot.

Every first Sunday in March the landing is re-enacted on a nearby beach. The crowd gathers round to welcome the striking Napoleon look-alike, splendid in white shirt and waistcoat, and white breeches tucked into long black boots. He wears a fine grey cloak with golden epaulets and sports a red, white and blue cockade on his wide black hat. He musters his men to the roll of blue and golden drums, and when everyone is gathered in their ranks, the returning emperor delivers his proclamation. Speaking of the glory of France, and the need to vanquish her enemies, he reminds them that they are united under the flag of a leader who shares their interests and whose honour and glory will also be theirs. And then the famous words which have become the motto of his return to Paris: 'The Eagle, with the national Tricolour, will fly from church tower to church tower, as far as the towers of Notre Dame.'

After a brief stop for refreshments in an olive grove where the Golfe-Juan to Vallauris road crossed, and still crosses, the route from Marseilles to Italy, Napoleon and his men set off to spend their first night eight kilometres away to the west, at

Cannes. In 1815 Cannes was a simple fishing village at the foot of the Suquet hill. None of the land where the Palais des Festivals and the fine hotels are now had been reclaimed from the sea then. There was a small chapel on the beach where the fishermen went on pilgrimages, and it was here that the army bivouacked that first night. It would be the first of many such brief and uncomfortable halts over the next 340 kilometres, before their triumphant entry into Grenoble six days later.

Today the slogan of the scenic drive from Golfe-Juan to Grenoble, *La Route Napoleon*, is 'He did it on foot: you can do it by car.' In fact, the modern N85 roughly follows the trail of Napoleon's seven-day march. Between Cannes and Grasse the Route is the same one that already existed on those earliest maps of France which were compiled by Cassini in the eighteenth century, and which Napoleon would certainly have had with him in 1815. Next to the Tourist Information Office in Grasse, a plaque records Napoleon's halt on the edge of the town: beside it, water still gushes from a spring. No doubt the *Grande Armée* refilled its water casks here too.

Beyond Grasse we finally have the chance to follow in the footsteps of those troops. With careful planning and appropriate preparation, Digne can be reached in four days. Frequently the modern highway deviates from, and runs parallel to or near the actual nineteenth-century route. Roman roads and ancient mule trails usually make for relatively easy walking. When the authentic route and the modern one overlap for long stretches and walking on the highway is impractical, alternative hiking trails wend their way across country, away from the traffic, to rejoin Napoleon's path – the *Voie Imperiale* – further along.

As we set out to follow in the footsteps of that little army, it's sobering to remember that they wore boots which had neither right nor left foot shapings, and which came in only three sizes. The men carried heavy packs: forty kilos when dry, considerably more when soaked by the rain.

If you prefer to stay on the asphalt, maybe you'll do it by car or motorbike. Rolling terrain makes for relatively easy cycling on the N85, and once a day the Nice to Geneva bus follows the N85 through Grasse and Castellane, to Digne and Sisteron, and on to Gap and Grenoble.

On the northern edge of Grasse, the road to Digne climbs steeply away from the town for several kilometres before reaching the so-called Plateau Napoleon. From here on, for the next sixty or so kilometres to Castellane, the road and adjacent paths meander across undulating countryside. In spring and summer the air is scented with wild broom and lavender, and the villages along the route record the emperor's passing with a plaque, a statue, an eagle with welcoming, outstretched wings, a Café Napoleon . . .

Escragnolles has hardly changed since those exhausted men trooped into its main square, stamping their aching feet to keep warm, blowing into cupped hands. They had covered forty kilometres since leaving Cannes, and still had another ten to go before they reached that night's halt at Seranon.

The twenty-five kilometres of N85 between Seranon and Castellane follow Napoleon's actual route fairly closely, sweeping across rolling open countryside. Long before we reach Castellane, the steeple of Notre Dame du Roc comes into view atop the massive outcrop of rock that gives it its name. The 184-metre-high rock is the site of the ancient Roman fort and the original village of Petra Castellana. The road curves around below the Roc and crosses the Verdon River into the village over a modern bridge parallel to the much older Pont Reine Jeanne which Napoleon and his men marched over. The village is the bustling gateway to the Verdon Gorge, at twenty-five kilometres long, the largest in Europe. It slices through the limestone plateau, varying in depth from 250 to 700 metres. The Verdon's greenish waters tumble along, sometimes as little as eight metres wide, at other points nearly a 100 metres across. The rim of the gorge spans from 200 to 1500 metres, and roads along both the north and south rims offer stunning views from various lookout points. The bed of the gorge can be reached on foot, and there are several possibilities there for kayaking and rafting.

Leaving Castellane's shaded main square, the Route Napoleon climbs north out of the valley and then threads its way through the narrow rocky gap that is the Col des Leques. Sheer, dramatic crags plunge dizzyingly down to the ribbon of water known as the Asse de Blieux. The road makes its way gingerly down to run parallel to the stream for the final ten or so kilometres across the plain into Barrême.

After a long but leisurely day, driving and strolling along sections of the route from Grasse via Castellane, we arrived in Barrême around 6 p.m. on a midsummer's eve. Camping Napoleon was a comfortable site to pitch our tents, and there are a couple of hotels in the village as well. Before dinner we strolled up to the railway station where there is a small fossil museum. Barrême's symbol is a gigantic uncurled ammonite. Their fossilised remains abound in the terrain around Barrême. (For real fossil enthusiasts, there is a trio of larger geological museums in Digne-les-Bains, Castellane and Sisteron.)

For the first 30 kilometres of the fourth day's march, Napoleon chose not to follow what was then, as now, the main road that curves around towards Digne in the Asse de Bilieux valley, in order to avoid the risk of being intercepted by royalist troops arriving from the south. He decided instead to revert again to the ancient Celto-Ligurian-Roman route up and over the mountains. This route runs parallel to the main road, north of – and through – the mountains that border the Asse de Bilieux valley. Thirty kilometres – the longest stretch so far of authentic *Voie Imperiale*: we aren't sure if we can do it in a day, so it's an exciting challenge. On our side we have the fact that we haven't been on the march for the previous three days, and have eaten and slept well the night before. Our shoes fit perfectly, and we'll be carrying only our maps, picnic, camera and, when we set out, 3.5 litres of water. This will prove invaluable, as we won't find a drinking fountain until we've covered half the distance. Against us is the worry that we aren't soldiers used to long marches: just a couple of reasonably fit, middle-aged, female teachers. We know that Napoleon and his men left Barrême just before dawn and reached Digne about midday. They were going as fast as they could: we'll be sauntering along, and we expect to take at least ten hours, maybe more. To give ourselves the best chance on this cloudless summer's morning we're up and on the road by seven o'clock: a hearty breakfast in the café in the village square, and picnic things stowed in our packs.

Following the signposts for the *Voie Imperiale* we start off up the hill behind the village. A steepish farm access road quickly becomes a forestry road, and as we leave Barrême behind and below us, the *Voie* narrows into a simple walking path. We know that it is roughly eight kilometres to the nearest settlement of Chaudon, but the signposts don't give us any indication of how long it might take: we calculate a maximum of four hours if it's rough going. The gradient eases. We're still going up, but very gradually, through pine woods alternating with more open scrub. Butterflies flit all around us and wild flowers vie, heather and lavender with broom and gorse; lupins with daisies and wild roses. Soon the path levels out and what we had thought might be a serious hike turns into a pleasant ramble as the trail skirts around the side of the mountain range rather than climbing directly over it. The path is clearly defined and just in case, regular white flashes of a white spread-winged eagle are stencilled onto the rocks and tree trunks to keep us on track. We amble along, enjoying the scenery, the birdsong, the scents and the absolute silence. We had expected to encounter other walkers, but not only are we alone, gloriously there is no sign whatsoever of other humans ever having come this way – not a single drink can or sweet wrapper.

After walking for nearly three hours, to within cooey of Chaudon, we come to a shale slope. Judging by the hoofprints digging away at the no-more-than-a-boot-wide path across it, boars have passed here recently. It seems that there is nowhere left for us to put our feet. And yet there's no other option here: we must go on or turn back; the shale drops away forbiddingly into a tumble of rocks and rubble. Like us, how many of Napoleon's men in clumsy, unfitted shoes, were tempted to give up and desert? And yet, faced with retracing our steps, we decide to press on. Slithering our way crab-like on our bottoms across no more than three metres seems to take forever. And then we are across, dusting the shale off our shorts: victorious! The worst is over: it is downhill into the tiny hamlet of Chaudon. As we ford one of the many streams that trickle down from the Barre de Chaudon and eventually flow into the Asse we meet a man and two dogs – apart from the boar prints and some droppings, this is the first sign of life since leaving Barrême. We stare at each other – evidently trampers don't come this way every day either. We turn north-west towards Digne – nineteen kilometres the sign says, and we feel optimistic.

Napoleon's authentic route deviates away to our left, but at the sight of more shale slopes down in the gully, we decide to keep to the asphalted D20. It's a quiet country road, and we stroll along until we find a shady picnic spot among the pine trees. Time to tuck into our chewy baguette with cheese and tomato: bliss! We've earned it, but it was easier than we imagined.

A further two or three kilometres brings us to the Col de Corobin. At 1211 metres it's the highest point on the day's walk, and we're soon loping down through a series of hairpin bends. Pine trees grip tenaciously to shale slopes on the upward side, while on the down side the terrain drops away into stony gullies. This is fairly barren countryside. Wild flowers and broom scrub scattered among the extravagantly shaped rock formations make for picturesque scenery, but it's extremely inhospitable country – we see not a hint of cultivation or habitation, and it's hard to believe that we're barely fifteen kilometres from the bustling town of Digne. Competitive cyclists have passed here though. Their fans have painted encouraging messages on the roadside retaining walls: *Allez Denis! Allez Auriol! Go Armin!*

With a swing in our stride we reach the hamlet of La Clappe. There has been a community here since Roman times, always struggling to coax a meagre existence from the stony ground. In recent years though, grants from the European Union, from the various regional and provincial tourist boards, banks and other organisations have contributed to the recovery and renovation of the hamlet's handful of buildings. Work is still in progress, but most of the buildings have been freshly re-plastered and painted in cream or a soft, warm sandy-salmony pink. New roofing, windows and shutters are making them weather-tight again; the debris of years of neglect has been cleared away, and a small restaurant and hikers' hostel are already functioning. What a lovely place to pause, or even to stay for a while. We order a pot of tea and relish it outside under the shade of a wild cherry tree.

The people are friendly – if Napoleon received a dubious welcome here, nobody at La Clappe is going to let anything mar the hamlet's reputation again today.

We reached La Clappe six not-too-strenuous hours after leaving Barrême, and although we still have thirteen kilometres to go to reach Digne, it's downhill all the way and we expect to make good time. Our rest in this hospitable and pretty spot has thoroughly refreshed us: another time we'd like to stay the night here too.

As we continue down into the valley, the vegetation becomes thicker and more verdant, and there are other walking trails in the pine forest here too. We're in the Forêt Domaniale de Cousson, and at Col de Pierre Basse the Grand Traversée des Pre-Alpes branches off towards the village of Entrages on the left, and towards Les Dourbes to the right. Napoleon took the trail towards Entrages, although he then skirted around below the village and rejoined the D20 where the lane from Entrages crosses the Eaux Chaudes stream. We're right down in the valley now, striding along beside the stream itself. In spite of its name, it isn't actually flowing with hot waters, although they do have therapeutic qualities. Soon after passing the bridge we stop to admire the Ferme Feston. This long, simple farmhouse has a certain grace thanks to the two semi-circular free-standing towers at either side of its front garden. In the afternoon sunshine it glows a peachy-pink under a tawny terracotta roof, and well deserves the title of Chateau Feston that has been used to describe it over the years.

One final kilometre further on, we reach the thermal spa area that gives Digne its name of Les Bains, The Baths. The spa buildings all post-date Napoleon's passage down the valley in 1815, but even then there was a modestly elegant establishment on the site where Napoleon's sister Pauline had come for a cure some years before. And in turn the emperor was also offered refreshments before continuing into the township.

The baths thrive today. A modern complex provides water, mud and massage-based treatments for rheumatism, respiratory problems, sports injuries and post-surgery trauma. It is an attractive centre for boosting general well-being. Situated in a cool wooded valley just three kilometres from the centre of town, it offers individual therapies and group activities such as aquatic aerobics classes. There's an outdoor gym in the green area along the banks of the Eaux Chaudes, and for on-site accommodation, there is even an aptly named 'Tonic Hotel'.

The urban bus service links the baths to the town centre, but even though we're feeling weary by now, we decide to press on on foot. On the outskirts of the town we come to Rue Mère-de-Dieu. In 1815 it was the main road into the town for anyone who had come over the mountains, and Napoleon and his men marched down it to the rhythm of drums beating. Nowadays it is a quiet lane, but because this is Midsummer's Day, the day of the annual Fête de Musique, three piano-accordionists are playing a lively tune under the plane trees as we plod by and pass the plaque that commemorates Napoleon's having stopped here for lunch on 4 March 1815.

Strolling along, we've arrived here just in time for dinner. We're full of admiration for Napoleon's men: they trudged on for another eighteen kilometres before stopping for the night at Malijai. Our march ends here in Digne and we agree that the Route's slogan could easily be 'Napoleon did it on foot. Why don't you do it too?'

Determined, plucky, indefatigable, indomitable, inspired . . . The adjectives that come to mind to describe people who set off on long, arduous treks to far-off goals could maybe even include 'foolhardy' and 'crazy', depending on your point of view. And if any of these adjectives could describe a 46-year-old Napoleon Bonaparte and his men, they could just as easily apply to another extraordinary walker who has left her mark on Digne-les-Bains.

Alexandra David-Néel fervently believed in always going as far as possible: in order to delve into a situation, to explore its every facet and to find its origins. She was twenty-two when she inherited enough money from her godmother to travel to India in 1890, the first year of a fascination with the Orient, with Tibet, and with Buddhism that would last for almost another eighty years.

On that first trip to India she was captivated by the sound of Tibetan music and the sight of the Himalayas. In 1911, and in spite of having married in the meantime, she set off again for the East. Perhaps she intended, as she promised her husband, to be away for only eighteen months. She returned fourteen years later, having become, in 1924, the first European woman to explore Tibet and to enter the Potala Monastery in Lhasa. When she returned to France she bought a small house on the outskirts of Digne-les-Bains and called it Samten Dzong, meaning Fortress of Meditation.

In spite of urban development, Samten Dzong is still on the edge of the town and retains its peaceful in-the-country feel, surrounded by tall trees, many of which Alexandra herself planted.

The Tibetan and French flags fly side by side at the gate, and Tibetan prayer flags flutter from bamboo poles in the garden. The modest, whitewashed house is trimmed with deep garnet-red eaves and shutters. A golden roof finial adds a definite oriental flavour, as do the two bronze snow lions in the garden. From 1955 Alexandra's companion-secretary was Marie-Madeleine Peyronnet, and although Alexandra died in 1969, Mlle Peyronnet has stayed on at Samten Dzong and still welcomes guests there today. The house is jointly a museum dedicated to Alexandra David-Néel's life and explorations, and a centre for Tibetan studies.

A battered aluminium pot in the museum's central showcase is, for me, one of the most fascinating exhibits. During the months that Alexandra trekked westwards to Lhasa, she melted snow and prepared her meagre soup and tea in this pot. Afterwards she smeared the soot over her face and wrists to complete her disguise as a Tibetan beggar.

Over the years the complex has expanded to accommodate more Tibetan exhibits. A separate building houses delicate Tibetan crafts – a carved teak altar, a mandala sculptured in sand and a tormas created with coloured butter – and photos of scenes of everyday life in the Himalayas. Recently a photographic display has been mounted chronicling Alexandra's life. She always carried the best of photographic equipment and many of the photos in the display are ones that she took. Early photos show Alexandra as a young woman with a faraway look in her eyes. Others range through her journeys across Asia on foot and by yak and horse, to when she was sitting happily in the grass in front of the Potala monastery with Yongden and a Tibetan child. The photo is dated February, 1924. Later still there are photos of her towards the close of her life – bright-eyed, alert and writing to the age of one hundred and one.

Route Napoleon

Getting there: suggested transport in **bold**
The Route starts in Golfe-Juan, and is well signposted as the N 85, Route Napoleon from Grasse northwards.

A **bus** from Nice to Grasse follows the Route via Castellane to Digne, Sisternon and Grenoble. It leaves Nice bus depot daily at 7.30 a.m.: reservations are recommended: (tel VFD in Nice, 0493 85 24 56). Digne and Barrême are also served by Chemins de Fer de Provence trains.

Eating and staying overnight:

Golfe-Juan
Hotel du Golfe, 81 Boulevard des Frères Roustan, tel 0493 63 71 22, fax 0493 63 24 71

Fish restaurant La Fourmigue, Port Camille rayon, tel 0493 63 62 72

Cannes
Centre International Marie Eugénie Milleret (CIMEM) – accommodation in a convent with peaceful garden just minutes from the centre of Cannes.
37 Ave du Commandant Bret,
tel 0497 06 66 70, fax 0497 06 66 76,
web – perso.wanadoo.fr/cimem/
e-mail assomption.cannes@wanadoo.fr

B&B Eve and Henri Daran, L'Eglantier, 15 rue Campestra.06400 Cannes,
tel 0493 68 22 43, fax 0493 38 28 53

Mougins – between Cannes and Grasse
Le Manoir de l'Etang, 66 Allée du Manoir, 06250 Mougins, tel 0493 90 01 07, fax 0492 92 20 70

Montauroux
B&B between Cannes and Grasse – Pierre and Monique
Robardet, Fontaine d'Aragon, Quartier Narbonne, 83440
Montauroux,
tel/fax 0494 47 71 39, e-mail p.robardet@wanadoo.fr

Barrême
Camping Napoleon,
tel 0492 34 22 70

Hotel-restaurant Alpes Hotel, Quartier Rochas,
tel 0492 34 20 09

La Clappe hamlet between Chaudon and Digne
La Clappe Centre d'Accueil, Nature et Decouverte
(Accommodation, Nature and Discovery Centre)

BP 26 – RD 20 Chaudon Norante, 04000 Digne les Bains,
tel 0492 34 21 69, fax 0492 34 41 20, 0492 32 41 21
e-mail laclappe.association@free.fr
Reservations are essential.

Digne-les-Bains
Hotel de Provence, 17 Boulevard Thiers,
tel 0492 31 32 19, fax 0492 31 48 39

Hotel restaurant Julia, Place Pied de Ville,
tel 0492 32 22 96, fax 0492 31 14 81
e-mail hotel.julia@wanadoo.fr www.hotel-julia.com

Tonic Hotel, 36 Ave des Thermes,
tel 0492 32 20 31, fax 0492 32 44 54,
e-mail TONIC.HOTEL.DIGNE@wanadoo.fr
perso.wanadoo.fr/tonic.hotel.digne

Maps for walking:
Depending on the sector – from Grasse to Digne,
choose IGN TOP25 3543 ET, 3542 OT, 3441 OT, 3440 ET,
1cm = 250m

Info and website:
Route Napoleon – www.route-napoleon.com

Office de Tourisme de Golfe-Juan, parking de Vieux Port,
tel 0493 63 73 12, www.Vallauris-Golfe-Juan.com

Cannes Office de Tourisme, Palais des Festivals, La Croisette,
tel 0493 39 24 53, e-mail tourisme@semec.com
www.cannes.fr

Castellane Office de Tourisme – Rue Nationale,
tel 0492 83 61 14, fax 0492 83 76 89

Digne-les-Baines
Digne-les-Bains Office de Tourisme, Place du Tampinet,
04000 Digne-les-Bains
tel 0492 36 62 62, fax 0492 32 27 24
e-mail info@ot-dignelesbains.fr
www.ot-dignelesbains.fr

Musée Alexandra David-Néel, 27 Ave Maréchal Juin,
tel 0492 31 32 38, fax 0492 31 28 08
e-mail neel@alexandra-david-neel.org
www.alexandra-david-neel.org
open daily for free guided tours at 10.30 a.m. and 2 p.m. all
year, and at 4 p.m. Oct-June, and at 3.30 and 5 p.m. July-
Sept.

Thermal Spa – Les Thermes de Digne-les-Bains,
tel 0492 32 32 92, fax 0492 32 38 15
e-mail Thermes_digne@wanadoo.fr
thermes.digne@eurothermes.com
www.eurothermes.com

Reserve Géologique de Haute-Provence www.resgeol04.org

Climate and when to go:
Check opening times at local tourist office before going.

Golfe-Juan – re-enactment of Napoleon's landing first
Sunday in March

Digne – Lavender Festival in June – the town has a busy
events programme – full details from tourist office. Thermal
spa open mid-February to end November

CHAPTER 22

The Massif de l'Esterel – bandit country

HENRI SETS OFF PURPOSEFULLY, SHOULD-
ering a voluminous lime green butterfly net. Odille calls an
affectionate *Bonne chasse* – happy hunting – to Henri, and
fastening Pitou's lead to his collar, she and the frisky terrier
step out in the other direction. Pitou tugs on the lead, picking
up the scent of hare and rabbit: like Henri and Odille, he's
obviously been here before. Their car has Fréjus number
plates: the Esterel forest park is their back garden. Some way
down the track by now, on the Route des Cols, Henri's
butterfly net is still clearly visible as it swoops and dives, for
the vegetation is sparse here on the southern slopes of the
Massif de l'Esterel, and the forestry roads provide easy
walking paths.

Looking west from Ventimiglia, the neat round humps of
the Massif de l'Esterel stand out seventy kilometres away on
the horizon. It's slightly further by car, but provided you

don't mind the hectic speed on the motorway, you can reach the Maison Forestiere du Malpey on the slopes of Mount Vinaigre in little over an hour. The Malpey Forester's House is one of a handful that remain of those built in the 1870s. Mauvey-pink with an inviting pergola draped in wisteria, it stands at the point where the Roman Via Aurelia can still be traced through the woods all the way to the outskirts of Fréjus. The access road that passes the house continues on to within 200 metres of the summit of Mount Vinaigre, while the century-old foresters' paths and tracks have been well maintained and are clearly signposted, so your walk can be as relaxing or as challenging as you like. The *Institut Geographique National*'s 1:25,000 map 3544ET shows all the paths and points of interest and has an English key.

At 614 metres, Mount Vinaigre is the highest point on the Massif de l'Esterel. In the mid-1980s fires devastated the forest on its southern slopes, so today the vegetation is still quite scrubby and the short walk to its summit offers sweeping views across the entire domain. The terracotta hues of Mount Vinaigre's porphyry slopes are the perfect backdrop for the greens of myrtle, heather and pine, and the silvery greens of rosemary, lavender with flowers of the deepest purple, thyme and sage. Let the scents and colours work their own magic.

The Massif de l'Esterel takes its name from the goddess Sterella. The Romans chose her to protect a shrine on the Via Aurelia at the point where, having left the coast to climb gradually up from Mandelieu, the road dipped down again towards the port of Forum Julii — modern-day Fréjus. Between Mandelieu and Fréjus, the National Route 7 — the N7 — still traces the Via Aurelia. Two thousand years ago it provided Rome's only access to the west: nowadays it is a secondary link. Through-traffic hurtles along on the nearby motorway, while a wider coastal road opened in 1903 is studded with such sun-drenched seaside drawcards as La Napoule, Théoule-sur-Mer, Agay and St-Raphaël.

Choose those thirty kilometres of the N7 between Mandelieu and Fréjus for a day out that will take you from Roman paths to back-to-nature hiking and biking and horse-riding trails; from perfumed marquis scrub to cork-oak forests; from a hermit's cave to a bandit's hideout; and from one spectacular scenic viewpoint to another.

Continuing their road-building enterprise westwards in those last hundred or so years before Christ, the Romans encountered one of the oldest land masses in Europe, the volcanic russet-red porphyry chunk of the Massif de l'Esterel. Skirting around it on the coastal side was impossible: rocky coves and inlets alternate with jagged lava-hard ridges and deep ravines. Today these are the features that make the 100-year-old coastal road so attractive to holidaymakers, but 2000 years ago an empire's traffic needed a much wider, more easily built and more readily maintained carriageway than could be constructed around a shoreline that barely provided scope for a narrow foot track. Turning away from the coast again, the Romans built their road around the northern side of the Massif. Up through cork and chestnut forests, counting off every *millia passum*, or every 1000 strides, with a massive stone block. These milestones were well over man-height, and engraved with details relating to the reigning emperor and consul of the day, as well as the distance from Rome. Over the centuries, some of them have been hauled away to be used in building elsewhere. Others have stayed in place, and one of these stands at the roadside in the cork forest near the Auberge des Adrets. Over the years cork harvesters have used it for a whet-stone to sharpen their cutting tools, chipping and wearing it away, indifferent to its ages-old history.

And so the road curves gradually up through the cork oaks, to the place just before its highest point, where the Romans built a simple shrine to Sterella. Early in the fifth century Saint Honorat sought tranquillity in the woods near here, but his hermit's cave was soon ferreted out by his over-zealous followers. Even in those days privacy invasion was a problem, and Honorat soon fled to the solitude of the islands of Lerins, off the coast from Cannes. In time the Christians replaced the shrine dedicated to Sterella with a chapel in honour of Our Lady of Esterel, and because wayfarers would pause at the shrine, an inn was built nearby. The inn flourished and became the strategically situated Logis de l'Esterel.

Not everyone who came this way was a humble pilgrim or harmless traveller. On the Massif's northern slopes the cork oaks and chestnuts grew thick, and dense. In the seventeenth century, these dark, dank places provided shelter for men evading the prisons and galley-slavery of Toulon's shipping yards. On the southern and seaward side, pine trees and scrubby brush clawed for a root-hold among the crags and crevices of the wind- and time-eroded rocks and pinnacles. Here, too, there were caves and crannies to slink into and remain concealed, and outcrops to crouch behind, hidden and ready to ambush an oncoming stagecoach load of weary, wary travellers.

A team of horses that had been fresh and strong as they left Fréjus would have been tiring almost fifteen kilometres later as they approached the Logis de l'Esterel, since it was usual to change the horses at that point.

Imagine the atmosphere inside the stagecoach as it nears the highest point on the road up from Fréjus. On a fine day

Mount Vinaigre glows golden, mottled with green, sky-blue above and patches of silver sea far below: a cameo of Mediterranean colours. On a dull day the mist lingers around the fingers of its wind-rounded pinnacles: spooky and mysterious.

Nowadays we have nothing to fear as the road skirts around just below the mountain's rugged summit. There's no one lurking behind an outcrop, ready to pounce and rob us of our belongings. We can sit back and enjoy the scenery. In the 1600s though, and well into the 1700s, you'd have been clutching your valise, perched on the edge of your seat and scanning every protruding rock for the first hint of a highwayman or brigand. By the late 1770s you'd have been praying that you would get through without meeting Gaspard de Besse.

Besse-sur-Issole is a charming country village about sixty kilometres west of Fréjus, and Gaspard was born there in 1759. As a young man Gaspard and his mates met one of the king's recruiting officers in a tavern, and impulsively enrolled themselves in the army. The next morning, realising what they had done, they deserted! They hid in the woods, hunting for food or stealing it, and steadily making their way towards the Massif de l'Esterel. Bright and optimistic Gaspard quickly became the band's leader. Astute and politically aware, even as they turned to banditry, Gaspard insisted on living by the cry of 'Terrify but never kill'.

Gaspard de Besse is often likened to Robin Hood – *Robin des Bois Provençal*. Highwayman without a doubt but never brutal: dashing and charming, cocksure in red breeches with a gold buckle and a sprig of broom stuck cheekily in his hatband. He stole riches and susceptible hearts with a flourish, and Robin Hood-like, gave to the poor. Alert to social injustice – the French revolution was barely a decade away – he ridiculed the nobility, and mocked the clergy. In those covert years of the late 1770s, as discontent and uprising fermented throughout France, the Auberge des Adrets became Gaspard's lair. A tiny stone figure guards the entrance from a niche over the lintel. Virginia creeper grudgingly concedes an opening for multi-paned windows and all-concealing solid brown shutters.

Try to hear the logs crackling in the enormous fireplace, stockinged feet padding hurriedly across the magnificent stone-paved floor, the clink of coins and valuables as the booty is discreetly counted and stashed into hiding. Imagine the furtive whispers, the secret signs, the bravado and the apprehension. Imagine scrambling down a secret passage and scurrying away to a cave deep in the hillside if danger knocked at the door. It's easy enough, early in the morning when the mist still lingers in the valley and around the peaks of Mont Viniagre: then, or in a storm or in the dead of night, the Auberge des Adrets, and the dark plum-purple stone stables opposite really are *Le Repaire de Gaspard* – Gaspard's Lair. Just after midday though, when the sun shines on the front, the Auberge is once again a fine and inviting hotel.

Before we look inside let's say goodbye to Gaspard de Besse. He lived true to his motto and never killed. None the less, when he was arrested in October 1781 the local government, having been the object of so many of Gaspard's mocking jibes, refused him even a hint of mercy. He was tortured to death – broken on the wheel – in the main square of Aix-en-Provence on 25 October 1781.

With the advent of rail travel – the scenic line runs close to the sea – the post house was closed down in the 1860s. Later on the inn was restored in 1898, and today the Auberge des Adrets is a four-star hotel. Ten sumptuous rooms where Gaspard's daredevil ghost is never far away are dedicated to him and to Dame Rose – like Gaspard, she was also from Besse: she was his mistress and the innkeeper's wife. Downstairs the logs still crackle in the fireplace until late at night. If you're just passing through, stop for a special meal – maybe sit outside looking down the daisy-speckled terraces towards the village of Les Adrets. Wisteria and an Esterel-red rose grow intertwined over the pergola. Close your eyes for a moment while the waiter draws the cork from the bottle, and remember: Romans, hermits and pilgrims, stagecoaches and brigands and . . . POP! . . . cork cutters. It's a much less important harvest now than it used to be, but cork is still cut from the trees that grow all along the roadside here. When the cork bark is removed the inner tree trunk is smooth and, taking its colour from the red Esterel earth, it looks raw and wounded: like a leg that has stayed too long in the sun. The stripped trunk oozes and forms a scab of new cork that builds up again, wafer by wafer, over the next ten years. A factory in Fréjus makes cork sheeting for insulation and handcrafts. And to safeguard the best wines that France can offer, they also make solid corks for that bottle of something special.

Massif de l'Esterel

Getting there:
The Massif lies to the west of Cannes. It's bordered on the seaward side by the coastal road from La Napoule to St Raphael (35 km) and the railway line serving the tiny sea resorts. The motorway passes to the north of the Massif, with easy access from exit 39 Les Adrets. The N7, roughly following the ancient Roman road, Via Aurelia, follows around the northern slopes of the Massif, south of the

motorway. The village of Les Adrets, consisting of a cluster of hamlets, is situated near the N7.

Two or three times a day there are **buses** between St Raphael/Fréjus and Lac Cassien/Fayence, Via Les Adrets, and between Mandelieu and Les Adrets.

The Massif is criss-crossed with walking and mountain-biking trails and there is road access to within a short walk of the summit of Mt Vinaigre. Take binoculars.

Eating and Staying:
Full list from the tourist information office.

Hotel restaurants:
Auberge des Adrets, N7,
tel 0494 82 11 82, fax 0494 82 11 80,
e-mail auberge@compuserve.com
www.auberge-adrets.com

L'Estirado des Adrets, Logis de Paris, near N7,
tel 0494 40 90 64, fax 0494 40 98 52
e-mail estirado@estirado.com
www.estirado.com

Le Relais des Adrets, Place de la Mairie,
tel 0494 40 90 88, fax 0494 40 95 17
www.logis-de-france.com

Maps for walking:
IGN TOP 25 3544 ET 1cm = 250m

Walking and mountain-biking map for paths around Les Adrets, from tourist information office.

Info and website:
www.mairie-adrets-esterel.fr

Office de Tourisme, Place de la Mairie,
tel 0494 40 93 57, fax 0494 19 36 69
e-mail lesadrets.esterel.tourisme@wanadoo.fr

Climate and when to go:
Pleasant all year round. Mimosa blooms in late winter, spring/summer wild flowers and butterflies, fabulous views from the top of Mt Vinaigre on a clear day.

CHAPTER 23

Odd jobs

'BUT WHAT IF ONE JUMPS OUT AND BITES me?' Michele had squeezed himself into Yvonne's cellar even though the door had jammed half open. Now he stood in the semi-darkness in a space that was just large enough for his working boots, the only part of the floor that wasn't occupied with rickety shelves and old furniture. He peered apprehensively into the darkest corners where anything could have been lurking. I wondered if he had already seen a furtive movement there among the old books, plates, flowerpots and chamber pots. He shook his head anxiously. Not yet, anyway.

'Surely a big strong man like you isn't afraid of a little mouse,' Yvonne teased him, while I wondered how anything that had left droppings the size of small olive stones could possibly be described as a mouse. Nightmare visions of a snarling, plague-carrying rat attacking the intruders flitted among the cobwebs and shadows as we began to plan our working-bee to clear the cellar. We had finally managed to open the door just a few minutes before. It had been securely locked for nearly thirty-five years, following the death of Yvonne's father in 1964, so we reassured ourselves that in the time it had taken to wriggle the keys in the locks and bunt open the door, any loitering rats would have retreated. Evidence of their occupation was everywhere. Enormous droppings covered every surface and the smell was stifling. An old straw-stuffed bed-base was clawed and chewed to shreds: a favourite nesting place had been a pile of raffia-covered Chianti bottles in one corner. Even the legs of some of the wooden shelves had been gnawed away. Most astonishing of all was the mountain of earth that spilled out from under the shelves. The rats had managed to burrow through the joins in the tiled floor and concrete walls in several places, and tunnelling down into the underworld of Ventimiglia Alta they had pushed bucketfuls of rubble up into the cellar. Michele and his mate shovelled for an hour, filling bucket upon bucket. After they went to the council rubbish dump I took over the shovelling for another hour, and still hadn't finished when they got back. If the same scene recurs in other abandoned cellars in Ventimiglia Alta, it's a wonder the whole town doesn't cave in.

Meanwhile, Yvonne was sorting through a pile of papers that had miraculously not been used for nesting. Her father had led an interesting, multi-talented life, and not long before his death at the age of eighty he had started to study German, as he had many German clients visiting his hotel-restaurant in Piazza Funtanin. Newspaper cuttings dating from before World War I recounted his sporting activities as a young man. The menus, guest registers and photos recording his career as a restaurateur-hotelier in England, Paris and the Piazza Funtanin were of interest to all of us. Some of the photos showed my place as it was in the early days before the gable end was raised, and Michele was captivated by the photos of the restaurant interior as it was in its finery before he was born. Now that he is the owner of its charred shell – it was gutted by fire some years ago – he was fascinated to see how it had been, fuelling his dream of how it will be again before long. Other treasures were the old menu boards, proclaiming that dinner could be had for 600 lire – less than the price of an ordinary postage stamp today – and an ice-cream on a stick for 50 lire – today it would cost 2000 lire. When Piero the plumber, Michele's older brother, stopped by to inspect our work he told us he remembered buying his ice-creams from Yvonne's father. The flags of Europe that had been flown across the front of the restaurant, and the goggles and helmet that Yvonne's father had worn as a racing driver, were among the day's finds too.

We formed a chain gang to heave old bed ends and discarded doors and shutters outside, and Michele and Marco loaded them onto the Ape – his dinky three-wheeled utility. Later they made another trip to the dump, the Ape almost swamped under the load, with an Italian flag from the day's finds flying proudly out the back.

Once we had cleared some floor space we faced the task of clearing the shelves: most of them would have to be dismantled and dumped as the combination of rats, time and damp had left them sagging and decaying. Grimy glasses for every type of drink that a fine restaurant can offer had to be packed and carried away for washing and sorting, and with them coffee cups, tiny milk jugs decorated incongruously with Venetian gondolas, white china plates, teapots and chamber pots. We picked our way through the glasses and crockery, plastic-hatted and gloved against the rat droppings that lay thick on each shelf. 'I wouldn't be doing this if it weren't for you,' Yvonne said. I wondered if I was being thanked or cursed. For me it was certainly another amazing experience: even shovelling rat dirt eventually brings the reward of a clean floor. Once the men had cemented up the holes in the walls, and we'd disinfected the shelves that were still usable, everything was neatly put back in its place again, ready to be inspected by prospective buyers.

As we basked in the spring sunshine at the café in Piazza Funtanin, enjoying a whisky to soothe our dusty throats, I imagined that the rats must have been furious when they tried to revisit this particular cellar and found their route barred by concrete mixed with coarsely broken glass.

And so I took stock of that first year in my new home since Michele had finished the renovations the previous spring. A year of discovery in many respects; a year of finding my own resources and using them to the fullest, a year of exploring my new surroundings, and a year of self-employment doing some ordinary jobs and some decidedly odd ones.

And then there were more and more friends, and friends of friends, coming to stay. It was beginning to look as though I would be lucky to get to the beach at all that summer.

Postscript

THE YOUNG WOMAN CLIMBED THE STAIRS reluctantly. Dark stairs dimly, sparingly lit. Up and up to the fourth floor. Not for the first time, she asked herself why she had decided to go to piano lessons in this gloomy, joyless house. In a green room with a big, black, forbidding piano, with the shutters always closed. She would never forget these lessons in this room.

Rosanna climbs the stairs quickly. It's her third lesson and she's looking forward to it eagerly. She studied English at school many years ago and didn't really like it, but now she's enthusiastic. And she likes the teacher's home; light and bright and sunny, overlooking the rooftops. Up to the fourth floor: the windowless stairwell is brightly lit and freshly swept. Climbing the stairs she looks at the names on the doors that she passes. Recognising none of them, she is convinced that her mother was wrong. She came to this house for the first time three weeks ago. 'You've been there before,' her mother had said, but she must have been mistaken.

The lesson passes quickly and Rosanna sits back in her chair, and tells me that she's so glad she has taken English up again. 'It's a pity I didn't like it very much when I was younger,' she says.

'Just like me and this house,' I laugh. 'I hated it the first time I saw it.'

'Was it awful?'

'So dark and uninviting, with green walls and a big black piano,' I shudder in reply.

'A big black piano?'

I tell her that the woman who sold me the house had been a music teacher.

Now Rosanna looks amazed, asks me the woman's name, and shakes her head in disbelief. 'So my mother was right all the time,' she says.

Over twenty years ago, she tells me, she came here for piano lessons, to a dim, pale green shuttered room dominated by a big black piano. 'I thought I'd never forget that room, but now I don't even recognise it.'

Even as I show her around the flat, she struggles to realise that it's the same place. It's a tribute to the men who worked here little more than a year ago to sand and paint the walls and ceiling, to level and tile the floor, to rewire, and to install the central heating: to transform this room and all the others, so that someone who knew them well no longer recognises them.

I decide it's time to invite the former owner and her family back for afternoon tea.

Practicalities

These brief suggestions are not intended as a substitute for a specialised guidebook.

Getting here

By plane: fly into Nice-Côte d'Azur airport, where you can pick up a rental car or take a long-distance bus to your destination, or a local one into the centre of the city where you can take the train to destinations along the coast in either direction.

Some budget airlines fly into Genova airport. The shuttle bus takes you into the city centre where you can take a train to your destination.

By train: regular, comfortable services reach all the coastal destinations mentioned here, except Portofino (nearest station Santa Margherita) and St Tropez (nearest station St Raphael or Fréjus). Destinations in the Var valley and the Roya valley can also be reached by train.

www.ter.sncf.com/paca

www.fs-on-line.com

By bus: all the destinations mentioned that are not served by train can be reached by local bus from the nearest coastal town.

www.rivieratrasporti.it

Gare Routière: de Nice (Nice bus station) 0493 85 64 44
de Menton 0493 35 93 60

Compagnie des Autobus de Monaco (Monaco bus company) 0493 50 62 41

By car: once you're here, unless you can be sure of free or low-cost parking, preferably off-street in coastal areas especially, a car can be more of a liability than a necessity.

Getting around
The outings and excursions described in this book can nearly all be done in a comfortable, relaxed day from a starting point somewhere on the coast near the Franco-Italian border: Ventimiglia, Bordighera and Menton all have accommodation to suit all tastes and pockets.

Italian and French trains serving the coast and Roya and Var valleys, and bus services to the inland villages and small towns, provide an excellent network of public transport with more departures, especially along the coast, during summer and school holidays. Bus drivers and train conductors tend to know their area and are helpful towards tourists.

Along the coast, traffic jams are a daily event, especially during the summer months. Parking can be expensive if you can find it. Weigh up whether you want to spend your time in a traffic jam in your own car; if the worst happens and you're in one on the bus, at least you'll be able to get chatting with a fellow passenger. Inland, roads are generally less congested, but as they're often winding it can be nerve-wracking if you're a nervous passenger, and frustrating for the driver who misses out on a lot of the spectacular scenery.

The ideal solution is a public transport-based stay, with maybe a hired car for a couple of days for greater flexibility if you want to pack more excursions into each day.

Walking trails are generally fairly well-kept and marked, so for a culture-nature combination, take local transport to your inland destination in the morning and perhaps walk back to base, preferably down hill, in the cool of the afternoon-evening.

After heavy rains the trails may sometimes be closed because of land-slips or rock falls – try to get local confirmation that the path is open before setting out, or else be prepared to turn back if it proves impassable.

Cycling: the cyclist is not very well provided for in this part of Europe, and inner-city cycle lanes are either non-existent or shared with buses and scooters. Once out of the cities, though, intrepid cyclists will generally find that motorists are courteous and patient, although being overtaken by a swarm of Sunday motorbikers can be a frightening experience. Country roads are often steep and winding, and although they are usually asphalted, regular excavating to lay cables and pipes has often left the surface rutted and bumpy.

When to come

Generally speaking, July and August are crowded and chaotic and it can take a while to get acclimatised to the heat. The Christmas/New Year and Easter periods are busy too, as are times of local carnivals or events such as San Remo Festival of Song in February or Monaco Grand Prix in May. If you are a celebrity spotter, these events are the ones to head for.

During summer many towns and even small villages organise special community events – concerts, dances, gastronomic evenings, open-air theatre, pageants and fairs. These are a great opportunity to meet and join in with local people and other holidaymakers alike.

Beat the heat and the crowds by getting an early start to your day: as much before 8 a.m. as you can. You'll be rewarded with the sight of fishermen coming in, locals out doing their shopping, clear sunlit photography conditions, less-congested roads and/or trains and buses, pleasant walking conditions, the aroma of freshly baked bread. Later on, treat yourself to a long, leisurely lunch, even if it's a picnic under a tree, and a rest in the shade, well away from the shimmering heat of early afternoon, before getting on with your day in the late afternoon.

Maps

For general big-picture reference, the Michelin *Provence-Côte d'Azur* 1cm = 2km, or Michelin Local 341 *Alpes-Maritimes* 1cm = 1.5km, and the Touring Club Italiano *Liguria* 1cm = 2km are all excellent. For walking use IGC (Istituto Geografico Centrale) maps 1cm = 500m in Italy, and IGN (Institut Geographique National) 1cm = 250m in France.

Weather and climate

It does rain on the Riviera – from mid to late summer sudden downpours and electrical storms can be as violent as they are short-lived. Afterwards the sky is often clearer than it has been for days and the air is cooler.

Winters tend to be dryish and mild on the coast, especially between Menton and Ospedaletti, although even here it does very occasionally snow. On the other hand, you can enjoy Christmas lunch out of doors here too.

Spring and autumn are lovely times of the year as well. Expect rain, but the temperature settles at around 15–20°C, and the days are long enough to get out and about and enjoy the sights, eat outdoors at lunchtime and delight in the flowers or, inland, in the bright autumn colours. Mimosa flowers as early as January, a traditional sign that winter is nearly over.

For updated weather reports, listen to English language Radio Riviera (106.3 and 106.5 FM) giving the weather after the news on the hour, or consult www.metroconsult.fr/temps and www.meteo.it/nord or www.tempitalia.it for five-day forecasts.

Clothing

This depends on your choice of Riviera. If it's a beach holiday, remember that many coastal towns outlaw swimwear off the beach. Cover your bathing suit to stroll along the waterfront and to go into shops and cafés. For glamorous places you'll feel more at ease in chic clothes, and dressing up is part of the fun.

Elsewhere, comfortable-smart casual applies, with nothing too skimpy acceptable in churches.

For visiting the villages, remember that many of the lanes and alleys are still cobbled and seldom flat – comfortable non-slip walking shoes are a must.

Special events

Some events always take place at the same time each year – on Easter Monday, on 14 July, on the third Sunday in September, etc. Other annual events drift around – early May one year, later in the month the next; and bad weather can mean that the event is put off until a later date. Many towns and villages publish a calendar of events month by month: obtain these from the tourist office or, in smaller villages, from the Pro Loco or the Commune/Municipio in Italy or the Mairie in France.

Learning the Language
Try a relaxed but professional full-immersion combination of lessons and culture.

For French
Contact Magali and Colin at Noves-de-Provence based 'Parlons en Provence'
Info@parlons-en-provence.com
www.parlons-en-provence.com

For Italian
Contact Carolyn at 'Un'esprienza italiana'
carolynmckenzie@libero.it

References

In English

Cameron, Roderick: *The Golden Riviera*

Chippindale, Christopher: *A Highway to Heaven – Clarence Bicknel and the Vallée des Merveilles*

Dall'Aglio, Gian Antonio: *Guide to Liguria: 25 excursions by car*

David-Neel, Alexandra: *My Journey to Lhasa*

Fedozzi, Giorgio; Scoffiero, Carlo; Deffarrari, Ettore: *Cervo*

Fricero, Emmanuel: *The Russian Orthodox Cathedral of St Nicholas in Nice*

Howarth, Patrick: *When the Riviera was Ours*

INSIGHT guide series: *Côte d'Azur – Monaco*

Lyall, Archibald: *The South of France*

Miller, Luree: *On Top of the World*

Müller, Dr George: *Menton and its Neighbourhood Past and Present*

Ruffini, Giovanni: *Doctor Antonio*

Bilingual English/Italian

Muratorio, Maura; Kiernan, Grace: *Thomas Hanbury e il Suo Giardino/ and his Garden*

In French, no English translation available

Editions Nice-Matin: *Èchappée Belle en Provence avec le Train des Pignes*
Banaudo, José, G.E.C.P.: *Guide du Train des Pignes*
Bartoli, Camille: *Vivre L'Authentique Route Napoléon*
Mouton, Henri: *La Route du Sel dans les Alpes-Maritimes*

In Italian, no English translation available

Bernardini, Enzo: *Le Incisioni Rupestri della Valle delle Meraviglie*
Besio, Armando: *Bordighera*
Cassini, Anna: *Un Avventura tra le stelle*
Durante, Bartolomeo: *Guida di Ventimiglia*
Ferraironi, Padre Francesco: *Le Streghe e L'Inquisizione*
Ferrero, Franco: *Questa Nostra Terra*
Meriana, Giovanni: *Valli di Sanremo e Ventimiglia*
Sista, Alfonso: *Da Ventimglia a Limone*

Italian/French, no English translation available

Calvini, Nino, and Cuggè Antonio: *Gli Antichi Percorsi del Sale/Les Anciennes Routes du Sel*